Barcode in Back

From Heritage to Terrorism

Critical in style, *From Heritage to Terrorism: Regulating Tourism in an Age of Uncertainty* examines the law and its role in shaping and defining tourism and the tourist experience. Using a broad range of legal documents and other materials from a variety of disciplines, it surveys how the underlying values of tourism often conflict with a concern for human rights, cultural heritage and sustainable environments.

Departing from the view that within this context the law is relegated to dealing with the 'hard edges' of the tourist industry and tourist behaviour, the authors explore:

- the ways that the law shapes the nature of tourism
- the need for a more focused role for law in tourism
- law's potential (and limitations) in dealing with tensions in tourism such as the panic created by the spread of global terrorism.

Addressing a range of fundamental issues underlying global conflict and tourism, this topical book is an essential read for all those interested in tourism and law.

Brian Simpson is Associate Professor of Law at the University of New England, Australia.

Cheryl Simpson is an Adjunct Lecturer in Archaeology at Flinders University, Australia.

From Heritage to Terrorism

Regulating tourism in an age
of uncertainty

Brian Simpson and Cheryl Simpson

Routledge
Taylor & Francis Group

a GlassHouse book

First published 2011
by Routledge
2 Park Square, Milton Park, Abingdon, Oxon, OX14 4RN

Simultaneously published in the USA and Canada
by Routledge
270 Madison Avenue, New York, NY 10016

A GlassHouse book

Routledge is an imprint of the Taylor & Francis Group, an informa business

Typeset in Times New Roman by
Taylor & Francis Books
Printed and bound in Great Britain by
CPI Antony Rowe Ltd, Chippenham, Wiltshire

British Library Cataloguing in Publication Data
A catalogue record for this book is available from the British Library

Library of Congress Cataloguing in Publication Data
Simpson, Brian.
  From heritage to terrorism : regulating tourism in an age of uncertainty /
Brian Simpson and Cheryl Simpson.
    p. cm.
  ISBN 978-0-415-42559-9
  1. Heritage tourism. 2. Culture and tourism. 3. Cultural property–
Protection. 4. Terrorism. I. Simpson, Cheryl. II. Title.
  G156.5.H47S54 2010
  338.4'791–dc22
                          2010003048

ISBN 13: 978-0-415-42559-9 (hbk)
ISBN 13: 978-0-203-84719-0 (ebk)

Contents

Preface   viii

PART I
Law in tourism   1

1   **Conceptualising tourism and the tourist as a
    legal problem**   3

    Law and the shifting objectives of tourism   5
    The relationship between the state, law and tourism   12
    Marketplace versus the public interest   13
    The different discourses of law and tourism   13
    National government and tourism   18
    The state, class and the human right to tourism   21
    The politics of tourism   22
    *Regulating tourism in an age of uncertainty: tourism as legal
       discourse   23*

PART II
Tourism as a just cause   29

2   **Establishing the exalted tourist**   31

    Constructing the tourist as a cultural terrorist   31
    Tourism as a noble pursuit   36
    We are all tourists now   38
    *The World Tourism Organization and the construction of the
       exalted tourist   39*
    Extending the exalted tourist   42
    *Regulating uncertainties: ethical travel in an age of terrorism,
       climate change and swine flu   46*

3   The urban tourist: inserting the tourist into the cityscape   **56**

Tourism and cities   56
Urban image and the promotion of tourism   58
Alternative layers of the city   59
Marketing the city and the loss of its (legal) soul   61
Defining and preserving heritage   64
Creating the image of the safe city   72
Special laws, special events and public order   78
The modern city as 'legilopolis'   81

4   The exalted cultural tourist: gazing on culture   **86**

Cultural property and tourism   87
*Cultural institutions and the city: the museum
    and art gallery   88*
The museum and the marketplace   88
The exalted tourist and the Indigenous dollar   91
Land rights, tourism and changing patterns of land usage   100
The preservation of Indigenous culture and tourism   102
Beneath the superficial   103
Meaningful tourism and Indigenous culture   104
Indigenous culture, competing meanings and rights   105

PART III
Tourism as transgression   **109**

5   The targeted tourist: the legal construction of fear   **111**

Tourism and injustice   112
Tourism and repression   112
Tourism as repression   115
The role of international law   117
Tourists as targets and the 'war against terror'   119
The loss of innocence: tourists as political targets   124
The politics and moral panic of travel advisories   128
Tourism and the construction of fear   133

6   The pleasure tourist: sex tourism as a legal dilemma   **137**

Sex, pleasure and tourism   137
Sex work and tourism   140
Prostitution as a tourist attraction   141
Sex tourism vs child-sex tourism   143
Tourism discourse and child-sex tourism   144

Laws on child-sex tourism 146
Codes of conduct as regulation 149
Tourism and legal discourse in sex tourism 154

7 Work and death in tourism: from darkness to voyeurism **159**

Regulating tourism work 160
Uncertainty and the global financial crisis 165
Hidden work and the law 166
Death as a tourist experience 167
Death as a tourist attraction 169
The role of transgression in tourism 172

PART IV
Tourism in law **177**

8 Conclusion: tourism as a legal problem **179**

Legal silence 182
Limiting the right to travel 186
Non-tourism as the new just cause 186

Bibliography 188
Index 193

Preface

The idea for this book grew from the course Law, Tourism and the State taught at Flinders University of South Australia by Brian Simpson from the late 1990s until his departure to take up an appointment at Keele University in the United Kingdom in 2002, and then by Cheryl Simpson from 2003 until 2005. The aim of that course was to engage in a critical examination of the law as it affected, and was affected by, tourism. Importantly, this was done in the context of the Legal Studies Discipline at Flinders University which we believed could provide an interdisciplinary and critical approach to the study of legal phenomenon. Unlike Law Schools, our view was that Legal Studies was not hampered by the narrow confines of professional admission requirements and the perceived need to address the 'practical' at the expense of the 'theoretical'. The existence of a course in Law, Tourism and the State at Flinders was itself some evidence of that, as to the best of our knowledge it is not an area of study in any Law programmes in this form. At the time of its creation, it was felt that a critical examination of tourism and its intersection with law would provide more useful insights into how the law in this area 'works' (and does not work) than a more standard (and dry) discussion of the laws which govern the tourism industry.

This background is of central relevance to the content of this book as from the outset we wish to make it clear that this is *not* a book about the manner in which the law regulates travel and tourism. If we were to explain the focus of this book in a few words it would be to say that it is an attempt to explore how law thinks about tourism. For the most part, and with few exceptions, we feel this is a neglected part of tourism studies for the simple reason that it is also a neglected part of law studies. Law tends to compartmentalise itself into 'areas' (such as contract, torts, property, crime) and has difficulty with subject matter that 'cuts across' these boundaries. In our view the connections which courses such as 'law and tourism' both demand and permit have the potential to make the study of law more relevant and interesting. From the perspective of tourism studies, where there is an absence of a body of scholarship in this intertwined area it would be unreasonable to expect tourism scholars to have much to say about law as a part of how tourism is constructed. This lack of breadth in writing on 'law and tourism' appears to be a significant gap in the field. We hope that this work aids in changing that a little.

However, the absence of much intersectional work on this point does present many difficulties, not least the dearth of material which might make those connections to which we have referred as important to make between the two disciplines. This has made our task at times arduous. There are discussions of tourism and power which come close to issues attached to law,[1] but even they acknowledge that in this related area there is much work to be done in tourism studies. As Andrew Church and Tim Coles have written, 'tourism studies still lack a full appreciation of the state's current role in relation to tourism and hence its power'.[2] This is comforting for us who stand outside the discipline of tourism studies attempting to discern the state of play in that other area of expertise. On the other hand it is daunting for the challenge it presents in attempting to provide a fresh perspective to that area of study. On the law side we hope that our approach and the literature presented opens up some new insights (and authors) for law scholars, although we appreciate that there is always a danger in interdisciplinary work of falling between two stools. For taking the risk we make no apologies.

This leads us to methodology. Our approach is eclectic and 'inter-jurisdictional'. In this we mean that we feel free in our approach to roam wide to establish continuities and discontinuities in order to discover how law thinks about tourism (and vice versa). This does mean that we cannot be bound to one jurisdiction, nor do we take an orthodox approach to what might constitute 'law'. Although we refer to some legislation and cases, the reality which we met in first teaching in this area was that in fact there are few actual laws that direct themselves to tourism *per se*. More importantly, many of the issues that concern those of us interested in the social and cultural impacts of tourism are not really addressed by law at all, but are contained in aspirational statements by international organisations, codes of practice and government strategies and discussion papers. These documents often construct a discourse which impacts hugely on how people interact with respect to tourism and its consequences and we feel that in this sense there is a strong argument that these are the 'laws' which affect people and so in effect regulate their behaviour in many areas of tourism. Of course, one aspect of this is the various international treaties and resolutions which relate to tourism. This body of international law is no doubt law in a more classical sense, although for some lawyers the inability to enforce such laws domestically renders them mute. Gladly, the legal system is moving away from such a narrow approach to the value of international law, but leaving aside that debate taking place within law, they still reinforce the manner in which regulation takes place in tourism – much of it is by way of a 'legal' discourse which is as much constructed by non-lawyers as it is by lawyers.

Finally, we would comment on the title of the book. In using the title *From Heritage to Terrorism* we wished to identify tourism as a diverse and contradictory area to regulate. It also suggests that a large area lies between issues of culture and identity and issues of death and destruction. At the same time there is a connection: terrorism is sometimes motivated by disputes over the value of particular views of which values should be retained and heritage preserved, while the keepers of our heritage often have to decide if past atrocities are to be part of the history that society should remember. In the middle of this sits the law, often called on to mediate a solution and find a position that allows such matters to be decided and permit society to still cohere. Of course, from a more critical perspective it may be that law is a device used to blur the issues, disguise the interests of the powerful and resolve the matter by way of a smokescreen built around rhetoric and the clever use of language. This in turn alludes to our concern with social injustice and inequality. While we hope we are detached sufficiently to ensure objectivity in our discussion, we also are of the view that any study of law should be informed by a concern for human dignity and respect. What is often found in the law's construction of tourism is a number of competing and conflicting views about the role of tourism, manipulated by powerful interests and resulting in little concern for the poor. The law has much to do in this area of tourism.

This is also the point at which the 'age of uncertainty' arises. We live in a time where from the vantage point of post-modernism there are no absolutes. At the same time, politicians and 'shock jocks' who provide simple solutions to complex social issues have high popular appeal. Confronted by terrorism, the mass movement of people around the world as refugees and tourists, and amid anxieties about identity at a number of levels, we all live in a world that seems uncertain and insecure. For a moment in the 1990s it seemed that international concern with tourism and its connection with human rights, poverty and social injustice might prevail over other concerns. Now all this seems uncertain as we deal with the fear generated by terrorism, climate change and pandemics. The question that seems to arise here is whether the law is to be used to maintain a position of respect and tolerance for others, or is to be corralled into protecting the status and privilege of the rich and powerful. In this context the law is but a tool that can only be understood in the hands of those who control it. Perhaps in this book we present some means to understand this process.

This then is our project and our aim in writing this book. We thank the many students from Flinders University who participated in Law, Tourism and the State over the years that it was taught by each of us. Without their input and thoughts this book would not exist. We also thank our respective partners and families for their support and encouragement and who, as always, make significant sacrifices to allow us to write.

We also thank the hotel housemaid who one of us met on our travels during the time this book was being written. Working in Sydney, she had come from Nepal, as she said, to provide her children with opportunities she perceived would be available to them in Australia, while indicating that her country was a beautiful place to visit. As she told her story it became apparent that here was part of the reality of modern tourism – women migrating, then commuting from outer suburbs to work long hours making other people's beds for a fraction of an academic's salary in order to advance her children's future, while still professing a deep pride for her country of origin and its culture. We hope that in writing this book we also do her story some justice.

Notes

1 See, e.g., A. Church and T. Coles (eds) *Tourism, Power and Space* (London, Routledge, 2007).
2 A. Church and T. Coles, 'Tourism and the many faces of power' in Church and Coles, *Tourism, Power and Space*, p. 278.

Part I

Law in tourism

Chapter 1

Conceptualising tourism and the tourist as a legal problem

The exotic holidays, which were becoming increasingly attractive to British tourists, may seem less so in a rather more dangerous world. This represents a real opportunity for the British tourism industry to sell its benefits to the British people. The more exotic holidays may also be less tempting to some of the foreign tourist markets, and we may also attract them. Most importantly, the British tourist industry and the relevant agencies should use this year to attract British tourists back to holidaying in Britain.

(Lord McNally, House of Lords, Hansard, 30 April 2003)

Tourism can bring pollution, traffic congestion, overcrowding, and sometimes downright environmental damage. The income generated by tourists all too often does not stay in the local area but is siphoned off to other areas, so local people are not benefited.

(Lord Patten, House of Lords, Hansard, 30 April 2003)

Tourism as a social phenomenon and as an area of state policy is rife with contradictions and confusion. Urry writes that the consumption of leisure activities 'cannot be separated from the social relations in which they are embedded'.[1] It should be no surprise then to discover that the laws and policies which seek to regulate tourism reflect the numerous tensions and other sources of social conflict present in society. While the more popular view of law in relation to tourism is to see it as a facilitator of both tourism and the business of tourism, our project is to present it as part of the 'problem of tourism'. By this we mean the manner in which tourism reflects power differentials in society and thus becomes a constantly shifting phenomenon which at different times takes on different and often opposed objectives. In this process the law does not become a mechanism for clarifying tourism, but instead becomes a force for disguising, concealing and thwarting the aims of different interests in relation to tourism.

The title of this book also speaks to the 'age of uncertainty' in which we find ourselves. While for many this had an apparent beginning with the events in New York City in 2001 (what has come to be known simply as '9/11'), it is clear that that day was more of a continuation of a process that had already begun in modern society. The age of uncertainty in travel and tourism did not begin in September 2001; it was merely underlined on that day, regardless of the fact that some airline security measures may be traced from the events on that day. Chris Rojek had already outlined in 1993 how tourism had been transformed in ways that reflected growing unease and anxiety in modern times. As he wrote then, 'de-differentiation has weakened the contrast between home and abroad'.[2] Mass tourism has come to ensure that travel is underpinned by a 'sameness' wherever one goes, thus creating a certain amount of confusion about where one is actually 'located' at any point in time.[3] Yet Rojek also appears to acknowledge that there are risks in travelling, perhaps through the 'on streets' encounters of a greater diversity of individuals now present in many urban destinations. In an age of concern with the risks associated with modern life he observed that 'television gives us a window on the world without incurring the risks and inconveniences that beset the traveller and the tourist'.[4]

For Rojek modern life is characterised by an 'artificiality' which 'creates constant anxieties about the nature of our real feelings'.[5] It is the shallowness of modern life created by modern consumerism and the dominance of the 'corporate agenda' that lies beneath this anxiety. Rojek argues that 'consumer culture encourages a positive, feel-good, keep fit, acquisitive attitude which marginalizes the traditional question of what life is for'.[6] One can already see the implications for tourism and fundamental questions about its consistency with equity and non-exploitative practices. As Rojek says, leisure and travel are ways of escape and their popularity reside in that they 'enable us to experience the rapid, hectic controls of Modernity in concentrated form'.[7] We live in an age where life is 'fast' yet routinised, where we are constantly 'busy' yet have no time for all we want to do, where the ten-second newsgrab has given way to the limited characters allocated on Twitter for what you are currently 'doing'. As Rojek wrote 16 years ago, long before Facebook, Twitter and Smartphones:

> ... popular leisure activity seems to thrive on fragmentary, contrasting and fleeting experience. Far from demonstrating a reaction to the routines of life as some commentators allege, leisure often involves the intensification and extension of those routines ... Leisure, one might say, is not the antithesis of daily life but the continuation of it in dramatized or spectacular form.[8]

Rojek's analysis may explain the manner in which many tourist attractions now seem to centre on the 'mundane'. How working-class estates can become tourist destinations and how 'shopping trips', for example, are recast as urban experiences and leisure activities. In fact, these are prime examples of how leisure and tourism is able to repackage any experience for consumption while also creating uncertainty about our lives. If work becomes leisure then where is the divide between our working life and our personal life? In the same way, if a tourist overstays and takes on menial work on low wages in pursuit of a dream of a new life, then is that a logical extension of the travel experience or the corruption of the purpose of tourism?[9] In a nutshell, where we have come to is the question of what is the purpose of tourism and the law's role in regulating it?

Law and the shifting objectives of tourism

From economic gain to sustainability

In 2003 the Australian Government issued a white paper on tourism policy.[10] This White Paper clearly adopts a business model of tourism which focuses on the need to repackage Australia in order to reap the economic benefits of (hopefully) increased tourism in the future. This culminates in the notion of 'Brand Australia' which is explained as a concept which extends beyond tourism to embrace a combination of Australia's 'spectacular natural environment, the distinctive personality of the Australian people and the free spirited nature of the country's lifestyle and culture'.[11] This in turn leads to Australia being described as a 'Platinum Plus' destination, one which will be able to increase its global market share of tourism through exceeding 'customer expectations in terms of the quality and value it provides; it is the concept of providing an exceptional experience with superior standards, from the moment visitors get on the plane to the time they return home'.[12]

The significance of this portrayal of Australia as a 'brand' is that it suggests the complete abdication of the reality and complexity of the nation state to the marketer's hype. As a consequence, those factors which inhibit tourism growth are presented as something apart from and not of the country which is being marketed. Thus the white paper notes that '[w]idespread security and safety fears have changed the environment for travel and tourism and threaten the predicted growth of tourism both globally and locally'.[13] Yet while on one level tourism is said to be endangered by the threat of terrorism, it is also applauded as a practice which 'provides the opportunity for cultural exchange and fosters understanding'.[14] Tourism may thus also be described as a force which might inhibit the conditions from which terrorism grows.

Clearly, the construction of tourism as being primarily about economic gain distorts the reality of tourism and its more complex connections with society. In this context 'sustainable tourism' becomes not a contradiction in terms, but a clever way of doing business. As the white paper puts it: 'Sustainable tourism is the development of an internationally competitive, ecologically sustainable and socially responsible tourism industry based on an integration of economic, social and environmental objectives and constraints.'[15]

Similar ways of thinking about tourism have also evolved in the United Kingdom. In 1999 the Department of Culture, Media and Sport outlined its strategy for tourism into the new millennium. After identifying the immediate benefits of tourism as 'the opportunity for rest, relaxation, adventure and enjoyment'[16] it states that tourism is much more than this as it 'generates wealth', 'creates jobs', 'promotes entrepreneurship', and 'provides social and environmental benefits, and supports local diversity and cultural traditions'.[17] This emphasis on the economic benefits of tourism leads to the need to grow the industry, albeit in a sustainable manner. This is never seen as a contradiction or having any real tensions. Thus this paper proposed that local planning authorities understand the

> needs of the tourism sector and do what they can to ensure that planning procedures do not constitute an unnecessary obstacle to tourism development. It is equally important that tourism developers appreciate the issues which planners have to face, and that they understand the system and are able to negotiate the complex procedures involved.[18]

It also proposed a more co-ordinated national approach to tourism with one body to advocate for tourism including the need to act 'as a voice for successful sustainable tourism in England'.[19] This translates – in the same vein as the Australian white paper – to a '"wise" growth strategy', that is, 'one which integrates the economic, social and environmental implications of tourism and which spreads the benefits throughout society as widely as possible'.[20] The difference between this and the later Australian document is that here the strategy is to integrate the economic, social and environmental *implications* of tourism, rather than the *objectives and constraints*. The question is whether much turns on the use of language here. It is our contention that much of this is designed to obfuscate rather than clarify how tourism is to be constructed, and that the manner in which documents slide from 'objectives and constraints' to 'implications' are examples of this.

The problem is that the 'integration of economic, social and environmental objectives and constraints' may suggest quite different objectives to different people. As with the notion of a 'Brand Australia', the notion that tourism can 'integrate' objectives or implications depends on an acceptance that ultimately social cohesion can be achieved. But as Urry suggests in relation to the notion of national icons, such icons are often vigorously contested, such as in his example of Australian bicentennial celebrations being viewed by indigenous people as the celebration of an invasion.[21] Urry writes of the 'end of tourism' focussing instead on the diverse manner in which we all travel. As he puts it, instead of tourism, 'rather there are countless mobilities, physical, imaginative and virtual, voluntary and coerced.'[22]

Taking Urry as a starting point, it seems to us that the important question then is how those laws which purport to regulate, facilitate and control 'tourism' fit with the notion that what we are actually addressing are diverse mobilities. As we shall see, viewed in this way, the 'problem of tourism' is perhaps better viewed as the 'problem with mobility' and its effects. The value of this approach can be demonstrated by considering the manner in which tourism generates not only the consumers of travel and its by-products, but also how it creates a movement of people towards areas where tourism provides employment. Such movements may be voluntary but also may be coerced (such as in the example of the trafficked sex worker). It may also spawn a host of other movements which surround what many may see as the 'core business' of tourism, such as the mobilisation of resources to underpin travel including physical resources and virtual spaces. It follows from this that what we should consider to be relevant in discussions of law and tourism should not be constrained by narrow notions of what constitutes tourism. We must ensure that our discussion connects law with the social forces and relations that are reflected in what we understand as tourism, social forces and relations that are constantly realigning and reshaping themselves.

This approach also assists in understanding the relationship between the notion of 'sustainable tourism' and law. As Farrell and Twining-Ward argue, the very term 'sustainable tourism' suggests that it is an achievable and determinable form of tourism.[23] Their thesis is based on the view that both nature and human activity must be viewed as parts of 'integrated, complex adaptive systems' or socio-ecological systems.[24] These systems structure behaviour but not always in a predictable way. As they describe the process, '[i]t is the forces generated within systems that produce continual uncertainty and unpredictability and confound those attempting management through rigid control'.[25] For them the notion that the economy, personal health, politics and tourism, for example, are normally in balance with occasional disturbances which if addressed return one to normality is a 'falsely optimistic principle [that] has long governed the scientific study of nature as well as most of the social sciences, including economics and tourism'.[26]

This approach is summed up in their description of how events occur in this context:

Events usually triggered by multiple causes have uncertain consequences, and because complex systems operate over a variety of *temporal* and *spatial scales*, little is likely to result simultaneously at the time expected or on the scale imagined. This is pivotal to any thoughts of achieving sustainability. Policy decisions may take from weeks to years for all goals to reach fruition. Those concerning human control of resources (like social policy) may cause cascades of surprising outcomes, some of which when they finally arrive may be quite out of proportion to the magnitude of the original inputs. Others, which take a long time to reveal themselves, may be recognised too late for us to do anything about them.[27]

Thus, the idea of sustainability has to be viewed as an ever-moving concept rather than one that is ultimately achievable. It has to adapt to time and place, not just in terms of the setting of the natural environment but also with respect to human culture and expectations. As Farrell and Twining-Ward put it, '[s]ustainable development then, must be viewed as an evolving complex system that co-adapts to the specifics of the particular place, *and especially to the aspirations and values of local people*'.[28]

This view of sustainable tourism seems to converge with those who argue that tourism can be made more responsive to the needs of people. Higgins-Desbiolles thus argues that the discourse of tourism which posits it as an 'industry' has come to dominate almost all discussions of tourism as a phenomenon.[29] She argues that tourism can also be regarded as 'a social force, which if freed from the fetters of "market ideology" can achieve vital aims for all of humanity'.[30]

Her argument centres around the dominance of the market in the current world economic order and the manner in which neo-liberalism has defined the prime purpose of government as promoting economic growth.[31] She then develops the connection of tourism with market ideology: 'The tourism sector is very important in these processes because the consumption of tourism experiences is a key "growth" sector in many contemporary economies. As a result, tourism has been radically changed by the hegemony of the market.'[32] The purpose of promoting tourism as part of the free-market economy is that it frees the commercial interests which profit from tourism to exploit countries and cultures. Higgins-Desbiolles cites authors such as Wearing who argue that:

> Tourism perpetuates inequality, with the multinational companies of the advanced capitalist countries retaining the economic power and resources to invest in and ultimately control nations of the developing world. In many cases, a developing country's engagement with tourism serves simply to confirm its dependent, subordinate position in relation to the advanced capitalist societies – itself a form of neo-colonialism.[33]

Her point then is that the 'mantra' that tourism is an industry that is only subject to the rule of the marketplace[34] serves the purposes of those interests that profit from it.[35] She argues that while this 'tourism as industry' discourse is here to stay, there are alternative discourses which do not focus on the economic objectives of the 'tourist industry'. These alternative discourses focus on the 'transformative capacity of tourism',[36] or as she defines them, the 'positive impacts'.[37] These include 'improving individual well-being, fostering cross-cultural understanding, facilitating learning, contributing to cultural protection, supplementing development, fostering environmental protection, promoting peace and fomenting global consciousness.'[38] She quotes McKean who says tourism can be viewed as a 'desire to know "others", with

the reciprocal possibility that we may come to know ourselves'.[39] Higgins-
Desbiolles then refers to the Manila Declaration on World Tourism as an
example of a statement of the positive aspects of tourism.

The Manila Declaration was made in 1980 following a conference convened
by the World Tourism Organization. That document proclaimed that:

> world tourism can develop in a climate of peace and security which can
> be achieved through the joint efforts of all States in promoting the
> reduction of international tension and in developing international
> cooperation in a spirit of friendship, respect for human rights, and
> understanding among all States.[40]

The Declaration also invokes tourism's ability to 'contribute to a new
international economic order' that would 'help to eliminate the widening gap
between developed and developing countries'.[41] Article 21 also reinforces the
importance of the spiritual factors in tourism:

> In the practice of tourism, spiritual elements must take precedence over
> technical and material elements. The spiritual elements are essentially as
> follows:
>
> (a) the total fulfilment of the human being,
> (b) a constantly increasing contribution to education,
> (c) equality of destiny of nations,
> (d) the liberation of man in a spirit of respect for his identity and
>   dignity,
> (e) the affirmation of the originality of cultures and respect for the
>   moral heritage of peoples.[42]

It also stresses the notion of tourism as a human right in article 4:

> The right to leisure, and in particular the right to access to holidays and
> to freedom of travel and tourism, a natural consequence of the right to
> work, is recognized as an aspect of the fulfilment of the human being by
> the Universal Declaration of Human Rights as well as by the legislation
> of many States. It entails for society the duty of providing for its citizens
> the best practical, effective and non-discriminatory access to this type of
> activity. Such an effort must be in harmony with the priorities, institu-
> tions and traditions of each individual country.[43]

While the approach of Higgins-Desbiolles has much to recommend it with
respect to the manner in which it suggests that tourism is much more multi-
dimensional than an 'industry' with the creation of profit as its *raison d'être*,
we would take issue that it can be simply presented as competing discourses

between market ideology on one side and tourism as a positive social force on the other. In our view, to do so is to ignore that the legal discourse which is reflected in the declarations issued by the World Tourism Organization and often repeated at national level in legislation and codes of conduct is produced by the same international and state apparatus which generates the discourse of the market and tourism as an industry.

That is to say that such declarations often contain within themselves the very problems that they are designed to address. For example, articles 13 and 24 of the Universal Declaration of Human Rights is said to underpin the broader aims of tourism proclaimed in the Manila Declaration above. Article 13 states:

(1) Everyone has the right to freedom of movement and residence within the borders of each state.
(2) Everyone has the right to leave any country, including his own, and to return to his country.

Article 24 provides that '(e)veryone has the right to rest and leisure, including reasonable limitation of working hours and periodic holidays with pay'.

We do not wish to engage with the trite criticism that the Universal Declaration is too general and vague to convey any meaningful rights. In our view the document is an important statement of principle with respect to the human rights it asserts. However, this does not make it immune from examination with respect to the actual content it might import into human rights. This approach also seems especially useful when we are discussing the various discourses that exist within tourism as opposed to narrow technical legal content. Thus article 13, while on the face of it appears to convey a broad right to travel, does not contain within it the problem of how one is to exercise one's right to leave a country if there is no corresponding right to enter other countries. Clearly, nations impose restrictions on who may cross their borders, which suggests the right to leave a country carries with it no guarantee of a welcome in another land.

While the history of article 13 may have something to do with a time when the restriction of movement by totalitarian regimes meant that *leaving* a country was more problematic than *entering* a country, in the current world there seems to be a greater emphasis on keeping out others than being concerned with enabling people to leave countries. The point is, of course, that article 13 in its own terms does not prevent that emphasis. Thus the whole notion that tourism is underpinned by the right to travel, and as a consequence to leave and enter countries, is much more problematic than this right would suggest.

The role of law in this process is important as it will be legal criteria that will be drafted to define what is to be regarded as 'acceptable movement' and what is to be regarded as unlawful entry into a country. For example, the

Acapulco Documents on the Rights to Holidays 1982 – another document which followed a World Tourism Organization meeting – refers to the importance of 'tourism as a vehicle for peace, harmony and mutual respect among peoples and for knowledge of the world and its truth'[44] and the 'right of access to holidays of all layers of the population and the least favoured in particular'.[45] It then asserts that such objectives cannot be achieved without a general framework of freedom of movement and travel.[46] At this point what is being claimed is quite radical and challenging – that the most dispossessed in society in particular are to be given free movement and travel for the purposes of tourism. This is indeed a challenge to traditional notions of what constitutes tourism. But if this occurs because it employs the legal discourse surrounding human rights and freedoms, then it also carries with it the further qualifications embedded in legal discourse. The Acapulco Documents on the Rights to Holidays 1982 immediately qualifies the aim of freedom of movement and travel with the qualification:

> any effort to foster freedom of movement and of travel must necessarily take into account the existing social and economic conditions of each country, its sovereignty, legislation and traditions as well as the rights and duties of its citizens.[47]

Thus the document concludes with respect to implementation of its aims that legislatures and other interest groups should seek to harmonise 'the easing, *wherever practicable*, of travel formalities in respect of entry into and exit from the territory, customs, and currency and health regulations'.[48] The qualification that this is to be done where practicable is the manner in which the use of legal discourse becomes problematic, for the right to free movement can always be constrained due to practicalities, such as concern with terrorism, the effect of tourist traffic on sites or other environmental effects. Indeed, the very documents which often speak to the social effects of tourism and seek to encourage it as a socially beneficial activity also acknowledge the negative impacts of tourism at the same time. In this sense, they provide both the justification for encouraging tourism and restricting it at the same time.

Article 24 of the Universal Declaration of Human Rights must also be qualified in its own terms. It purports to assert a human right to rest and leisure, logically contingent on a limitation of working hours and paid holidays. But this contingency is itself qualified by the term 'reasonable' which suggests that this right will be contested by different interest groups with respect to what is reasonable in this context. An example of how this plays out at a national level is contained within the workplace legislation brought in by a conservative federal government in Australia. Under the relevant law an employee is entitled to public holidays,[49] but an employer may request an employee to work on a public holiday,[50] and the employee may refuse to do so 'if the employee has reasonable grounds for doing so'.[51] Whether a refusal is regarded as reasonable is to be adjudged by reference to a range of considerations which include the nature of the work, the type of work performed, the nature of the workplace, the employee's reason for refusing, the employee's personal circumstances including family responsibilities, whether additional pay will be provided, notice of the work, and whether work on public holidays could have been expected.[52] The only conclusion from this is that while the legal issue has been drafted as a matter of the reasonableness of the refusal to work, it is no longer a matter of whether the employee has a right to the public holiday. Thus article 24 guarantees very little. An employee required to work on a public holiday because there are no 'reasonable' grounds to refuse to work would appear to have little to support an argument that this is an unreasonable expansion of her working hours. The only argument would be that the Australian law is itself an unreasonable intrusion into the rights of workers to holidays. But this only illustrates the manner in which the discourse constructed around a more socially oriented view of tourism is subject to contest.

The relationship between the state, law and tourism

It is thus important to consider the role which the state plays in regulating tourism. It is possible from the above discussion to identify a number of ways in which tourism concerns the state. These include: the manner in which tourism promotes economic growth, the extent to which tourism is consistent with the preservation of local culture and traditions, whether the practice of tourism is consistent with accepted standards of behaviour within local communities and the international community, the right of people to access tourism, how tourists behave when touring, and the moral and ethical standards adopted by the tourism industry.

It is clear that the state – and as a consequence the law – is not simply concerned with the 'micro' issues of standards of behaviour within the tourism industry and by tourists. While criminal acts committed by the tourism industry or tourists will often attract the attention of the state (in the form of police and courts) it is also the case that the state has a concern with 'macro' issues. That is, the state is also concerned, within the context of tourism, about matters which transcend the behaviour of individuals and relate to national and international development.

This immediately raises many issues and dilemmas. For example, a group of tourists might engage in behaviour which is harmful to a local community. This might be thought to be the basis of action by the state to stop this behaviour. It might even be criminal activity. But this group of tourists may also be responsible for bringing into that community a large amount of money through their expenditure while visiting. Such a case raises the possibility that the economic value of the tourists will override official concern with some aspects of their behaviour.

The most obvious example of this issue is that of child sex tourism. In that instance there are some nation states which have quite clearly decided to allow such tourism to flourish in order to attract the economic benefits which accrue from it taking place. But there are other examples in the area of tourism. Tourist developments which require the bulldozing of the homes of local people, the commodification of cultural artefacts resulting in the loss of authentic culture and the use of child labour in the tourism industry instead of ensuring such children attend school also raise the same questions about the role of the state.

Where these issues arise they indicate the complexity of the 'state' and its role in regulating tourism. Clearly, the state is made up of many parts which can lead to inconsistent stances in relation to the same issue. This is most apparent when one considers the tension between the state as guardian of the public interest versus its role as protector of the economic system.

Marketplace versus the public interest

Part of the problem in defining what is 'appropriate' within tourism it seems is that the state is in the position of both defending the marketplace as the primary mechanism of distribution within society while at the same time attempting to curb the excesses of the market. Thus 'the struggle is not just between the state and the marketplace but also within the state'.[53] In other words it is not just a matter of the state determining what is in the public interest in the area of tourism and drawing the boundaries of tourism accordingly. In this context what is to be regarded as in the 'public interest' is itself greatly contested. Thus it might be more accurate to say that there is no one clear role for the state but many different roles which it is expected to perform. As a consequence the law's role in regulating tourism is likewise vexed and ambiguous. To the extent that law aims to provide coherence and unity to society it is often framed in terms of a 'balancing' of the various competing interests. But this does not in itself create coherence, particularly when these interests are often in conflict with each other.

The different discourses of law and tourism

While the above discussion illustrates that there is an 'industry' discourse on tourism and an alternative 'social force' discourse it is in law that both discourses come together. This convergence, however, is multilayered and complex. At the level of international law, the emphasis is on the social effects of tourism and appropriate responses. At the domestic or national level on the other hand it is the tourism as industry discourse which tends to prevail.

To begin with international law in this area it is apparent from the references cited above from the Universal Declaration of Human Rights that tourism is interwoven with various human rights including free movement

and the right to leisure.[54] The Statutes of the World Tourism Organization
(WTO Statutes) also assert that the state is obliged to do more than simply
consider the economic benefits of tourism. Thus article 3(1) of the WTO
Statutes state:

> The fundamental aim of the Organization shall be the promotion and
> development of tourism with a view to contributing to economic devel-
> opment, international understanding, peace, prosperity, and universal
> respect for, and observance of, human rights and fundamental freedoms
> for all without distinction as to race, sex, language or religion. The
> Organization shall take all appropriate action to attain this objective.

Article 3(2) of the WTO Statutes also links the above aim with the need to
'pay particular attention to the interests of the developing countries in the
field of tourism'. The World Tourism Organization must also work closely
with the United Nations Development Programme in this regard.

The Manila Declaration on World Tourism in 1980 and the Acapulco
Documents on the Rights to Holidays 1982 have also been discussed above.[55]
These documents proclaim the importance of tourism as a force for understanding and are also concerned that tourism occurs in a non-exploitative
manner. Subsequent documents have built upon these foundations. The
Tourism Bill of Rights and Tourist Code 1985 refers to the positive effects of
tourism 'and the contribution it can make in the spirit of the United Nations
Charter and the Manila Declaration on World Tourism, to improving
mutual understanding, bringing peoples closer together and, consequently,
strengthening international cooperation'.[56] Basing itself on the right to rest
and leisure asserted in the Universal Declaration of Human Rights and in
the International Covenant on Economic, Social and Cultural Rights and
the aims of the Manila Declaration which connected tourism with the
establishment of a new international economic order[57] it also affirmed
the right of everyone to 'travel freely for education and pleasure and to enjoy
the advantages of tourism, both within his [sic] country of residence and
abroad'.[58] It then proceeded to articulate a 'tourism bill of rights' which as
its title suggests embraces the language of legal discourse. While the
immediate concern with this Bill of Rights is to define tourism as much more
than an industry solely concerned with commercial gain, it is also apparent
from the problematic nature of the terms used that this aim can be readily
submerged or confused by the manner in which competing interests may
interpret the language.

Thus while the 'right to rest and leisure' claimed in article 1 is relatively
coherent it is in the following articles that it is less clear as to how one is to
comply with their terms. Article 2, for example, speaks to the need for States
to 'formulate and implement policies aimed at promoting the harmonious
development of domestic and international tourism and leisure activities for

the benefit of all those taking part in them'. Of course, in seeking to reconcile all interests involved in tourism one may ask whether this is possible or mere rhetoric. The document then proceeds to articulate a range of proposals to achieve this outcome. Article 3 requires States to 'integrate their tourism policies with their overall development policies at all levels – local, regional, national and international – and broaden tourism cooperation within both a bilateral and multilateral framework, including that of the World Tourism Organization'. This article also refers to the need to 'protect the tourism environment, which being at once human, natural, social and cultural, is the legacy of all mankind'.[59] The document also expects States to not only facilitate tourism but also ensure that it is not used 'to exploit others for prostitution purposes'[60] or that it connects with the illicit drug trade.[61]

The Tourism Bill of Rights also stresses the importance of the free movement of tourists,[62] the prevention of discrimination towards tourists,[63] and the need to provide tourists with information in order to foster 'understanding of the customs of the populations constituting the host communities at places of transit and sojourn'.[64] It also stresses the importance of host communities receiving tourists with 'the greatest possible hospitality, courtesy and respect necessary for the development of harmonious human and social relations'.[65] In turn the host communities can expect certain standards of behaviour from tourists. In particular the Tourism Bill of Rights entitles host communities to expect from tourists 'understanding of and respect for their customs, religions and other elements of their cultures which are part of the human heritage'.[66] The Tourist Code contained within the same document likewise emphasises the importance of tourists respecting local customs and traditions including the need to 'refrain from accentuating the economic, social and cultural differences between themselves and the local population'.[67]

The Hague Declaration on Tourism 1989 followed an inter-parliamentary conference sponsored by the Inter-Parliamentary Union and the World Tourism Organization. While it reiterates similar principles to earlier documents it is notable for the stress it places on the free movement of people and the breadth of this movement. It notes that tourism 'encompasses all free movements of persons away from their places of residence and work, as well as the service industries created to satisfy the needs resulting from these movements'.[68] There is the suggestion here that the free movement of labour is as important as the free movement of tourists in order to sustain tourism. The Declaration then continues to speak as tourism within the industry discourse identified above. Principle 2, for example, stresses that 'tourism can be an effective instrument for socio-economic growth for all countries'.[69] This creates the need for 'a sound infrastructure'[70] training of personnel,[71] the integration of tourism into the development plan for countries,[72] the development of domestic tourism as a base for international tourism,[73] and that a balance is struck between the growth of tourism and the impact it will have on the natural, physical and cultural environment.[74]

Such declarations contain the tensions within the development of tourism. The idea of 'balancing considerations' is well known in the law, but it is a phrase which is open to severe criticism as it may simply disguise the manner in which certain interests tend to prevail over others. The point is that while the law appears to be providing the solution to the tension between tourism and its social impact, in fact it is the use of such legal terms which facilitates that tension being submerged instead of resolved. This is furthered by the tendency to connect with the broad message contained in such documents, instead of analysing the detail of the actual words used.

Thus the Hague Declaration on Tourism 1989 calls for 'effective measures' to ensure that tourism is based on the concept of sustainable development including if necessary the restriction of access to certain sites and to 'ensure that tourism development plans take special account of aspects related with environmental protection and the need to promote awareness among tourists, the tourism industry and the public at large of the importance of safeguarding the natural and cultural environment'.[75] At first glance such statements are worthy and inspiring, but then one realises that the qualifications 'if necessary', 'take special account' and 'safeguarding' are ambiguous and provide little guidance as to how such steps will actually be implemented.

In May 1997 a World Tourism Leaders' Meeting on the Social Aspects of Tourism was held in the Philippines. This meeting addressed the need for tourism to be equitable and socially responsible. In particular the meeting resulted in the Manila Declaration on the Social Impact of Tourism 1997. This Declaration seeks to maximise the 'positive' effects of tourism while eradicating the 'negative' consequences. This Declaration commits to widening the participation of communities 'in the planning, implementation, monitoring and evaluation processes of tourism policies, programs and projects within the context of national objectives and priorities, and for this purpose introduce community awareness campaigns to inform people of the benefits to be gained from tourism development'.[76] This immediately raises the question of why such education programmes will sing the benefits of tourism development when the import of such declarations is that tourism has positive and negative impacts on communities. Is the purpose of such education to promote a critical awareness of tourism or is it to ensure that the priorities of government align themselves with those of the tourist industry?

The Manila meeting agreed to work towards the creation of a Global Code of Ethics for Tourism, which was established in 1999. As Higgins-Desbiolles notes this document was created after the fall of communism and in its preamble states that 'the world tourism industry as a whole has much to gain by operating in an environment that favours the market economy, private enterprise and free trade and that serves to optimise its beneficial effects on the creation of wealth and employment'.[77] Higgins-Desbiolles' comment is that this aim of balancing 'economic development with environmental protection and alleviation of poverty ... is informed by the sustainability discourse of the 1990s'.[78] Her analysis is decidedly upbeat, that tourism as a social force can be constructed in a way which advances human rights. For her it is surprising and so presumably speaks to the strength of the social discourse of tourism that it has survived into the age of marketisation. As she argues:

> While the neo-liberal era demands that tourism's benefits are to be allocated according to the 'invisible hand' of the market, the discourse of tourism as a 'human right' demands the involvement of communities and governments in ensuring a just distribution of its bounties (as well as its ill effects).[79]

Yet even in making this case Higgins-Desbiolles demonstrates the weakness of the case. This is about the distribution of positive and negative outcomes from tourism which raises questions of values – what is positive and what is negative in this context? – as well as how to determine what is the appropriate balance. In the Global Code of Ethics for Tourism the 'right to tourism' is expressed in terms which seem markedly aspirational – and translates into:

> [t]he prospect of direct and personal access to the discovery of the planet's resources constitutes a right equally open to all the world's inhabitants: the increasingly extensive participation in national and international tourism should be regarded as one of the best possible expressions of the sustained growth of free time, and obstacles should not be placed in its way.[80]

Where in this expression of the right to tourism is the balance between travel and sustaining the environment? The problem is that in fact the balance which such documents purport to engage in is one which is struck between considerations which are not comparable. The trap which Higgins-Desbiolles has fallen into is one of acceptance of the legal discourse (or social discourse as she would perhaps describe it) that posits a choice between the discourse of industry which sidelines the negative impacts of tourism, and the social/legal discourse which emphasises human rights and environmental sustainability. On the face of it the international declarations and codes discussed above do seem to create this binary effect; however, a more critical legal analytical approach would question this simple divide.

Underpinning this whole discussion of the regulation of tourism are important matters of values which are often not articulated. As authors such as Gladstone[81] argue, tourism and the discourse of tourism is often constructed in western terms as if people in Third World countries do not travel for leisure. As he writes, 'people in low-income countries somehow do not seem to qualify as tourists'.[82] This of course is far from the truth, yet many of the Tourism Codes seem to accept implicitly that tourism is something that is 'done' by the rich to the poor, that the problem is one of how western tourism can be controlled to ensure that its impacts do not cause those in poverty hardship. Thus at an international level there is the recognition of the need to import into the practice of tourism necessary balances and controls and that it is not just a simple matter of identifying the economic benefits of tourism as the major human-rights issue (economic growth after all is an important factor in ensuring an increase in standard of living) but also recognising that left to the dictates of the market those economic benefits may not flow equitably.

But this all accepts the divides constructed by what may turn out to be a western discourse of tourism which suggests that there is one universal position on what is 'good' and 'bad' in tourism. Beyond a concern with the distribution of the income earned from tourism there are also issues connected with the protection of the environment, the preservation of culture and the promotion of human rights and freedoms which will be judged differently from different cultural and ideological perspectives. This is where legal discourse as used in the various documents discussed above can play a binding role at one level, as it often speaks to the 'public interest' which few will disagree should be the ultimate test. The problem is that the meaning given to such words will vary greatly from group to group. In the end result, it may be that while the legal/social discourse operates at an international level rhetorically, at the level of national law, the powerful interests that sit behind the ideology of the marketplace control more directly the manner in which tourism is both constructed and as a consequence regulated.

National government and tourism

How do these concerns at the international level translate to the national level where, after all, laws are enforced? The Australian Tourist Commission Act 1967 (Cth) at one point stated that the principal objects of the Commission were to 'increase the number of visitors to Australia from overseas; maximise the benefits to Australia from overseas visitors; and to ensure that Australia is protected from adverse environmental and social impacts of international tourism'.[83] One of its additional functions was 'to closely monitor and report the effects of international tourism on Australia's natural environment and society'.[84] Although rarely referred to, such provisions served to remind that tourism was not just about profit.

The complex role that the Australian Tourist Commission performed was also seen from the composition of the Board. Section 13(13) required that at least one of the members appointed by the Minister 'shall be a person who has environmental or sociological expertise relevant to the tourism industry'. The government member must have expertise in 'the formulation of public policy and public administration' (s.13(5)). Such expertise is clearly intended to inject into the administration of the Board the ability to address the wider role of the Commission identified above. Thus while the public face of the Australian Tourist Commission was that of tourist promoter, one can see that its statute required it to address a number of concerns already identified on the world stage. In this sense the tourism industry discourse did not completely dominate the legal framework.

Of course, such broader concerns are not always identified in law. It can be argued that the dominance of market ideology in contemporary society not only dilutes the importance of 'public interest' concerns in those instances where it is expressed (such as the Australian Tourist Commission legislation above) but it also leads to laws which barely touch on these concerns. Thus the South Australian Tourism Commission Act 1993 simply states in section 3:

> The object of this Act is to establish a statutory corporation to assist in securing economic and social benefits for the people of South Australia through –
>
> (a) the promotion of South Australia as a tourist destination; and
> (b) the further development and improvement of the State's tourism industry.

While perhaps broad enough to encompass the social and cultural impacts of tourism these concerns are not explicit as they are in the Commonwealth legislation. The South Australian legislation appears to be primarily concerned with economic growth from tourism and the social benefits derived from such growth. The Act does not consider, however, whether such economic and social benefits will flow equitably to all people and does not sketch out a mechanism to track whether this occurs. This is most apparent with the functions of the Commission which are contained in section 18. While some of the functions listed might be construed as authorising investigation of the social impacts of tourism, it would appear to be so justified as an adjunct to the exercise of some other function. The emphasis is clearly on tourism promotion, development of economic plans and enhancing the ability of tourism businesses to provide for tourists. Likewise section 9 of the South Australian Act does require the Board's membership to include persons who have 'appropriate expertise in the operation of tourism businesses, regional tourism, business and financial management, marketing, environmental management and industrial relations'. It seems noteworthy that the terms 'social' and 'cultural' do not appear in this list.

This approach seems to resonate in other jurisdictions. For example, the Canadian Tourism Commission Act 2000[85] states the object of the Commission is: 'to (a) sustain a vibrant and profitable Canadian tourism industry; (b) market Canada as a desirable tourist destination; (c) support a cooperative relationship between the private sector and the governments of Canada, the provinces and the territories with respect to Canadian tourism;

and (d) provide information about Canadian tourism to the private sector and to the governments of Canada, the provinces and the territories'. Likewise the Hong Kong Tourism Board Ordinance includes as the objects of the Board 'to endeavour to increase the contribution of tourism to Hong Kong' and 'to promote Hong Kong globally as a leading international city in Asia and a world class tourist destination'.[86] There is little evidence of the incorporation into such laws of the social discourse of tourism mentioned in the World Tourism Organization documents discussed above.

Following the 2003 White Paper referred to earlier in this chapter, the Australian Tourist Commission was restructured into Tourism Australia and the enabling Act redrafted the objects of the new body:

(a) to influence people to travel to Australia, including for events; and
(b) to influence people travelling to Australia to also travel throughout Australia; and
(c) to influence Australians to travel throughout Australia, including for events; and
(d) to help foster a sustainable tourism industry in Australia; and
(e) to help increase the economic benefits to Australia from tourism.[87]

The new legislation thus removes any reference to 'adverse' impacts of tourism, and while it does mention the need to foster a sustainable industry, it seems likely that this has as much to do with ensuring that the industry can sustain itself to make ongoing economic returns than it has to do with actually limiting tourism at all. In relation to the functions of the new national tourism body the shift in the legal framework is subtle but telling. In effect in place of a concern with monitoring the effect of international tourism on the natural environment and society, Tourism Australia is 'to increase awareness throughout Australia of the contribution of tourism to Australia's economy, society and environment'.[88] It is almost as if by legislative fiat tourism has moved from having an impact (possibly adverse) on society and the environment, to now being constructed as making a *contribution* to both, with the significant inclusion of the economy at the forefront.

It is important because the law here reflects the manner in which the battle over the articulation of the 'public interest' is currently being fought. If one accepts that the state has some obligation to articulate a broader vision of society than one which is simply concerned with the accumulation of profit and that in some way this in other words represents a 'public interest' position against which to judge the operation of the market, then what occurs when the line between the market and the state blurs?

The difficulty is that at present the role of the state as defender of the public interest has been diminished on a number of fronts. On one front, the state has depleted resources to monitor and investigate negative impacts and thus its role as defender of the public interest is often derided because it can be said that it is 'simply not doing the job anyway.' Thus in the context of the Australian Tourist Commission one may ask whether the previous legislative object of considering the social impacts of tourism was effective if the amount of money to engage in that research was low in any effect. Thus the legislative changes which occurred can be said to have simply brought the law into line with 'reality' in any event. Of course, this is a reality constructed by the imperatives of the market.

To a certain extent the problem is one of emphasis. But this emphasis is important in determining the direction of tourism law and policy. As one can see even from a comparison of the Australian Tourist Commission Act and the South Australian Tourism Commission Act important matters can be subtly removed (or placed) on the agenda by failing to make them explicit considerations. While there sometimes may be a way of reading other considerations into the legislation this requires a Board with the preparedness and the self-direction to do so. But the composition of the respective Boards also reflects certain emphases.

The state, class and the human right to tourism

Shaw and Williams note access to tourism can be considered as a fundamental human right.[89] But in a climate of economic rationalism, sustained attacks on an expansive role for the state, and an emphasis on economic growth how can the state fulfil its obligation to ensure that the human right to tourism and leisure is recognised?

Shaw and Williams draw attention to those World Tourism Organization documents mentioned above which stress the right to tourism and holidays. They state:

> Goals such as the provision of the right to holidays are usually encompassed by the term 'social tourism'. This refers to the situation in which deprived, disadvantaged or economically weak sections of the society are provided with the means of taking a holiday. In one sense it highlights the increasing importance placed on tourism as a leisure activity and its duality in many societies, where it is perceived both as a luxury and as a basic right of each individual.[90]

They then identify the various ways in which the state can support social tourism. The role of voluntary associations in providing holiday centres and camps is stated but Shaw and Williams comment that most government support is indirect. For example, the state may ensure that employees are guaranteed paid holiday leave or provide the manner in which aspects of tourism is taxed. In some countries support is much more direct; sometimes it takes the form of state-subsidised holidays.

Shaw and Williams identify the class, gender and ethnic differences with respect to access to tourism and leisure. They note that it has often been stated that class divisions combined with a government approach (in the UK) which has tended to subsidise leisure activities rather than tourism. As a result, 'many central governments have traditionally aided the arts, heritage and cultural sectors, while leaving improvements in access to other leisure activities to local government'[91] (Shaw and Williams: 1994: 64). This raises direct questions for tourism. If there are class divisions with respect to the types of leisure pursued by members of a community, and if it is the case that certain cultural pursuits (such as theatre, opera, classical music, museums, for example) are accessed by wealthier people within a community then the subsidisation of such forms of leisure may mean less support for the leisure activities of less wealthy groups in society.

The dilemma for the state is that the recognition of 'cultural tourism' as a potentially lucrative market within tourism – due to presumably the higher amounts of money possessed by those interested in 'culture' – leads to calls for increased subsidisation of such cultural activities in order to attract that form of tourism. But such subsidy may only benefit the affluent tourists and local people who indulge in that form of leisure activity. While this occurs less money is available for the leisure activities of the less affluent. From the perspective of those who define the state's interest in protecting the market and advancing economic development the issue is clear – the state must act to increase the economic benefits to the community from this form of tourism. But for those who see the state as having a role in balancing various interests in the community the concern is that such subsidisation will in fact only benefit a small part of the community at the cost of those less able to pay for their leisure.

The politics of tourism

It should be apparent that there are many choices which face the state when it is pursuing a tourism strategy or policy. Will it give priority to economic benefits? Will the social and cultural impacts of tourism be considered? Should local communities be protected from new tourist development? Should the market determine the nature and pace of tourism development?

Richter has shown how tourism in the Philippines was developed to fulfil various political agendas.[92] At one level public subsidies for hotel development meant less money for public housing. At another level the Department of Tourism gained increased powers at a time when other parts of government administration were being decentralised.

In part the strategy pursued by the Philippines government was to ensure that it shared in the growing market in international tourism. But it was also the case that increased tourist traffic leant what many considered to be an oppressive and corrupt government a form of legitimacy. It also lined the pockets of many individuals. The comments of Richter may well have meaning beyond the example she writes about:

> in a system as centralized in fact as the Philippine government is, the distinction between international, national, and personal political uses of tourism is often blurred. Yet, there have been specific instances in which tourism policy has been used directly to affect personal fortunes without any apparent long-range considerations ...
>
> It is sometimes said in the Philippines there is no such thing as 'conflict of interest', merely 'convergence of interest'. The development of the tourism industry tends to substantiate that observation. Many of the top policymakers have large economic interests in tourism. Not surprisingly, then, many of the new hotel owners were able to secure government funding far in excess of the generous ceiling the president endorsed, though small inns and pension owners could not get even standard bank loans. Now that Manila is severely overbuilt with luxury hotels constructed with cheap and seemingly limitless credit, the same people are complaining in their role as hoteliers that they must renegotiate their loans or they will be unable to meet their payments, leaving the country's banking institutions with 14 hotels to manage.[93]

Of course, whether short-term political and financial gains or corruption is the basis for such tourism 'strategy', the problem is that there is in fact little strategy at all. In such a context the social and other impacts of tourism are not factored into decision making and it is likely that many in the community will unnecessarily suffer as a result.

Regulating tourism in an age of uncertainty: tourism as legal discourse

The defining characteristics of the early twenty-first century appear to be mobility and concern about the sustainability of the environment on the one hand, and the fear attached to confronting 'others' (which somewhat ironically increased mobility delivers) as well as constantly rising expectations with respect to economic well-being globally. In other words we live in an age where on many levels we lead constantly contradictory and confused lives. In this confusion it is often the law that is looked to for cohesion and certainty, or at least the language of the law. It is our contention that the law, although portrayed as the solution in such times, must be seen as part of the problem and its role in facilitating ongoing power inequalities, whether by design or obfuscation, should be a proper basis for critiquing the law's role in understanding the problem of tourism.

In many respects the role of the law is to focus on the individual. Thus while there is a tourism industry, business or policy, it is the individual tourist that tends to gain the attention of the law. We would argue that within this framework there is the partial reconciling of the problem of tourism in that the law suggests that while 'tourism' is a 'good', it is the individual tourist that often creates the problem. But this is the law simply atomising what is essentially a problem with tourism and disguising the process by which tourism constructs its reality. In fact it is more to the point that the tourist can be constructed as either 'exalted' in both tourism discourse and in the law or as part of an underbelly of tourism that calls on the law to both disown and proscribe such behaviour. In effect, these competing definitions of the tourist to which the law in particular directs its focus in regulating tourism simply reaffirm the underlying argument of this book that tourism is a contradictory practice. It is this theme which we particularly wish to carry through this book.

The other theme that is central to the following chapters is the role that discourse plays in regulating and controlling behaviour of tourists and those affected by tourism. Keith Hollinshead has identified Urry's work as indicating – although not always explicitly – how a Foucauldian analysis can be brought to understanding and critiquing the practice of tourism.[94] One of the central problems which has confronted us in writing this book is the apparent lack of 'law' in relation to tourism. Yet we are aware that tourism and its related mobilities are heavily policed, controlled and regulated. Orthodox analyses would contend that the law creates the framework within which tourism is allowed to 'flourish'. But that neo-liberal sense of the role of the law is neither convincing nor credible when we live in an age of surveillance and increased state control of our everyday lives. Simply, there is too much at stake for powerful interests to let tourism 'flourish' or 'wilt' within a basic legal framework.

Hollinshead argues that Urry's work indicates the manner in which Foucault's use of the power of discourse to control and regulate life can also be applied to tourism and leisure activity. In particular he focuses on Urry's *The Tourist Gaze*[95] and explains the manner in which gaze there described renders some aspects of society dominant while others are ignored.[96] As he explains the significance of Urry's work:

> the outlook that Urry tenuously presents is that of a contemporary world increasingly traversed by the disciplining and constraining power of the gaze of urban-industrial expectancy, where an ever widening range of cultural activities and leisure pursuits around the globe are significantly reordered through the taken-for-granted conformities of mass, packaged and brochured travel. Accordingly, one could read Foucauldian Urry as a prophet of the world now very much in part *in custody to tourism*. One could argue that the universalising surveillance (which Urry suggests inhabits the spread of urban-industrial travel) is decidedly fascist in the force of its ethnocentric and essentialising

sublimities and it is notably dangerous, because it is so under-recognised and thereby so easily tolerated. There, quietly and implicitly, lies one's Foucault in one's Urry.[97]

The value of this for our purposes is that it suggests there are various 'subtle' forms of regulation and control at work within tourism. Hollinshead writes of the manner in which 'contemporary people are born into a myriad of regulations, and into a mire of meticulous rules and fussy inspections as the supervisory force of the gaze is contextualised within the smallest fragments of detailed life ... and conceivably within the tourist attractions and travel programmes of that society'.[98] It is this notion of surveillance that underpins the tourist gaze and the manner in which individuals become almost self-policing as they internalise the expected ways of behaving that both explains at times the lack of 'hard law' (it is not needed) while also suggesting a state that is 'supra-legal' in effect. Hollinshead claims:

> the consequence of the structuring presence of such a gaze in, over, and through tourism is the possible development of tourism as its own juridical space, and thereby also the generation of distinct and/or networked subsidiary juridical spaces within tourism. Thus by introducing Foucault's concept of surveillance into tourism, Urry does not so much enable or encourage 'host' or 'foreign' populations to be studied almost as if they were the foreign population acting within the domain of tourism.[99]

Thus the matter becomes one of asking 'what do we repeatedly and systematically privilege in tourism representations and what do we respectedly and systematically deny and frustrate?'[100] This leads Hollinshead to identify a number of implications of the 'tourism panopticon' that he constructs. These include considering how tourist industry discourse controls the lives of host populations through embedded messages about their role, position and status which they then self-impose and the similar process through which tourist guides and brochures also carry such messages to populations and may subjugate them. As Hollinshead puts it, citing Dann,[101] 'the way the use of various languages in and of tourism regulate people and things'.[102]

Thus this must be one aspect of any study of the regulation of tourism. It would be folly to think that only the formal laws of the land would deliver an answer to the question of how tourism is regulated. But we would also take it one further step and suggest that the law itself can form part of this Foucauldian discourse or tourist gaze in that law and legal culture send many messages about mobility, rights and 'others' that are not always directed to tourism but become internalised by individuals and are carried with them as forms of self-discipline during their travel and leisure times. It is that thought also that informs the following chapters.

Notes

1 J. Urry, *Consuming Places* (London, Routledge, 1995), p. 195, cited in G. Shaw and A.M. Williams, *Critical Issues in Tourism: A Geographical Perspective* (2nd edition) (Malden, Blackwell, 2002), p. 3.
2 C. Rojek, *Ways of Escape: Modern Transformations in Leisure and Travel* (London, Macmillan, 1993), p. 200.
3 Ibid.
4 Ibid.
5 Ibid., p. 212.
6 Ibid.
7 Ibid.
8 Ibid., p. 213.
9 On the blurring between work and leisure see Rojek, *Ways of Escape: Modern Transformations in Leisure and Travel*, p. 188.
10 Australian Government, *The Future of Australian Tourism: A Medium to Long Term Strategy for Tourism* (White Paper, Commonwealth of Australia, Canberra, 2003).
11 Ibid., p. 6.
12 Ibid., p. xiii.
13 Ibid., p. xiii.
14 Ibid., p. xvi.
15 Ibid., p. 42.
16 Department for Culture, Media and Sport, *Tomorrow's Tourism: A Growth Industry for the New Millennium* (London, 1999), p. 5.
17 Ibid., pp. 5–6.
18 Ibid., p. 11.
19 Ibid., p. 15.
20 Ibid., p. 61.
21 J. Urry, *The Tourist Gaze* (2nd edition) (London, Sage, 2002), p. 158.
22 Ibid., p. 161.
23 B. Farrell and L. Twining-Ward, 'Seven steps towards sustainability: tourism in the context of new knowledge', *Journal of Sustainable Tourism*, 13(2): 109–22 (2005), at 118.
24 Ibid., p. 109.
25 Ibid.
26 Ibid., p. 110.
27 Ibid. (original emphasis).
28 Ibid. (our emphasis).
29 F. Higgins-Desbiolles, 'More than an "industry": the forgotten power of tourism as a social force', *Tourism Management*, 27 (2006): 1192–1208.
30 Ibid., p. 1193.
31 Ibid., p. 1194.
32 Ibid.
33 S. Wearing, 'Re-centering the self in volunteer tourism' in G.S. Dann (ed.) *The Tourist as a Metaphor of the Social World* (Oxford, CABI, 2002), pp.237–62, p. 238, cited in Higgins-Desbiolles, 'More than an "industry"', p. 1195.
34 Higgins-Desbiolles, 'More than an "industry"', p. 1195.
35 Ibid., p. 1196.
36 Ibid.
37 Ibid.
38 Ibid., pp. 1196–97.

39 P. F. McKean 'Towards a theoretical analysis of tourism: economic dualism and cultural involution in Bali' in V.L. Smith (ed.) *Hosts and Guests: The Anthropology of Tourism* (Philadelphia, University of Pennsylvania Press, 1998), pp. 119–38, p. 133, cited in Higgins-Desbiolles, 'More than an "industry"', p. 1197.
40 Manila Declaration on World Tourism, Preamble.
41 Ibid.
42 Ibid., article 21.
43 Ibid., article 4.
44 Acapulco Documents on the Rights to Holidays 1982, Preamble.
45 Acapulco Documents on the Rights to Holidays 1982, para. 5.
46 Ibid., para. 9(d).
47 Ibid., para. 9(d)(iii).
48 Ibid., para. 17(d) (our emphasis).
49 Workplace Relations Act 1996 (Cth), s.170AF(1) as amended by Workplace Relations Amendment (Work Choices) Act 2005, schedule 1. This legislation was repealed in 2009 by the new Federal Labor Government however similar sections remain in the new Act: see Fair Work Act 2009 (Cth.), ss. 87, 114.
50 Ibid., s. 170AF(2).
51 Ibid., s. 170AF(3).
52 Ibid., s. 170AG.
53 B. Simpson, 'The legal boundaries of tourism: the state versus the marketplace in defining the tourist' in N. Ravenscroft, D. Phillips and M. Bennett (eds) *Tourism and Tourist Attractions: Leisure, Culture and Commerce* (LSA Publication No. 61, 1998), pp. 79–97, at 80.
54 See above pp. 9–12.
55 See above pp. 9–11.
56 Tourism Bill of Rights and Tourist Code 1985, preamble.
57 Ibid.
58 Ibid.
59 Ibid., article 3(e).
60 Ibid., article 4(e).
61 Ibid., article 4(f)
62 Ibid, article 5 (a), though 'without prejudice to any limitative measures taken in the national interest concerning certain areas of the territory'.
63 Ibid., article 5 (b).
64 Ibid., article 5 (d).
65 Ibid., article 7.
66 Ibid., article 6(2).
67 Ibid., article 11(b).
68 Hague Declaration on Tourism 1989, Principle 1(a).
69 Ibid., Principle 2.
70 Ibid., Principle 2(2)(a).
71 Ibid., Principle 2(2)(b).
72 Ibid., Principle 2(2)(c).
73 Ibid., Principle 2(2)(d).
74 Ibid., Principle 2(2)(e) and (f).
75 Ibid., Principle 2(2)(d).
76 Manila Declaration on the Social Impact of Tourism 1997, para.1.
77 Global Code of Ethics for Tourism, preamble.
78 Higgins-Desbiolles, op. cit., p. 1198.
79 Ibid., p. 1199.
80 Global Code of Ethics for Tourism, article 7(1).

81 D.L. Gladstone, *From Pilgrimage to Package Tour: Travel and Tourism in the Third World* (Abingdon, Routledge, 2005).
82 Ibid., p. 195.
83 Australian Tourist Commission Act 1967 (Cth), s.6.
84 Ibid., s.7(e).
85 Canadian Tourism Commission Act 2000, s.5.
86 Hong Kong Tourism Board Ordinance, s. 4.
87 Tourism Australia Act 2004 (Cth), s. 6.
88 Ibid., s. 7(i).
89 G. Shaw and A.M. Williams, *Critical Issues in Tourism: A Geographical Perspective* (Oxford, Blackwell, 1994), chapter 3.
90 Ibid., p. 61, citing P. E. Murphy, *Tourism: a Community Approach* (London, Routledge, 1985).
91 Ibid., p. 64.
92 L. Richter, 'The political uses of tourism', *Journal of Developing Areas*, 14 (1980): 237–57.
93 Ibid., p. 252.
94 K. Hollinshead, 'Surveillance of the worlds of tourism: Foucault and the eye-of-power', *Tourism Management*, 20 (1999): 7–23.
95 J. Urry, *The Tourist Gaze: Leisure and Travel in Contemporary Society* (London, Sage, 1990).
96 Hollinshead, 'Surveillance of the worlds of tourism', p. 9.
97 Ibid., p. 12.
98 Ibid., p. 13.
99 Ibid., pp. 14–15.
100 Ibid., p. 15.
101 G. Dann, *The Language of Tourism – A Sociolinguistic Perspective* (Wallingford, Oxford CAB International, 1996).
102 Hollinshead, 'Surveillance of the worlds of tourism', p. 17.

Part II

Tourism as a just cause

Chapter 2

Establishing the exalted tourist

Open your mind to other cultures and traditions – it will transform your experience, you will earn respect and be more readily welcomed by local people. Be tolerant and respect diversity – observe social and cultural traditions and practices.

(The Responsible Tourist and Traveller, endorsed by
United Nations World Tourism Organisation resolution
A/RES/506(XVI), December 2005)

Of course, the whole thing is, once you cease to be a master, once you throw off your master's yoke, you are no longer human rubbish, you are just a human being, and all the things that adds up to. So, too, with the slaves. Once they are no longer slaves, once they are free, they are no longer noble and exalted; they are just human beings.

(Jamaica Kincaid, *A Small Place* (New York, Farrar,
Straus and Giroux, 1988), p. 81)

Constructing the tourist as a cultural terrorist

It is often said that it is better to be a traveller than a tourist. This statement has much to do with the evolution of mass tourism and the notion of 'authentic' versus 'inauthentic' tourism experiences. Travellers presumably engage with the 'reality' of places, while the tourist consumes a sanitised, and no doubt crass, version of where they happen to be. Crick[1] notes the difference between 'tourism' and 'travelling' as expressed by Boorstin and Fussell:

> Boorstin ... stresses the difference between 'travelling' [with its etymological connection to the notion of work (*travail*)] and 'tourism' (the apotheosis of the pseudo, where passivity rather than activity reigns). Tourism is a form of experience packaged to prevent real contact with others, a manufactured, trivial, unauthentic way of being, a form of travel emasculated, made safe by commercialism. ... For Fussell, to write about tourism is necessarily to write satire, for the 'travel industry' is a

contradiction in terms: Exploration is discovering the undiscovered; travel is at least intended to reveal what history has discovered; tourism, on the other hand, is merely about a world discovered (or even created) by entrepreneurs, packaged and then marketed.[2]

This tends to create a certain amount of confusion about what tourism really is and whether tourism is centrally concerned about 'authentic' experiences after all. It may be questioned whether it matters more that the tourist feels they have 'consumed' what they expected according to the tourist marketing brochures, or that they have experienced something that is 'genuine'. Part of the problem will be whether an authentic experience will be even recognised as one, and indeed whether tourists actually want to be confronted by 'reality':

> Critics of mass tourism point to the manufacture of tourist spectacles, the 'stage authenticity' that extends from contrived 'native' dances in the Third World to the multibillion dollar theme parks in high-income countries. Tourists' search for authenticity is ultimately confounded, however, by the commodification of tourism in modern societies: Authenticity is replaced by staged authenticity – by inauthentic production for the market – and the alienation tourists seek to escape is reproduced in their experience as tourists.[3]

The irony, as Gladstone points out, is that in using tourism as a form of escape from the everyday routine of their lives, tourists in effect escape into other contrived spaces.[4] There is a significant body of literature that highlights the negative consequences for host communities subjected to pleasure-seeking tourists. Tamara Ratz writes:

> The tourist–host relationship is characterised by four major features: it is transitory, unequal and unbalanced, lacks spontaneity and is limited by spatial and temporal constraints. The tourist usually stays in the destination for a short time, so there is no opportunity to develop the superficial relationship into a more meaningful one. The traditional spontaneous hospitality turns into commercial activity. Tourists are on holiday, served by locals, which results in different attitudes and behaviour. The obvious relative wealth of the tourists often leads to exploitative behaviour on the hosts' side.[5]

Ratz identifies the main impacts of the tourist–host relationship as: the 'demonstration affect' – when the hosts' behaviour is modified to imitate tourists; change in language usage in the destination; growth of alcoholism, crime, prostitution and gambling; transformation – revitalisation or commoditisation – of the material and non-material forms of local culture.[6]

She also notes the following impacts of the development of the tourism industry apart from the impact of the tourist–host relationship: the creation of new employment but much of which is seasonal, unskilled and low-paid; abandonment of traditional work patterns can be affected, through, for example, the decline of agricultural occupations; changes in size of demographics of host population; alteration of community structure; increased mobility of women and young adults; development of local infrastructure and increased supply of services and thus increased quality of life for local people.[7]

Ratz would support the proposition that becoming a tourist destination can result in the loss of culture as the type of culture which one will want to present is one which appeals to the tourist – perhaps a case of 'who pays the piper calls the tune'. If the culture that appeals to the tourist is not the same as the traditional fare then there is likely to be pressure to adapt the local version. The consequence of not doing so will be the loss of valuable foreign exchange.

This latter point is important as it indicates where the pressure might come from to change the culture. While individual artists might resist this pressure to adapt, government agencies and other parts of the tourist industry (airlines, hotels, etc.) might apply different forms of pressure to force the process of change. Thus who gains government support for their art, who is provided with exhibition space, where visitors are taken may also be end products of a process which begins with a view of 'what the tourist wants'. In this sense it is about the market – if the aim is to increase foreign exchange then how can one justify any kind of support for those who do not assist in that process?

Kaleo Patterson[8] identifies the way in which the tourism industry in Hawaii has destroyed reefs and fishing grounds as the result of golf-course irrigation and hotel sewage. He also writes about traditional foraging areas from which indigenous people have been prohibited from entering. Rights of access to certain areas can result from the need to create 'safe tourist enclaves' and in so doing remove rights from local people. Patterson also speaks of the desecration of sacred sites.

For Patterson the marketing of Hawaii is that of 'Hula marketing' – the romanticisation of the culture 'to appeal to the fantasies of world travellers'. It becomes difficult to distinguish the 'authentic cultural experience' (often the line contained in marketing brochures) and the real thing:

> Popular images show smiling, flower-adorned girls and hula dancers, exotic moonlit feasts with natives serving hand and foot. This kind of marketing and promotion perpetuates racist and sexist stereotypes that are culturally inappropriate and demeaning. It sells an artificial cultural image with complete disregard for the truth.[9]

It is the reinforcement of the racist and sexist stereotypes that perhaps impact most on local people. The incentive of economic gain is a reason for internalising these roles. The difficulty is then that local people may be very happy to act in the way the brochures project the culture to be. Over time one then has the problem of distinguishing the 'real' culture from the 'artificial' one. But perhaps one thing is certain – a different culture has resulted. The dilemma is to establish whether it is a positive or a negative change.

This might suggest that we do need criteria for evaluating this process and that a sense of history is clearly important to identify what might constitute 'traditional' or 'authentic' practice or experience. It also suggests that to the extent that the 'new' culture (or the culture presented in tourist marketing) is alleged to be racist or sexist some definition of racism or sexism is required. Centrally for a discussion of the power of discourse, there also needs to be consideration of who controls the images which form the basis of marketing campaigns – although this may mean little if local people have internalised a 'false' culture and adapted their roles accordingly.

Patterson asks in relation to Hawaii how tourism can be reshaped according to the community's needs. He quotes from an international conference on tourism sponsored by the Third World Ecumenical Coalition on Tourism:

> Contrary to the claims of its promoters, tourism, the biggest industry in Hawaii, has not benefited the poor and oppressed native Hawaiian people. Tourism is not an indigenous practice; nor has it been initiated by the native Hawaiian people. Rather, tourism promotion and development has been directly controlled by those who already control wealth and power, nationally and internationally. Tourism ... expands upon the evil of an economy which perpetuates the poverty of native Hawaiian people and which leads to sexual and domestic violence and substance abuse among native Hawaiian people. In addition, sexism and racism are closely interlinked with tourism. In short, tourism, as it exists today, is detrimental to the life, well-being and spiritual health of native Hawaiian people. If not checked and transformed, it will bring grave harm, not only to the native Hawaiian people, but to all people living in Hawaii.[10]

Shankland[11] provides an example of what Ratz might describe as host people transforming their culture to accommodate the tastes and desires of the tourist. He writes about Indian villagers in Paraguay who have changed their traditional dances for the benefit of tourists. He also points out that those who voice this concern represent official stances on tourism which on the one hand wants to market indigenous culture while at the same time indigenous people are being dispossessed of their lands.

He also cites the example of a Carnival in Bolivia where the cost of 'authentic' costumes has become so high that traditional indigenous dancers can no longer afford to take part. In Rio the Carnival included more and more white models and imported soap stars (what Shankland refers to as the increase of 'flesh' on display) – to appeal to the increasingly middle-class audience – resulting in the exclusion of Afro-Brazilian residents of the shanty towns. It thus became less of a popular festival and more one linked to the marketing of a particular image of the city. It led to a change in the nature of the city. As Shankland observes, the exclusion of many local people led to increased crime in Rio and the scaring away of many visitors allowing the Carnival to be reclaimed by the local population.[12]

Shankland also refers to the complexities surrounding the manner in which the Green movement has co-opted certain indigenous peoples as symbols of a more appropriate approach to tourism. On the one hand the idea of appealing to environmentally aware tourists through attempts to better understand indigenous people and their relationship with their natural environment has many positive features. It might be that such awareness can be the key to limiting the damage caused by international tourism. But it is also easy to resort to half-baked understandings of such people and their cultures.[13] Shankland notes the irony of holding an international conference on ecotourism in the middle of a region where government is systematically destroying rainforest and does not acknowledge indigenous land rights. He also refers to the 'invasion' of one tribe's area by visitors clamouring to see indigenous people in authentic dress – when in fact the dress came to them from an earlier period of colonisation.[14]

Importantly Crick notes the lack of social-science research on tourism. This raises questions about the amount of thought that has been invested in thinking about the various impacts of tourism on local communities. He identifies, citing Boissevain, 'four biases' in the images of tourism which exist:[15] the 'grossly inadequate framework of economic analysis'; the lack of the local voice; the failure to distinguish the social consequences of tourism from other processes of change going on in a society independently; and the noble-savage syndrome.

Crick also questions some of the supposed benefits thought to accrue from tourism, such as increased cultural understanding of the tourist's culture. He writes that because tourism has more to do with hedonism and conspicuous consumption tourists are poor cultural carriers. He notes:

> Tourism is very much about *our* culture, not about *their* culture or our desire to learn about it. This explains the presence in guide books of sites and signs that have little genuine historic or living connection to a culture but that exist simply as markers in the touristic universe. As Barthes remarks, perceptively, travel guidebooks are actually instruments of blindness. They do not, in other words, tell one about another culture at all.[16]

Crick responds to the claimed 'peace and understanding' benefit of tourism by referring to a 1980 conference in Manila where the need to preserve

Philippine culture was asserted while at that time the city was said to have 10,000 prostitutes 'at the disposal of international tourists and members of the local elite'.[17]

He also refers to the suggestion that international tourism narrows the mind rather than broadens it. The claim here is that travellers are indifferent to the social reality of their hosts and empirical evidence is that individual perceptions are replaced with stereotypes. Crick suggests that the mystifying images promoted by the tourism industry are part of the industry itself and should not prevent a 'realistic and empirical analysis of this industry and its consequences'.[18] Thus the image can be easily accepted by the nation that promotes it and so stunt its own development and culture. The images are not real. As Crick points out poverty does not sell. Paradise does. But the Paradise does not exist: he refers to brochures that proclaim the Caribbean as 'the Best of the Mediterranean on Mexico's Pacific'. The Victorian Tourist Commission markets Victoria as different parts of the world. South Australia is marketed as Australia's Mediterranean. Crick might say this is all nonsense. No such place exists, except in the minds of the promoters and those who believe the images.

When the United Nations Conference on Environment and Development (the Earth Summit) in 1992 adopted Agenda 21 to create a more sustainable future, the travel and tourism industry responded with its support. The then Secretary-General of the World Tourism Organisation remarked:

> Tourism growth is one of the greatest success stories of our times but, in recent years, there have been increasing warning signs: the over-saturation and deteriorations of some destinations, the overwhelming of some cultures, bottlenecks in transport facilities, and a growing resentment by residents in some destinations.[19]

This may represent the extent to which the notion of the pleasure-seeking tourist had become embedded in the discourse of tourism. The challenge of climate change may have accelerated the shift to conceptualising tourism in terms more noble, although as we shall see the existence of other discourses of tourism and the tourist were not invented at that time.

Tourism as a noble pursuit

There is a broader basis for understanding the nature of the tourist experience that relates to the various types of tourist that can be identified and at least calls into question the various critiques discussed above. As Gladstone notes, the idea of the 'pleasure tourist' – essentially a Western tourist – is in its own terms problematic as many people also travel for business or to visit family and friends.[20] His project though is to highlight tourism in the Third World and he points to the large number of non-Western pilgrim and religious travellers.[21] Gladstone also acknowledges that the purpose in travelling for the pilgrim and that of the pleasure-seeking tourist may be very similar – to step outside their usual lives.[22] This leads to broader typologies that centre on how tourism relates to the person's commitment to the values of Western society.[23] Thus 'recreational tourism' might evidence a commitment to such values and the purpose of tourism for such a tourist is to rest and re-energise, to re-enter the 'capitalist' fray.[24] The 'diversionary tourist', on the other hand, uses tourism to escape their mundane and alienating life.[25] 'Experiential tourists', while alienated from the values of their society, utilise tourism to find 'meaning in the lives of others' and reassurance that others live authentically.[26] 'Experimental tourists' are similar but actually engage in the lives of those others in a search to find a new way to live for themselves,[27] while 'existential tourists' commit a new set of values in that other place, perhaps similar to the pilgrim.[28]

One can see that in identifying these various motivations for travel there are in effect many types of tourist and thus the notion of the 'ugly' tourist who visits other places with little regard for the cultural norms and practices of those places is but one face of tourism. In the alternative typologies not underpinned by the pleasure motivation one can see the genesis of the exalted or noble tourist – one that travels not for pleasure but for purpose. Thus the Preamble to the Global Code of Ethics for Tourism[29] recites the case for tourism as a noble pursuit that recognises:

> the important dimension and role of tourism as a positive instrument towards the alleviation of poverty and the improvement of the quality of life for all people, its potential to make a contribution to economic and social development, especially of the developing countries, and its emergence as a vital force for the promotion of international understanding, peace and prosperity …

Nevertheless, in spite of these noble sentiments it will be questioned whether this discourse has been significantly influential in regulating the behaviour of both tourists and hosts. While that is a common refrain advanced by those such as Crick above, it is also easy to underestimate the power of discourse in regulating behaviour. Only a few years prior to the adoption of the Global Code of Ethics for Tourism the national body responsible for promoting tourism in Australia was still identifying the need to convince the population of the value of tourism. The Chairman of the Australian Tourist Commission wrote in the Commission's 1996–97 Annual Report:

> The nation is still to fully appreciate the value of tourism, and raising tourism's profile at home will be a key focus in years ahead. Australia must realise that close to 700,000 people are directly dependent on jobs from tourism and that inbound tourism is our largest foreign exchange

earner, injecting \$16.1 billion of foreign exchange into our economy in 1996/97.[30]

This statement is significant as it indicates that the Australian Tourist Commission then saw its role as not just that of promoter of Australia as a tourist destination but also as being charged with educating the Australian community about the value of tourism. One could be critical and suggest that this statement only speaks to the economic benefits of tourism and in that sense is narrowly framed. While this is true, it does nevertheless indicate a process by which the tourism body indicates that a tourism discourse that presents its benefits will necessarily change – and regulate – behaviour in the tourism context.

We are all tourists now

In Australia, an important part of the transformation towards creating tourism as a noble pursuit was the co-option of all members of society into the tourism agenda. While in the year 2008–9 Australia managed to sustain growth in earnings from international tourism in spite of economic downturn and the swine flu outbreak,[31] it was a downturn in domestic tourism that caused the national tourism body to promote the benefits of taking a holiday. This was marketed as 'No Leave, No Life' and was based on the recognition that Australian workers had accumulated 123 million days in unused annual leave.[32] Much of the campaign focussed on the important health benefits of a proper work/life balance and was directed towards employers as well as employees.[33] Of course, such a campaign falls squarely within the remit of Tourism Australia under the Tourism Australia Act 2004 (Cth) as the Act states its functions to include that of increasing 'awareness of potential domestic travellers of Australia as a place to travel'.[34] Clearly much of the tenor of this authority's activities is to create and maintain economic benefits from tourism and the domestic campaign can be viewed as a simple attempt to cushion the industry from a possible decline in inbound international tourism by generating more local tourism.

But this campaign also creates a discourse around tourism that focuses on the importance of leisure travel for workers while saying nothing about the broader human right to leisure mentioned in Chapter 1. In part this is caused by the legal constraints placed on Tourism Australia by its enabling legislation, although there is nothing in the terms of the Act that would in itself limit the meaning of 'potential traveller' to only the affluent or those in paid employment. However, the sense that tourism is an 'industry' that is measured in terms of its economic benefits – as they *can* be measured – while its social contribution is more difficult to measure has arguably led to the 'right to leisure' of all people to be absent from tourism discourse in

Australia. In other words, there is little in the current discourse on tourism that constructs tourism as a human right.

That said, the invisibility of those not in the paid workforce (or in low-paid and casual employment with limited access to paid holidays) has still led to a discourse which suggests that we are 'all' tourists or potential tourists. Implicit in the 'No Leave, No Life' campaign is that to become a tourist in one's own country is almost patriotic as it benefits the country, the economy and one's family. In other words, the right to tourism is transformed from a right to a duty and so a new discourse is born.

The World Tourism Organization and the construction of the exalted tourist

This shift in how tourism is constructed is most evident in the creation of the Global Code of Ethics for Tourism.[35] As mentioned in Chapter 1, the Tourism Bill of Rights and Tourist Code which can be regarded as a predecessor to the more recent Global Code of Ethics stressed the right to leisure, the manner in which tourism can promote world peace and international understanding, free movement of tourists, and mutual respect between tourists and hosts.[36] This was then followed by the Manila Declaration on the Social Impacts of Tourism 1997[37] which stressed the need to eradicate the negative impacts of tourism and also carried with it an agreement to work towards a Global Code of Ethics. The Global Code of Ethics in its very name suggests a shift away from 'rights' towards ethical duties. Thus while the Code's preamble reiterates the role of tourism as a force for peace and international understanding it is the recognition of the effects of tourism on the environment[38] that then introduces a new discourse into the expectations placed on tourist behaviour. Thus the Global Code of Ethics states the new aim to promote responsible, sustainable and universally accessible tourism in the framework of the right of all persons to use their free time for leisure pursuits or travel with respect for the choices of society of all peoples.[39]

As also discussed in chapter one[40] this is to occur within the context of a 'market economy, private enterprise and free trade' in a manner which creates wealth and employment.[41] The potential for contradictory outcomes has also already been made in the previous chapter with respect to the assertion of the right to travel on the one hand and the sustainability of the environment on the other.[42] But in its own terms the Global Code of Ethics clearly strengthens the notion of the *responsible* tourist – as opposed to the tourist who claims rights – as a means to legitimate the obvious tension between travel and sustainability. This is the creation of the exalted tourist, who travels for noble purposes and who does so in a manner sensitive to the needs of the environment.

Thus the Global Code of Ethics itself is not even written in a 'Bill of Rights' format. Instead it appears as a series of articles which simply state and then discuss various 'aims' of tourism all within the context of responsible and ethical behaviour. The order of the articles is also significant as it begins with 'tourism's contribution to mutual understanding and respect between peoples and societies'[43] then addresses 'tourism as a vehicle for individual and collective fulfilment'[44] before moving to 'tourism, a factor of sustainable development'.[45] The right to tourism and the liberty of tourist movements appear towards the end of the document in articles 7 and 8.

Clearly, the significant change in recent years for tourism has been the challenge presented by an increased concern with the environment and climate change. Thus the Global Code of Ethics constructs tourism as not just concerned with sustainability, but as one with it. In article 2 therefore, tourism is presented as being 'a factor of sustainable development' and not as being in possible conflict with it. A close reading of the article also indicates the manner in which tourism is constructed, not simply as something that has to accommodate sustainable design, but as something which is almost a necessary pre-condition for its achievement. Thus while article (3) begins by stating the overarching principle that 'all stakeholders in tourism development should safeguard the natural environment with a view to achieving sound continuous and sustainable economic growth geared to satisfying equitably the needs and aspirations of present and future generations'[46] the rest of the article proceeds to extol the manner in which tourism can actually save the environment. Article 3 (2) thus proclaims:

> All forms of tourism development that are conducive to saving rare and precious resources, in particular water and energy, as well as avoiding so far as possible waste production, should be given priority and encouraged by national, regional and local public authorities.[47]

Likewise, article 3(3) calls for the staggering of tourist and visitor flows 'so as to reduce the pressure of tourism activity on the environment and enhance its beneficial impact on the tourism industry and the local economy'.[48] But this is ambiguous. This may be read as acknowledging that tourism degrades the environment and that staggering visits will slow this process down and hence keep the industry in a location viable for a longer period than would otherwise be that case. Or it could be interpreted to mean that staggering visits will preserve the environment. It is suggested that the latter reading is how the dominant discourse[49] would prefer it to be read. This is evident from the last two paragraphs of article 3 which stress the role tourism can play in the protection and preservation of natural heritage. Thus it is stated:

> Tourism infrastructure should be designed and tourism activities programmed in such a way as to protect the natural heritage composed of ecosystems and biodiversity and to preserve endangered species of wildlife; the stakeholders in tourism development, and especially

professionals, should agree to the imposition of limitations or constraints on their activities when these are exercised in particularly sensitive areas: desert, polar or high mountain regions, coastal areas, tropical forests or wetlands, propitious to the creation of nature reserves or protected areas.[50]

Of course, it seems accepted that there will be little discussion of the meaning of 'protect' or 'preserve' in this document in the context of tourist development. What we mean by this is not the refrain of the cynical – that such documents as the Global Code of Ethics pander to well meaning but ultimately unattainable sentiment. Such a critique misses the point of such documents and simply accepts that they are actually designed to achieve change – in this particular passage the preservation and the protection of the natural environment. This might be partly achieved by default, but the real purpose of such documents as the Global Code of Ethics is to provide a discourse that establishes a positive relationship between tourism and the environment through legal 'tricks of the trade'. In this instance the 'trick' is the transformation of the process of 'protection' and 'preservation' from apparently scientific evaluations to matters of legal interpretation. Thus, if a tourist development relocates wildlife to a new location nearby, the question of whether that action has actually 'protected' and 'preserved' it becomes a juridical point.

By making the actions of the tourism industry accountable to a legal document the matter becomes not just one of interpretation but also permits the possibility of a positive construction being placed on the role of tourism and the tourist in protecting the environment. This can be achieved even by one carefully placed word in a paragraph. For example, article 3(5) states:

> Nature tourism and ecotourism are recognized as being *particularly* conducive to enriching and enhancing the standing of tourism, provided they respect the natural heritage and local populations and are in keeping with the carrying capacity of the sites.[51]

The insertion of the word 'particularly' elevates the role of tourism in environmental tourism, and indeed as the paragraph states quite explicitly, 'enriching and enhancing the standing of tourism'. This is the interesting aspect of this statement in the Global Code of Ethics in that it regards the outcome from the pursuit of certain forms of tourism (most usually associated with preserving and protecting the environment from the impacts of tourism) as the standing of tourism being raised, not in a better environment.

All of this reflects to some extent the manner, as Burns suggests, in which tourism now attempts to meet the paradoxical roles 'of eradicating poverty and delivering development through growth and redistribution'.[52] In response to the notion that good tourism planning can maximise the benefits and minimise the negative impacts of tourism he comments '[i]n a broad sense this fails to take account of the complexities of globalizing markets'.[53] Burns also posits two models of tourism development. The first model, the 'tourism first' approach regards development as primary and tourism as an industry based on an underpinning philosophy of the free market as the driver of distribution.[54] The opposing model is that of 'development first'. This regards tourism as a system underpinned by an approach which places culture in tourism rather than commodifying it and which regards 'tourism as part of a package to improve economic alternatives enabling equitable distribution'.[55]

These two approaches are clearly in potential conflict. As Burns says:

> one of the key tensions of tourism discourse [is] the viability of alternative forms of tourism such as ecotourism taking place without the presence of other, more intensive forms of tourism. In this case, viability refers not only to commercial sustainability of individual enterprises, but to the long-term potential of an industry comprised of a number of small-scale, village-located tourism enterprises to deliver what most governments want from tourism, including foreign exchange earnings, tax revenues, employment, and a measure of stability.[56]

What one needs to ask is the extent to which the Global Code of Ethics is designed to obscure this tension rather than resolve it. Indeed, the underlying principles of the Code would appear to suggest a commitment to the free market and the notion of tourism as an industry, while Burns' analysis would suggest that this is the very model that makes a more sustainable and equitable form of tourism difficult to achieve. Yet the language of the Global Code of Ethics displays a confidence that tourism can be elevated to the status of (almost) saviour of the environment.

Extending the exalted tourist

The Global Code of Ethics is not alone in creating the discourse of the exalted state of tourism. In 2004 the World Tourism Organization created an Inventory of Codes of Practice and Similar Charters in the Tourism Industry Addressing Ethical and Sustainability Issues.[57] The inventory listed fifty such documents. These codes cover a range of areas, from environmental protection and sustainable development to codes of ethics for tourists and those organising tours. In broad terms they reflect the same concerns and issues raised by the Global Code of Ethics. But they also confront the same criticism – are they to be read as aspirational and educative statements that do more to enhance the standing of the tourist than change practices, or do they actually become a part of a process of advancing a 'better' society?

It is difficult to disagree with the sentiment of many of these codes, but we would also argue that they need to be read as part of a wider discourse which seeks to exalt the tourist. In this context the emphasis on certain words can be stressed. For example, the National Audubon Society in the United States has a travellers' ethic that all its tours must subscribe to. This ethic includes statements such as:

Wildlife and its habitat must not be disturbed

Fragile habitats must not be stressed. Trails will be followed. Plants will be left to grow.

In delicate habitats, vegetation destruction and rock slides can easily be caused by the trampling of too many people. Mosses, lichens, and certain wildflowers and grasses must not be walked upon – they may take as much as 100 years or more to regenerate. It is the obligation of the tour company and the naturalist leaders to promote a "stay on the trail" policy. No responsible tour operator or naturalist should allow the removal or picking of plant specimens or other ground cover. Introduction of exotic plant species must be avoided.

Coral reefs take anywhere from several years to several decades to regenerate. Therefore, the National Audubon Society insists that all of its tour operators provide the broadest protection possible for this underwater life form. Destruction of any part of any coral reef calls for the greatest censure.

Animal behavior will not be inhibited. Because many of the most well subscribed tours are operated during various animals' breeding seasons, tour operators and leaders should establish and always maintain at least minimum distances from these animals ... [58]

It is the direct and assertive manner of this document that sets its tone. 'Trails will be followed. Plants will be left to grow.' This has more the sense of a graduation address where the wise elder is sending the young on their life crusade than a document that is seeking to address the reality of tourist behaviour. For this is the paradox of such documents. While they suggest that tourism can (and will be!) done responsibly, their existence owes much to the recognition that many tourist practices have failed (and still do!) to meet these expectations.

Another passage from the National Audubon Society travel ethic states:

The experience a tourist gains in traveling with Audubon must enrich his or her appreciation of nature, conservation, and the environment.

Every trip to a wilderness area must be led by experienced, well-trained, responsible naturalists and guides. These naturalists should have a solid background in the various habitats to be visited, the flora and fauna contained there, and the sensitive nature of those habitats. These naturalists and guides must be able to provide proper supervision of the visitors, prevent disturbances to the area, answer questions of the visitors regarding the flora and fauna of the area, and present the conservation issues relevant to the area.[59]

Clearly, this can be read as an attempt to address the criticism that tourism provides an escape for affluent people from their everyday existence and does little to enhance their understanding of the places they visit. In that case, tourists fail to achieve an increased understanding of the world as a precursor to agitating for change in the living conditions or practices in those places they visit. They colonise rather than engage with those areas. But is there an alternative reading of this ethical statement? The clue may be in the word 'traveling' for it is the opportunity that this society presents in its tours to provide a more 'enriching' experience that distinguishes it from mass tourism. Here we have travellers, not really tourists at all who visit places 'responsibly' and who gain from the insights of the guides. This is the exalted tourist pure and simple, who ironically needs the mass tourist, the cultural 'terrorist' with which we began this chapter in order to define what he or she is not. In many ways the exalted tourist is the 'anti-tourist'.[60]

The International Institute for Peace Through Tourism's Credo of the Peaceful Traveler has the tone of an evangelical epistle:

> Grateful for the opportunity to travel and experience the world and because peace begins with the individual, I affirm my personal responsibility and commitment to:
>
> Journey with an open mind and gentle heart
> Accept with grace and gratitude the diversity I encounter
> Revere and protect the natural environment which sustains all life
> Appreciate all cultures I discover
> Respect and thank my hosts for their welcome
> Offer my hand in friendship to everyone I meet
> Support travel services that share these views and act upon them and,
> By my spirit, words and actions, encourage others to travel the world in peace.

This is not to suggest that such a credo is in itself negative, but does it have any meaning without a sense that many, or even most, tourists travel with little understanding about the role tourism might play in promoting world peace? Clearly to 'sign' this credo is to affirm a commitment to certain forms of behaviour and in doing so gain entry into the status of the exalted tourist.

Similar approaches can be taken to deconstructing the codes initiated by commercial organisations such as hotel chains. A common critique of those codes is that they make good business sense and are perhaps cynical attempts to capture a sector of the market that is concerned about sustainability, social justice or equitable development. Yet even if we put to one side the rejoinder that this critique may be partially untrue (to the extent that corporate social responsibility does assist in creating more just outcomes) the motives may be secondary in either case if for the corporation involved the 'feel good' factor of attaining some exalted status plays a more central role than the outcome. Corporations, after all, are made up of people.

One example of the application of corporate social responsibility at work in tourism is that of ACCOR, one of the largest hotel corporations in the world with 4000 hotels in 100 countries and reported annual sales of $US12 billion.[61] ACCOR under the banner 'as guests of the earth, we welcome the world' has an Environment Charter which lists a number of areas where they seek to limit the effects of their hotels' operations on the environment. It begins with a section on 'informing and raising awareness' ('raise the hotel's staff awareness of the environment', 'integrate the preservation of the environment in all jobs', 'make our guests aware of environmental issues') and then proceeds to specify various specific practices to reduce energy use. These include 'use energy-efficient refrigerators in bedrooms', 'use energy-efficient air-conditioning systems' and 'install solar panels for heating swimming pools'. Other sections of the charter relate to conserving water, recycling waste, eliminating appliances that contain CFCs and reducing the use of insecticides and weed killers.[62] ACCOR also states a commitment to supporting local development (such as sourcing its produce locally), protecting children (it is a signatory to the Code of Conduct for the Protection of Children from Sexual Exploitation in Travel and Tourism), has committed to fighting HIV and malaria, and seeks to provide hotel guests with healthy meal options to fight obesity.[63]

The extent to which such a Charter or commitments are successful may be debated. Indeed, ACCOR's commitments to local development did not prevent it being criticised in February 2009 for building a new hotel in Sarawak, Malaysia with a company that has been involved in logging in the area and attacks on indigenous communities.[64] Nevertheless, after ACCOR was criticised for failing its own standards it was then reported to have set conditions for its future involvement in the project.[65] But this is secondary to the effect such standards have on the construction of tourism regardless of their success in achieving their stated aims. Aspirations such as those committed to by ACCOR have the immediate effect of suggesting that tourism can do good and can be done in a positive manner. There is after all no suggestion that the hotel chain will encourage people not to travel. In a real sense continued travel is integral to its business success. And for those that travel, to do so with a sense of their exalted status as travellers who do so with sensitivity to social and environmental justice will reap rewards not just for ACCOR but also for the traveller's self-worth.

Regulating uncertainties: ethical travel in an age of terrorism, climate change and swine flu

As we approach the end of the first decade of the twenty-first century there is, however, the potential for the notion of tourism as a noble pursuit to unravel. Ironically, perhaps, it is the increased mobility which authors such as Urry use to proclaim the end of tourism – in a conceptual sense – that has spurned the possibility of the end of the noble tourist in a real sense. This has led to new uncertainties in the world which seriously undermine the philosophical underpinnings of the exalted tourist.

The first uncertainty is the 'rise' of terrorism since September 11, 2001. Of course, terrorism did not begin on that day but there is little doubt that in an age of mass tourism any strike at the major means of conveyance of tourists in the modern age, the jet airliner, will cause anxiety to both tourist and the tourism industry.[66] As a consequence, record amounts of money have been poured into aviation security – $40 billion in the United States alone according to one recent report.[67] The problem for the tourist industry has been that even after such expenditure the risks seem no less large, as an attempt to bring down a plane on Christmas Eve, 2009 over Detroit illustrated. While some areas of security have been improved this event caused some to comment in the United States that:

> a review of government audits and interviews with experts inside and outside the government also shows that the system has been slow to make even bigger changes because of a balky bureaucracy, fickle politics and, at times, airline industry opposition. It has also squandered tens of millions of dollars on faulty technology, like high-tech "puffer" machines that repeatedly broke down and flunked the most basic test: they failed to detect some explosives.[68]

The same news report also suggested to aim for total security was unrealistic:

> "It is a fool's errand to try to make the aviation system terrorist proof," said Mr. Hawley, who helped start the T.S.A. [Transportation Security Administration] and then ran it until this past January. "The only way to do that is ground the airplanes."[69]

The idea that the airline system can *never* be safe must be anathema for the tourism industry. The ideology of the security services must be to aim for safety and the Transportation Security Administration sets out its philosophy on its website:

> We are your neighbors, friends and relatives. We are 50,000 security officers, inspectors, directors, air marshals and managers who protect the

nation's transportation systems so you and your family can travel safely. We look for bombs at checkpoints in airports, we inspect rail cars, we patrol subways with our law enforcement partners, and we work to make all modes of transportation safe.[70]

But as with our earlier discussion of corporate commitment to ethical travel, it would be folly to judge the effects of such security services simply in terms of their stated aims. Clearly, one effect of a heightened concern with terrorism is to create a 'suspicious' tourist that now elevates the security officer – 'we are your neighbors, friends and relatives' – to an exalted position over the foreign cultures and practices one encounters travelling. The credo of the peaceful traveller has been replaced with the credo of the TSA official:

> I am the face of TSA.
> I use innovation, my experience, and state-of-the-art technology to protect the traveling public.
> I respect the individual needs of each traveler, carrying out my duties with dignity, courtesy and integrity.
> I am intensely committed to ensuring fair treatment in the screening process.
> I am the frontline of defense, drawing on my imagination to creatively protect America from harm.
> I am a Transportation Security Officer.[71]

Respect for the values of other cultures has been replaced with the need to respect the role of the security official. That is not to say the values of the peaceful traveller have been abandoned – they have become incorporated into the values of the security official. The core values of the TSA are:

Integrity

We are a people of integrity who respect and care for others.
We are a people who conduct ourselves in an honest, trustworthy and ethical manner.
We are a people who gain strength from the diversity of our cultures.

Innovation

We are a people who embrace and stand ready for change.
We are a people who are courageous and willing to take on new challenges.
We are a people with an enterprising spirit, striving for innovations, who accept the risk-taking that come with it.

Team Spirit

We are a people who are open, respectful and dedicated to making others better.

We are people who have a passion for challenge, success and being on a winning team.

We are a people who will build teams around our strengths.[72]

Cultural diversity thus shifts from what one learns from others to the source of a more imaginative security service. The insights from having different cultural perspectives are now presumably an aid in assessing suspicious behaviour in others rather than acknowledging difference. There is also the likelihood that the fear of terrorist attack while travelling will turn many towards staying in their own countries for leisure.[73] Thus in times of uncertainty there seems to be some acknowledgment that people will turn inwards rather than look outwards motivated by peace and tolerance. But even this fear of the 'external' threat that leads to a disinclination to travel must be weighed against the fear of domestic terrorism. Such fears are already well known in the United Kingdom, Europe and the United States. In Australia, the 'Sea–Air Gap' which in the past has reassured Australia that distance from world centres offered protection has now been said to no longer exist.[74]

Strong border control measures are essential in securing Australia against external terror threats. But the terrorist threat to Australia does not only come from external sources. It can also come from people living and working in Australia.

Although we have much greater control of our security at home than abroad, the threat of the unknown remains. We have identified and successfully disrupted the activities of some groups but we must remain alert and adaptable to deal with new threats should they emerge.[75]

The 'threat of the unknown' can have two effects on travel and tourism. There is, on the one hand, the fatalist who may take the view that one may as well travel anyway, that the terrorist 'should not be allowed to win'. On the other hand, as many reports acknowledge, terrorism does affect tourism, causing many people to avoid travel or alter their destinations. But it is rare in the current climate to consider the cultural impact of the 'threat of the unknown'. To the extent that many of the terrorist attacks of recent years have been associated with extreme Islamic groups, there is the obvious potential for this threat to be equated with a fear of those who are non-Western. Thus for the Western tourist this is not a climate conducive to regarding tourism as a mechanism for increased cultural tolerance. Tourism can readily become a context for cultural suspicion. This is in spite of official statements which call for tolerance as, while they blame 'extremists' for advocating terrorism it places the debate in terms of extremism as practised by certain groups:

> In defending our values, we must make it clear that we will not resile from our commitment to tolerance, openness, freedom and equality. We must not let the terrorists turn Australians against each other. The government will continue to make it clear that this is not a campaign against Muslims or against Islam. There is a clear distinction between the vast majority of moderate and tolerant Muslims and the tiny minority who carry out acts of terrorism in the name of Islam.[76]

It is a catch-22 for tourism. To regard tourism as a vehicle for world peace requires tolerance and understanding of difference. But it is a (small) part of that different group (to Westerners) that represents the threat. The problem is that when travelling, how do we know which part the 'other' person is from?

While terrorism makes it difficult to maintain support for the exalted tourist based upon cultural tolerance, climate change possibly creates an even bigger challenge to the exalted tourist based on environmental sensitivity. While many tourists may feel threatened by terrorism, few in reality will be affected. But all travellers affect the environment. The act of travelling contributes to environmental degradation in some way, given current awareness of climate change and its causes.

In 2007 the Davos Declaration[77] called upon governments, the tourism industry and consumers to take various actions towards limiting the effects of tourism on the climate. For the tourism industry this included taking action to 'promote and undertake investments in energy-efficiency tourism programmes and use of renewable energy resources, with the aim of reducing the carbon footprint of the entire tourism sector', to 'seek to achieve increasingly carbon free environments by diminishing pollution through design, operations and market responsive mechanisms' and 'raise awareness among customers and staff on climate change impacts and engage them in response processes'.[78] There is the temptation to label this as well-meaning rhetoric (engage customers in 'response processes'!) but again we return to our contention that such documents do actively affect the discourse of tourism. Here again is the exalted view of tourism – if only the industry can take the correct action, then it may actually assist in the reduction of global warming.

For consumers, the Davos Declaration was more limited:

> In their choices for travel and destination, tourists should be encouraged to consider climate, economic, societal and environmental impacts of their options before making a decision and, where possible, to reduce their carbon footprint, or offset emissions that cannot be reduced directly.
>
> In their choices of activities at the destination, tourists should also be encouraged to opt for environmentally-friendly activities that reduce

their carbon footprint as well as contribute to the preservation of the natural environment and cultural heritage.[79]

There is here still the refrain of choice, consistent with the commitment to market responsive mechanisms. And how much more exalted can the tourist be than to be expected to do the right thing in relation to reducing global warming? Certainly, there is no suggestion here that the 'right' action might be not to travel at all. That this is not an action governments can currently promote is illustrated by a speech given by the United Kingdom's Minister for Culture and Tourism, Margaret Hodge, to the UN World Tourism Organization's Ministers' Summit in 2007. In that speech she said:

> It is absolutely not for the Government to deny people the right to travel or to deny the industry the opportunity to respond to that demand for travel. So we face the very difficult task of trying to square the circle between people's desire to travel and the opportunities this brings, the need to reduce and minimise the adverse impacts of aviation use and indeed growth ...
>
> And people travelling around the world, jetting off on holiday contributes to climate change. The tourism industry fuels around 5% of global CO2 emissions. And it is often at the sharp end of bad publicity about the effects that flying, for example, has on the climate. But for every negative news story, there should be a positive one too because a lot of work is being done by the tourism industry to reduce its greenhouse gas emissions and the industry's carbon footprint ...
>
> Of course it's a huge challenge. But it is also a huge opportunity for the tourism industry and for all of us. It's an opportunity to create new jobs in for example, the sustainable energy sector; to address energy security; for our economy to become more productive as it becomes more energy efficient; and to improve quality of life as we find less polluting ways of getting around ...
>
> We have also been working hard with our tourism businesses to reduce their impacts on the environment. Buildings are responsible for approximately 40% of the carbon emissions in the UK, with non-residential buildings responsible for approximately half of this and we are actively encouraging those who provide accommodation and visitor attractions to take a long hard look at their activities to see how this can be reduced ...
>
> But in taking this work forward we must not lose sight of the fact that tourism is a major contributor to economies, especially in developing countries.
>
> In 2006, international tourist receipts totalled 733 billion US Dollars.
>
> That is important business. What we must ensure therefore is that tourism grows – as it inevitably will – in a sustainable way.[80]

This is the paradox in discussions about tourism and climate change. In seeking to reduce greenhouse-gas emissions, the state is not prepared to support a reduction in growth. Instead, it must present the tourism industry as 'smart' and able to accommodate growth within a framework of environmental responsibility. This also requires the state to present growth in tourism as essential for poverty reduction. Yet this has been a long-standing criticism of tourism, that many of the profits are repatriated away from the non-developed countries which receive tourists and back to the affluent nations. Of course, the World Tourism Organization has attempted to interrupt that from continuing, but it has not been suggested, as far as we are aware, that equitable distribution of tourism profits has been achieved.

What remains is a bundle of aspirational discourse and 'concern'. Research by Tourism Australia in 2008 suggested that while many tourists professed concern about environmental degradation, only a small proportion actually acted on that concern although it was becoming increasingly influential:

> While there is clear evidence of consumers' increased concern with climate change and environmental degradation throughout the world, this is yet to translate into clear actions, particularly when it comes to changing their holiday habits.
>
> To date, the majority of consumers are playing their part through day-to-day actions such as reducing water usage and recommending more responsible practices to their friends and relatives. However, the proportion of people who claim they will eventually change their habits (e.g. participating in offset schemes and purchasing more environmentally friendly transport) is growing.
>
> The Japanese market is yet to act on any environmental concern with only 1 in 5 people reducing their personal water usage and less than 1 in 10 having taken any action on any other of the issues measured.[81]

In the case of Australia the need for aviation as a means of travel to support the tourism industry is perhaps more pronounced than in other parts of the world given the distance of Australia from other affluent countries. This creates considerable tension given the reality that the extent to which technology can deliver reductions in emissions to offset the 'inevitable' growth in tourism is questionable. As one government report noted:

> Australian tourism is dependent on transport for tourist access to destinations. The aviation sector continues to implement measures to reduce aviation GHG emissions. Aircraft are 70 per cent more efficient than they were 40 years ago, and further efficiency improvements can be made through aircraft design, engine efficiency and operational practices. However, the growth in demand for aviation is forecast to

exceed technological improvements and, therefore, aviation emissions as a share of total emissions are expected to increase.[82]

But this report also identified the exaggeration of the contribution tourism makes to climate change:

> Consumers in many of our key tourism markets are increasingly focusing on climate change. High profile interest group campaigns in some of our key tourism markets, particularly in the United Kingdom, have been targeting long-haul air travel. This may have contributed to the exaggerated perceptions of the contribution of tourism, and air travel in particular, to climate change. Changing consumer perceptions relating to climate change have the potential to affect the destination choice of travellers, and therefore the economic contribution to the Australian economy from these markets.
>
> There is a need to monitor changing consumer perceptions and behaviours in relation to climate change and to reposition Australian tourism marketing strategies to meet the challenges and opportunities presented by climate change.[83]

Thus climate change now becomes an 'opportunity' for new marketing strategies, suggesting that the problem of climate change is as much an ideological one as it is a scientific one:

> Tourism contributes significantly to the Australian economy, to job creation, to wealth generation and to regional economic development. To sustain the economic, environmental and social benefits the tourism industry currently generates for Australia, the impacts of climate change on tourism and how they are managed will require ongoing research and analysis and long term policy responses. The National Tourism Strategy, which will be developed over the next 12 months, will provide the mechanism for governments and industry to ensure that responding to long term climate change challenges is integral to long term tourism policy and consistent with state and territory tourism strategies.[84]

In such a case the notion of the exalted tourist may well resurface as it supports the view that tourism can be managed in such a way – within a market-based economy – to be environmentally sustainable. The problem of course is that various environmental interest groups may be constructing the anti-tourist as the new hero, as one that disavows the need to travel as the ultimate act of responsible behaviour. When this is aligned with fear of terrorism or the fear of contracting disease (as the SARS outbreak caused) and more recently with concern about the global spread of swine flu, then there are indeed in the minds of many, good reasons to stop travelling, even if there is an element of moral panic in their standpoints. In this case the philosophical underpinnings of the 'exalted tourist', in a final act of irony, could possibly contribute to the ultimate demise of mass tourism as we know it.

Notes

1 M. Crick, 'Representations of international tourism in the social sciences: sun, sex, sights, savings, and servility', *Annual Review of Anthropology*, 18 (1989), pp. 307–44.
2 Ibid., p. 308.
3 D.L. Gladstone, *From Pilgrimage to Package Tour: Travel and Tourism in the Third World* (Abingdon, Routledge, 2005), p. 21 citing D. MacCannell, *The Tourist: A New Theory of the Leisure Class* (New York, Schocken, 1976).
4 Ibid.
5 T. Ratz, 'The socio cultural impacts of tourism' (http://www.geocities.com/Paris/9842/impacts.html).
6 Ibid.
7 Ibid.
8 K. Patterson, 'Aloha! "Welcome to paradise",' *New Internationalist*, 245, (July 1993): 13–15.
9 Ibid.
10 Ibid.
11 A. Shankland, 'The natives are friendly!' *New Internationalist*, 245 (July 1993): 20–22.
12 Ibid.
13 Ibid.
14 Ibid.
15 Crick, 'Representations of international tourism in the social sciences', p. 311
16 Ibid., p. 328.
17 Ibid.
18 Ibid., p. 329.
19 Antonio Enríquez Savignac, Secretary-General, World Tourism Organization, Foreword, *Agenda 21 for Tourism Industry*, p. 3.
20 Gladstone, *From Pilgrimage to Package Tour*, p. 4.
21 Ibid.
22 Ibid., p. 5.
23 Ibid., p. 5, citing Erik Cohen, 'A phenomenology of tourist experiences', *Sociology* (1979), 13(2) 179–201.
24 Ibid.
25 Ibid.
26 Ibid., pp. 5–6.
27 Ibid., p. 6.
28 Ibid.
29 Adopted by resolution A/RES/406(XIII) at the thirteenth WTO General Assembly (Santiago, Chile, 27 September–1 October 1999).
30 Australian Tourism Commission Annual Report 1996–97.
31 See Tourism Australia, Annual Report 2008–9, p. 2.
32 Ibid., p. 12.
33 Ibid., pp. 12–13.
34 s.7.

35 Adopted by resolution A/RES/406(XIII) at the thirteenth WTO General Assembly (Santiago, Chile, 27 September–1 October 1999).
36 See above pp. 14–15.
37 See above p. 16.
38 Consistent with the principles expressed in the UN Earth Summit in Rio de Janeiro 1992 and the adoption of Agenda 21 (see Preamble to Global Code of Ethics).
39 Global Code of Ethics, Preamble.
40 See above p. 16.
41 Global Code of Ethics, Preamble.
42 See above p. 17.
43 Global Code of Ethics, article 1.
44 Ibid., article 2.
45 Ibid., article 3.
46 Ibid., article 3(1).
47 Ibid., article 3(2).
48 Ibid., article 3(3).
49 By this we mean the discourse promoted by those who exercise significant power in society: the state, the tourism industry and others that benefit from a liberal free-market economy.
50 Global Code of Ethics, article 3(4).
51 Ibid., article 3(5) (our emphasis).
52 P. Burns, 'Paradoxes in planning: tourism elitism or brutalism?', *Annals of Tourism Research* (1999), 26(2): 329–48, p. 329.
53 Ibid., p. 330.
54 Ibid., p. 333.
55 Ibid.
56 Ibid., pp. 333–34.
57 WTO, February 2004.
58 National Audubon Society, *Travel Ethic for Environmentally Responsible Travel*, http://web1.audubon.org/travel/ethic.php.
59 Ibid.
60 See J.K.S. Jacobsen, 'Anti-tourist attitudes: Mediterranean charter tourism', *Annals of Tourism Research* (2000), 27(2): 284–300.
61 http://www.city-of-hotels.com/165/hotel-chains-en/accor-hotels-en.html, visited 28 December 2009.
62 Accor Hotels Environment Charter.
63 See http://www.accor.com/en/sustainable-development/ego-priorities.html.
64 See http://news.mongabay.com/2009/0223-accor_sarawak.html.
65 Ibid.
66 See, e.g., 'Terrorism hitting trade and tourism hard', *Sydney Morning Herald*, 26 February 2003.
67 'U.S. Struggles anew to ensure safety as gaps are revealed', *New York Times*, 28 December 2009.
68 Ibid.
69 Ibid.
70 http://www.tsa.gov/who_we_are/index.shtm.
71 http://www.tsa.gov/who_we_are/i_am_tsa.shtm.
72 http://www.tsa.gov/who_we_are/mission.shtm.
73 See, e.g., OECD Directorate for Science, Technology and Industry, *National Tourism Policy Review of Australia*, July 2003, p. 53. Other fears such as disease (SARS, swine flu) will also cause this to occur, ibid.

74 Australian Government, *Transnational Terrorism: The Threat to Australia* (Commonwealth of Australia, Canberra, 2004), p. 72.

75 Ibid., p. 73.

76 Ibid., p. 104.

77 *Climate Change and Tourism: Responding to Global Challenges*, Davos, Switzerland, 3 October, 2007.

78 Ibid., p. 3.

79 Ibid.

80 Margaret Hodge's Speech to the UNWTO's Ministers' Summit on tourism and climate change, 13 November 2007: http://www.culture.gov.uk/reference_library/minister_speeches/2009.aspx.

81 Tourism Australia's Brand Health Monitor, *Environmental Concerns* (September, 2008)

82 Australia Department of Energy, Resources and Tourism, *Tourism and Climate Change – A Framework for Action* (Canberra, July 2008), p. 8.

83 Ibid., p. 11.

84 Ibid., p. 13.

Chapter 3

The urban tourist
Inserting the tourist into the cityscape

It's impossible to imagine Liverpool without music, or music without Liverpool.
(Liverpool and the City Region Visitor Guide '09)

There's no place in the world like Sydney.
(The Official Guide, Sydney, 2009)

The place to be ... Burnley Town Centre.
(Tourist Map)

You Can Ride Your Skateboards and Bikes ... But Not Through the City Centre.
(Gosford, New South Wales, Safe City Poster)

Tourism and cities

While many tourists speak of visiting a 'country', in reality of course they usually enter that country through a major city and often stay for lengthy periods in that city. The notion of the global city has also given rise to the city as the destination. Thus many tourists visit cities with this status, such as London, Paris or New York. In such cases it is probable that few of those visitors actually travel across many other parts of the United Kingdom, France or the United States. In part this reflects the urban nature of modern society. Museums, theatre, shopping and sporting events tend to be located in cities and so there seems a natural fit between the city and the tourist. There will always be tourists who wish to stray 'off the beaten path' but there will be many more who enjoy the delights of the urban landscape exclusively.

What this has given rise to is the potential for the city to be recast as a 'product' that can be marketed to tourists. As John Hannigan describes it, this involves a process – largely begun in the 1980s and 1990s – of 'theming' the city where various activities converge:

In the theme park cities of the 1990s, shopping, fantasy and fun have further bonded in a number of ways ... shopping has become intensely entertaining and this in turn encourages more shopping ... This convergence is described as 'shopertainment' ... [1]

A critique of this process is that cities are as a consequence produced as landscapes of pleasure for visitors. Residents of the city are then either marginalised to the outer circles of cities, where they might emerge to service the tourist centre, or become themselves part of the tourist trail – the resident that makes the urban landscape 'real'. This is all part of the manner in which cities both attract inbound capital and regenerate. As Holcomb notes:

As tourism has become an ever more vital strategy for urban regeneration, governments and the tourist industry have invested greater amounts of resources on campaigns to 'sell' the city to potential 'consumers'. This increasingly is how cities are marketed ... Public funds are spent on marketing campaigns, and the city 'product' is both redesigned and reimaged for visitors rather than for residents. [2]

The question this poses is who the regeneration of cities is actually supposed to benefit. One of Sharon Zukin's central concerns is the manner in which 'the politics of representation plays a significant role in conflicts over [the] economic revitalization' of cities. [3] According to her, 'the politics of representation is ... shaped by concrete questions of who owns, occupies, and who controls the city's public spaces'. [4] As we will see, such debates become pronounced when mega events are attracted to cities as part of their tourist and regeneration strategy. For example, the gaining of the right to host the Olympic Games seems to be now often followed by legislation which enables the 'clearing' of the streets of the homeless, poor and others that might 'affront' the sensibilities of visitors. [5]

The manner in which cities are recast for the purposes of tourism does not simply give rise to spatial dislocation for local people. Their urban culture and history can also be rewritten. Abrahamson notes that in effect to make cities more attractive for visitors:

[t]his may, of course, require some manipulation or reinvention of culture and history that will leave some locals feeling left out of the public representation of the place. Farmers, unemployed laborers, and others may feel that the selling of an industrial museum in their city presents an inauthentic cultural representation, or at least one that seriously departs from the meaning of the place that they share. [6]

The tourist city is a contested city. As we have discussed in earlier chapters this is in effect acknowledged in various documents initiated by the World

Tourism Organization which seek to transform the practice of tourism into more responsible behaviour. For example, the Manila Declaration on World Tourism 1980 recognises the impact that tourism can have on social and economic development by aiming to connect tourism with a commitment to social justice and world peace. The 1982 Acapulco Document notes that 'domestic tourism enables the individual to take possession of his own country' and that 'States should improve their understanding of the role of domestic tourism and give more attention to its social, educational and cultural terms.' The 1985 Tourism Bill of Rights and Tourism Code highlights the need for such matters as the need for tourists to respect the 'customs, religions and other elements of [the] cultures' of host communities,[7] and behave in a manner which 'foster[s] understanding and friendly relations among peoples'.[8] Such statements can only be understood through the recognition that tourism does create contests for both material and cultural space in cities.

The Global Code of Ethics for Tourism, as we have noted, also emphasises the importance of 'responsible tourism' in Article 1(1):

> The understanding and promotion of the ethical values common to humanity, with an attitude of tolerance and respect for the diversity of religious, philosophical and moral beliefs, are both the foundation and the consequence of responsible tourism; stakeholders in tourism development and tourists themselves should observe the social and cultural traditions and practices of all peoples, including those of minorities and indigenous peoples and to recognize their worth.

Again, such documents can only be understood as a recognition that tourism has often been an *irresponsible* force as the tourist industry pursues profit and tourists pursue pleasure. In attempting to create a new discourse of tourism which casts tourism in more noble terms, such statements also remind us that tourism is a process which creates tensions and contests within urban spaces.

Urban image and the promotion of tourism

Imagery which is used to promote cities helps to create various urban 'realities'. While such images can provide important symbols which assist in focussing the marketing and promotion of cities (as well as creating a certain 'feel good' factor amongst the populace) they also carry the risk of distorting the real nature of the urban scene through concealing other realities. This distortion is no doubt more likely to occur if there is perceived to be economic gain to be realised from using a particular image over others. Thus given the acceptance that mass tourism offers real financial rewards if one can attract those tourists, there is immense pressure on cities to market

themselves through images which project the city in a way which is thought
to be attractive to those tourists.

As Boniface and Fowler remark:

> 'Urban heritage', manifestly eclectic and elastic, has been sharpened as
> an economic tool, for towns, as always, need their trade.
>
> Tourists, however, do not see themselves merely as trade tokens. They
> want quite a lot of a town, and this is where the clashes of interest can
> begin to develop. In the first place, a city or town has to *seem* to be
> attractive from a distance in order to attract the attention of the poten-
> tial visitor. While the serious scholar will go wherever his or her original
> sources in art gallery, museum or archives lie, no one essentially bent on
> leisure will willingly go somewhere perceived as being 'worse' than
> domestic circumstances. For the same reasons, it is difficult to take a
> positive decision to go somewhere if the attraction to make one do so is
> not clearly defined. Furthermore, there's not much point in going to a
> town that no one back home has heard of: where are the social-status
> Brownie points in visiting 'anywheresville' (unless you can elevate it over
> suburban sherry to *the* undiscovered place where everybody will be
> touring two years hence).[9]

We argue that the pressure to create a particular image can have two significant consequences. The first is the non-representation and subsequent
denial of other views of the city; and second, the tendency to preserve only
those parts of urban heritage which are consistent with the marketing
image resulting in the loss of those parts of the urban scene which are not so
consistent.

Alternative layers of the city

In one sense what makes a city a place worthy of visiting is what makes it
'different' but as Boniface and Fowler point out there tends to be a certain
sameness in what tourists are fed as part of the tourism experience. They
remark:

> What a paradox if, all over the world, tourists are travelling to visit cities
> and towns that are different and yet, unless they make the effort to
> eschew the tourist and 'do their own thing', everywhere everyone is
> being fed the same soup – 'heritage' minestrone: the contents differ in
> detail but the concoction is still minestrone. As one travel brochure
> rather surprisingly asked, making the point that its tours induced
> 'delightful confusion: a half-remembered kaleidoscope', 'Did we feed the
> ducks in Geneva or Lausanne?'[10]

Such an approach ignores the many other layers which contribute to the make-up of cities. But it is also clear that Boniface and Fowler are saying more than this. What they are critical of is the way in which such ways of packaging cities ignore what tourists often want to experience. In their view tourists come to a place with complex motivations and desires – they want to see what is different about a place – but this complexity is usually ignored when cities are presented to tourists. They continue:

> Understandably, every urban place needs its local heroes for its own self-esteem; better still if it can glow with pride at an association with someone of national or greater standing. Nevertheless, such figures tend to be inflated in significance to meet the needs of the 'mostest' type of tourism – who after all wants to visit the home or museum of a nobody? – while, at this level of mini-bus heritage tourism, interesting but controversial issues such as social variety, ethnic diversity, and social and ethnic deprivation are clearly not part of urban heritage. Pity: such are among the traits which make cities different and dynamic as well as interesting.[11]

This leads to the question of whether tourism should ignore such diversity in the urban environment. Of course, to confront these 'other' faces of the city means that the tourist will often come into contact with less fashionable images of the city – at least as far as powerful interests who inhabit the city are concerned. That is, there is clearly every reason why those who wield power and influence within a city have little to gain from tourists leaving the city with the view that such power and influence is not exercised for the benefit of all who live there.

Boniface and Fowler thus ask whether tourism should investigate such issues:

> Does tourism have an educational role? If not, fine, let's just enjoy ourselves and confine our perceptions of heritage to pleasantries; but if it does, – and many tourists do travel for self-education – then perhaps the tourist menu, the very concept of urban heritage indeed, should be broadened.[12]

The notion that the concept of urban heritage should be broadened is most challenging. For what a city chooses to preserve as its heritage is closely tied to its self-image and thus the way it wants to present itself to visitors. If a city regards its various layers as important components of its heritage then such a city will preserve (and thus present) a far different image of itself than a city which regards the deeds of the rich and powerful as what makes it a worthy place. When a city has a significant part of its heritage destroyed either willingly through government action or through the deliberate destruction of heritage through civil war, such as that in the former Yugoslavia, part of the soul of the city is gone for ever.

Marketing the city and the loss of its (legal) soul

A case study – the construction of modern Brisbane and the Gold Coast

One example of a city losing much of its built heritage and how the layers of meaning of a city can be quickly eradicated is that of the City of Brisbane, Australia, which underwent a rapid remaking of its image during the 1970s. Brisbane is the State capital of Queensland and was fast becoming a 'growth' state much in the image of California. The promise of warm weather and the abolition of death (inheritance) taxes attracted retirees from Southern States. But wealth could not just be built on the backs of an ageing population. The then (conservative) Bjelke-Petersen State government had a desire to present an image of a modern Brisbane which would also attract capital to the State for industrial growth. Its climate also attracted tourists and its proximity to natural attractions (such as the Great Barrier Reef) positioned it as a major centre for tourism. But until this time Brisbane had a visual image as that of a 'large country town'. Simply, it did not have the appearance of a modern city which in itself represented a 'destination'. It was yet to become 'Brisvegas', the 'fantasy city' in Hannigan's terms. In creating a 'modern' city in those terms the Government then set about destroying a large amount of its built heritage.

The changing image of this city at this particular historic point in time provides a snapshot of the power of governments to change the image of a city and in particular the power of governments to act where there is little legislative restraint to protect heritage. Under the long reign of the Queensland Premier Joh Bjelke-Petersen from 1968 until 1987 Brisbane was promoted as a clean, safe and modern city. It was marketed as a friendly, welcoming place for both domestic and international tourists. Bjelke-Petersen has been attributed with putting Queensland on the tourist map and in doing so creating a 'new Brisbane'. What we are concerned with here as an aspect of this process is the manner in which the visual image of the city was recast to meet this agenda. Thus in an attempt to better portray this image many old-style Queenslander build-ings[13] and other old long-standing buildings were demolished in central Brisbane and new buildings put up in their place creating an instant 'modern Brisbane'.

Whereas heritage in all its facets has long been recognised internationally as a draw card for tourists, in comparison with many other countries Australia has been slow to recognise the value of protecting its built heritage for tourism. It was not until the 1970s, when UNESCO officially adopted the term 'heritage' to encompass both the built and natural remnants of the past,[14] that a number of states in Australia introduced protective legislation for the built heritage.[15] Prior to this time the National Trust had been the only major group which had shown any determined interest in the preservation of 'old buildings'.[16] It was during this time when other Australian states were introducing legislation to protect their built heritage that the State of Queensland undertook to demolish many of its most significant heritage buildings. In fact it was not until the 1990s with a new government in place that Queensland enacted heritage legislation.

The image of a modern Brisbane that the then government wanted to construct was not thought to be consistent with old Queenslander-style buildings and so the Bjelke-Petersen government demolished as many of those buildings as it could. Fisher's description of the period leaves the reader with a sense of the destruction during this time: 'Between the mid-1970s and early 1990 over 60 significant buildings bit the dust in central Brisbane, as the pre-war town was transformed into a nondescript high-rise city.'[17] The demolition of these buildings did not take place with the full support of the community. On the contrary many of the buildings were listed by the National Trust and there were many concerned protestors, but the legal redress available to the community was minimal. With no state heritage legislation in force, a government with a particular vision of the modern city, and with close private business connections that supported this vision, had little to prevent it from achieving its aims. One particular example, the Bellevue Hotel, would have qualified as a highly prized heritage attraction today. A detailed description of the Bellevue Hotel provided by Fisher gives us some idea of what a glorious building it once was:

> this delightful three-storeyed rendered brick hotel, listed by the Australian Heritage Commission as part of the National Estate, had been designed by J.J. Cohen in colonial renaissance style at the height of the 1880s boom, its street awnings and verandah balconies dripping with filigree cast iron. Built in 1886 at the corner of George and Alice streets each façade was further enhanced by a central mansard-roofed turret echoing the roofline of parliament house across the way.[18]

The building was razed late one evening in 1979. The demolition crew was brought in under police protection as angry members of the community protested to no avail.[19] This hotel, under the since-enacted state heritage legislation would no doubt have been protected on a number of grounds such as its aesthetic, architectural, historic and social significance to the present generation or past or future generations.[20]

The ongoing destruction of heritage buildings was to a large extent inevitable under the Bjelke-Petersen era as the government held considerable power and was able to continue demolishing buildings late at night in an attempt to avoid protestors. Private wrecking operators such as the Deen brothers were also only too willing to help out. Fisher points out that their then business card summed up the situation nicely: "Moreover the Deen brothers – George, Ray, Happy, Louie and Funny – like the legendary dwarfs were available for hire at all hours according to their business card, their motto being 'All we leave behind is the memories'."[21]

Marketing Brisbane as the modern city was not the only project the government had in its quest to capture the tourist dollar. Establishing the Gold Coast city as a highly desirable destination was another major feat for the Bjelke-Petersen government which had many similarities with the redevelopment of Brisbane. This project, although not involving the demolition of heritage buildings, nevertheless, as with Brisbane, had as its focus the construction of a 'modern' city through the building of numerous high-rise self-serviced apartments, together with luxurious hotels and a number of golf courses to cater for the anticipated tourist boom. Patrick Mullins neatly coins the creation of this massive Gold Coast development as 'Tourism urbanization is the process by which cities and towns are built or re-developed explicitly for tourists'.[22]

The State of Queensland has for many years been active in attracting a tourist market promoting just such an image. While part of the lifestyle image promoted for Queensland has included a number of beach towns, it is the Gold Coast city which has been promoted to both the internal tourist market as well as the international tourist. Marketing of the intangible such as the promise of the beach lifestyle has been a very effective draw card for this city. Holcomb points out that so far as the image creation of the city is concerned much of what cities offer throughout various parts of the world have the same sorts of qualities. He asks: 'How, then, does the generic city, one with a range of suitable but not extraordinary attractions, market itself to compete with other similar cities?'[23]

One way he suggests this can be achieved is for a city to have a landmark. For the Gold Coast it has been the accessible Australian beach combined with the relaxed 'Australian way of life' and 'unique' cultural landscape. In a similar vein, various coastal cities in Spain have been packaged to the English tourist in almost the exact same manner with 'Spanish lifestyle' replacing that of Australia. But another enduring symbol and 'landmark' of the Gold Coast is the 'modern' skyline of high-rise buildings. It is this that possibly delivers the visual image that marks the place as worthy of becoming a destination. This image, together with that of the 'new Brisbane' would not have been possible without the legal vacuum which existed at the time many of its heritage sites were being removed.

Nor are the events in Brisbane unique. Cities globally are re-inventing themselves in this manner. Blackpool in the United Kingdom is undergoing a transformation from 'the Mecca of the English working class' during the nineteenth century and into the twentieth century[24] to a place now described as 'trendy'.[25] This is explained in tourist literature:

> Blackpool has and is undergoing so much change. Blackpool now has a whole host of boutique accommodation, dispelling the myth of the land-lady in her rollers. Blackpool's attractions are also getting a makeover as well as the tram system. The new headland in front of Blackpool tower will attract huge concerts, and the new seafront is beginning to take shape.[26]

So much about reconstructing the city for tourism also involved de-constructing. The question this raises is exactly which parts of the past should be preserved in this process?

Defining and preserving heritage

A view of heritage which explores the many layers of the city and seeks to preserve them is arguably much more likely to produce a richer tourism experience for those who visit. And importantly, it may be that such a city goes much further in satisfying the complex needs of tourists than a city which serves up the 'standard fare': 'Towns and cities are actually much more interesting than the tourist is often allowed to appreciate – and there is no need for the visitor's experience of *urbanitas* to be effectively short-changed.'[27]

The urban heritage is of course largely constructed through legislative regimes and remains a highly political arena where developers and heritage professionals often remain locked in conflict. Both may have some (among other matters) regard to tourism with their ultimate objective but may have very different expectations as to how the tourist will engage with the built heritage. A building which is to be retained for business purposes with a focus first on profit may be dealt with very differently from a building that is to be saved for its heritage value alone. When it comes to defining heritage the interpretation of relevant legislation becomes all important for developers and heritage professionals alike.

In Australia, at the Federal level, the Australian Heritage Commission Act 1975 (Cth) until recent years created the 'national estate'. Once registered as part of the national estate various processes allowed for the protection of places registered as part of the national estate. The criteria for determining whether a place was part of the national estate was set out in section 4 of the Act as stated:

> 4(1) For the purposes of this Act, the national estate consists of those places, being components of the natural environment of Australia or the cultural environment of Australia, that have aesthetic, historic, scientific or social significance or other special value for future generations as well as for the present community.

This Act has now been repealed and replaced by the Environmental Protection and Biodiversity Conservation Act 1999 (Cth) but the broad definitions of the repealed legislation have been retained in the current Act. The heritage value of a place is defined to include: the place's natural and cultural environment having aesthetic, historic, scientific or social significance, or other significance, for current and future generations of Australians.[28] Section 341D of the Act provides that the criteria for a place having heritage values shall be prescribed by the Regulations under the Act.

The Environment Protection and Biodiversity Conservation Regulations 2000 provide the criteria for determining heritage for the Commonwealth:

> The Commonwealth Heritage criteria for a place are any or all of the following:
>
> (a) the place has significant heritage value because of the place's importance in the course, or pattern, of Australia's natural or cultural history;
> (b) the place has significant heritage value because of the place's possession of uncommon, rare or endangered aspects of Australia's natural or cultural history;
> (c) the place has significant heritage value because of the place's potential to yield information that will contribute to an understanding of Australia's natural or cultural history;
> (d) the place has significant heritage value because of the place's importance in demonstrating the principal characteristics of:
>
>> (i) a class of Australia's natural or cultural places; or
>> (ii) a class of Australia's natural or cultural environments;
>
> (e) the place has significant heritage value because of the place's importance in exhibiting particular aesthetic characteristics valued by a community or cultural group;
> (f) the place has significant heritage value because of the place's importance in demonstrating a high degree of creative or technical achievement at a particular period;
> (g) the place has significant heritage value because of the place's strong or special association with a particular community or cultural group for social, cultural or spiritual reasons;
> (h) the place has significant heritage value because of the place's special association with the life or works of a person, or group of persons, of importance in Australia's natural or cultural history;
> (i) the place has significant heritage value because of the place's importance as part of indigenous tradition.[29]

A broad definition of heritage has thus remained the legislative model for the Commonwealth for over 30 years.

It is important to note that nothing in the current or repealed legislation identifies the importance of a place as a tourist attraction (or likely tourist attraction) in determining whether a place should become part of the national estate. The Hawke Report which reviewed the Federal heritage legislation also did not mention tourism. But, of course, it is well understood that the national estate has such a strong connection. This follows from the comments of Boniface and Fowler who identify the extent to which it is assumed that tourists want to experience 'mostest' tourism – that is, visit places that have special significance. It is noteworthy that both Acts utilise terms such as 'special', 'importance' and 'strong' in setting down its criteria for entry into the register of the national estate. A review of the Australian legislation in 2009 also recommended that the law be re-enacted and renamed the Environment Act with a new set of objects including the protection of 'matters of national environmental significance and, consistent with this, seeks to promote beneficial economic and social outcomes'.[30] This was recommended because:

> establishing an object that promises strict environmental protection when it is clear that in certain circumstances social and economic considerations will legitimately be brought into decision-making, risks drawing the legislation into disrepute and should be avoided.[31]

Clearly, one of the economic benefits to be derived from heritage is that earned through tourism. While the Hawke Report does not expressly refer to tourism, the tourism White Paper issued by the Australian Government in 2003[32] had 17 references to 'heritage'. Some of these stressed the economic benefits:

> Around 77 million hectares or nearly 10 per cent of Australia's land area is designated as protected. In addition, a large portion of Australia's 16 million square kilometres of ocean are under the jurisdiction of the Australian Government and much of this is being managed as marine protected areas. National parks and world heritage areas are the heart of this system and are essential to Australia's tourism industry.[33]

The White Paper noted that visits to national parks alone constituted 84 million visits generating $54 million on revenue in 2001–2 but that 'despite the obvious importance of such visitation to both the tourism industry and the national park sector, these players are often seen as having divergent interests rather than working together to pursue common goals'.[34] This is again the tension between sustaining the environment on the one hand and making it available for economic gain. This presents particular challenges in the case of significant natural heritage sites such as the Great Barrier Reef. In that context the White Paper made the comment that:

> The role of privately owned tourism infrastructure in publicly owned protected areas has received only limited attention to date in the identification and planning of tourism product. Industry involvement is important in helping to address issues such as congestion and opening up new areas for visitation, which can both facilitate tourism dispersal from congested areas and expand the opportunities for 'presentation' of natural heritage and biodiversity.
>
> The Australian Government will work with state and territory governments to identify barriers to private-sector involvement and investment in parks and will also seek to review tourism industry representation and input to protected area management with a view to identifying ways to strengthen involvement.[35]

Such comments allude to the political content of defining heritage. The notion in the White Paper that heritage sites are also 'tourism products' would alarm those who are primarily concerned with conservation of such places. It also may suggest that while significant natural heritage sites generate debate, urban sites might not. The Barrier Reef has iconic status in the realm of conservation, but one old building in a city might not be so protected by the regulation created by the process outlined above. Witness the history of Brisbane discussed above.

What the relevant laws also fail to explain is on what basis one should define such terms as 'significant heritage value'. Who should such sites be important to? In what way should a place have a 'special' association with a particular community or group? How 'strong' do the connections have to be? What if the same place has significance for indigenous and non-indigenous persons for very different reasons? It is likely that strong disagreement may arise in situations such as this. In resolving such matters the politics of heritage will come into play, with the economic benefit derived from tourism no doubt being one of the considerations.

In other words there is a high degree of discretion contained within the law when interpreting the heritage criteria. In this context there will be many pressures to connect what is entered into the national estate to the type of image Australia wishes to present to the world (and tourists). Boer and Wiffen, commenting on the history of national-heritage laws in Australia, suggest that Australian heritage professionals take a broad view of what constitutes national heritage for the built environment and that this may be due in part to the age of the built heritage:

> This suggestion of a broad view implies the possibility of a narrower view, and indicates the scope of the definition of heritage may be

contentious. Nations with a longer tradition of permanent building may have a narrower view of what in that tradition constitutes heritage, and not only concentrate on the built environment, but also within that, preserving monuments. Australian heritage professionals take a wider view.[36]

We thus return to the question posed by Boniface and Fowler above – will this result in the preservation of places which represent the many layers of urban life, including those parts of that life which are reminders of the inequalities and injustices of cities? To some extent these matters might seem difficult to sustain as issues on national heritage. As many aspects of urban development and the design of cities fall within the province of State governments in Australia, it is to State legislation that we need to turn to determine whether there is more scope at a local level to preserve a more inclusive heritage of the city. In the State of South Australia, for example, under section 16 of the Heritage Places Act 1993 (SA) a place has 'heritage value' if:

(a) it demonstrates important aspects of the evolution or pattern of the state's history; or
(b) it has rare, uncommon or endangered qualities that are of cultural significance; or
(c) it may yield information that will contribute to an understanding of the state's history, including its natural history; or
(d) it is an outstanding representative of a particular class of places of cultural significance; or
(e) it demonstrates a high degree of creative, aesthetic or technical accomplishment or is an outstanding representative of particular construction techniques or design characteristics; or
(f) it has strong cultural or spiritual associations for the community or a group within it; or
(g) it has a special association with the life or work of a person or organisation or an event of historical importance.

The New South Wales legislation provides that 'State heritage significance' 'in relation to a place, building, work, relic, moveable object or precinct, means significance to the State in relation to the historical, scientific, cultural, social, archaeological, architectural, natural or aesthetic value of the item'.[37] The Victorian legislation defines 'cultural heritage significance' as 'aesthetic, archaeological, architectural, cultural, historical, scientific or social significance'.[38] Such definitions of 'heritage' are commonplace in such laws. But as the recent review of the Australian federal law illustrates the real tension lies in the extent to which in defining a place as of heritage value its economic benefits in relation to such matters as tourism should be considered. In Queensland the purposes of the relevant Act actually refer to the need to exercise the powers under the Act having regard to the need to achieve 'the greatest sustainable benefit to the community from those places and artefacts consistent with the conservation of their cultural heritage significance'.[39]

What this may indicate is that while the laws have always permitted the consideration of the economic returns from preserving heritage due to the vagueness of the criteria and breadth of the language, there seems to be a move to more explicitly connect the economic return – which must specifically often relate to tourism – with the need to define and preserve heritage sites. This also seems to be a move in the United Kingdom where a White Paper on the heritage system concluded that it was complex and needed to be streamlined for clarity.[40] The need to reform the process was because:

> The historic environment contributes to a broad range of local priorities. Local heritage can underpin sustainable communities, drive regeneration and tourism, and support sustainable development. It is a vast and valuable educational resource for both formal and informal learning. And it has its own intrinsic value as an expression of our past and of our identity.[41]

It seems of note that the economic returns appear before the intrinsic value of heritage preservation here. Clearly, in seeking to reform the heritage system as part of the reform of the planning system to ensure sustainable communities the concern is that 'sustainable' means that communities can regenerate and still develop. Inbound tourism has strong connections with the notion of regeneration. This also has the effect of linking tourism, regeneration and sustainability – key components of the exalted tourist discussed in the previous chapter. Just as tourism can deliver sustainability according to this construction, so too heritage also can deliver this outcome:

> Heritage has a crucial role to play in delivering sustainable communities. For many people, it is heritage that provides their community with a sense of character, distinctiveness and identity and makes it somewhere they want to live. In towns and cities, heritage has provided the starting point for imaginative and successful regeneration. In the countryside it plays an important role in rural regeneration. As pressures on the planning system grow, it is often heritage that provides a focal point for engaging communities in decisions about preservation and development.[42]

The notion of heritage as something with economic value is reinforced in the draft Heritage Protection Bill released in the United Kingdom following the White Paper. It provides for the registration of 'heritage assets' which includes 'heritage structures', 'heritage open spaces', world heritage sites and marine heritage sites.[43] The basic criteria for listing a structure, for example, as a heritage asset is that it is considered to be of 'special archaeological, architectural or artistic interest'.[44] English Heritage has responsibility for developing criteria to determine what is of interest in this context and although the legislation has yet to be passed there is already in train a process of reform of the system following the White Paper. One part of that process has been the issuing of a Draft Planning Policy Statement on heritage protection[45] and Planning Practice Guide[46] (the latter of which is described as a 'living draft' in order to develop best practice in determining what 'assets' should be deemed worthy of heritage protection).

The Draft Planning Policy Statement is explicit in connecting heritage protection with economic returns from tourism:

> The historic environment is central to our cultural heritage. It contributes to our sense of national, local and community identity, through the memories of events and phases in our history that it holds. It has aesthetic value and provides local distinctiveness that is so important to a sense of place. It can help us support the economic development and regeneration of our communities, particularly through leisure and recreation. Through all this it enhances the quality of our daily lives.[47]

The construction of heritage as an 'asset' also reinforces the notion that it is their marketable value which is an important part of their actual designation. Thus the UK Government's principles for heritage protection embrace the notion that:

> by ensuring that policies and decisions concerning the development and use of land take account of the positive benefits of conserving and, where appropriate, enhancing heritage assets (such as encouraging sustainable tourism to support economic growth or re-using existing heritage assets for example as part of regeneration).[48]

Policy HE2 in the draft Planning Policy Statement requires that regional planning authorities develop a regional spatial strategy. This strategy is to 'ensure a consistent approach across the region to the conservation, enhancement and enjoyment of the historic environment'.[49] In other words this document would be central in determining which sites to preserve. The formulation of this strategy is then linked directly with the economic benefits of tourism:

> In determining its strategy, the regional planning body should take full account of the positive contribution that the historic environment can have for regeneration, encouraging tourism, and enhancing the quality

of the environment and the region's sense of place, alongside other objectives such as economic growth and housing supply. Their approach should be consistent with securing progress against the UK's carbon emissions targets.[50]

This is also supported by supporting data in the consultation paper which stresses the value of heritage 'assets':

> In addition to its cultural value, the historic environment makes a considerable contribution to economic well-being. For example, tourism accounts for around 5 per cent of GDP – in 2007, £16 billion was spent by overseas visitors and £11.5 billion by UK citizens on holidays in the UK (Visit Britain) – and heritage forms an important part of the 'draw'. In 2006, 9.8 million (30 per cent) of overseas visitors to the UK visited castles, churches, monuments or historic houses, spending £5.4 billion (34 per cent of all overseas spend) while they were in the UK ...
>
> By delivering more effective conservation and enhancement of heritage assets through the planning system, it is reasonable to assume that the new PPS will result in a better quality historic environment, and that this in turn may lead to an incremental growth in the revenue generated by tourism. However, it has not been possible to quantify this.[51]

The Planning Practice Guide also supports this objective when noting that when drawing up a Regional Spatial Strategy one consideration should be how the historic environment 'makes a positive contribution to achieving sustainable development' through 'increasing tourism and leisure opportunities'.[52] One suspects that the stress here is more on the development than the sustainability.

The concern with the legislation discussed above is that while it may seem broad enough to include a vast array of places which might reflect the diversity and character of a city, the outcomes are heavily influenced by a discourse that values 'assets' of clear marketable value for tourism. This is more than leaving the matter to the judgements of those who administer the Act. It is clear that the state has increased its hold over the definition of 'heritage' to include a discourse that itself will limit the framework within which such decisions will be made. Thus the decision to classify a place as having heritage value will be contentious as it will not only seek to preserve that place for future generations but will also contribute to the manner in which the city presents itself to the world. In the context of the importance of tourism the pressure to present a 'marketable image' will be immense. As Conforti states in the context of urban heritage, '[p]reservation is clearly a selective process and what is selected usually reflects the interests of those making the choice'.[53]

Creating the image of the safe city

Constructing tourism through spatial regulation

While the marketability of the city may depend to a great extent on the preservation of a heritage that fits with visitors' expectations, the ability to move about the tourist city has probably become the foremost concern of many tourists in an age of terrorism and increased fear of street crime. Much of this is built upon the fear of the 'other' – usually code for non-white, non-European and non-middle class. The manner in which this manifests itself has recently occurred following the failure to detect explosives on a passenger who attempted to bring down a flight over Detroit in December 2009. One consequence has been the suggestion that racial profiling might be used to determine which passengers to search more thoroughly, for as one United Kingdom MP commented: 'Certainly some people will be aggrieved but the fact is that the majority of people who carry out these terror attacks do happen to be Muslims.'[54]

The notion of targeting travellers with particular backgrounds has only gained further momentum. In February 2010 the Australian Government released a White Paper on counter-terrorism and the risk of 'home grown terrorism'.[55] Although the focus of this paper was on the risk from 'within' it was accompanied by an announcement that Australia would be applying more stringent visa checks on people travelling to Australia from ten countries. These countries would also not be immediately announced to prevent people 'slipping through the net',[56] although Somalia, Yemen, Pakistan, India and Indonesia have all been mentioned as likely inclusions on this list.[57]

The fear of terrorism then is quickly translated into a fear of 'others' which resonates well with a populace already wary of those who are different. But we have to consider whether the exclusion and fear of 'others' is the cause or effect of the manner in which tourism is constructed. Tom Mordue notes the manner in which cities now compete for 'footloose global capital'.[58] In seeking to gain an advantage, cities have recast themselves spatially as Mordue observes:

> Edensor describes how local authorities in conjunction with powerful commercial interests develop 'tourist enclaves' that are subjected to high degrees of spatial regulation. So often found in urban settings, tourist enclaves are purified spaces that are aesthetically and socially set apart from everyday life, where 'undesirable elements' and social practices are likely to be deterred.[59]

Importantly such spaces give rise to new forms of regulation through the practice of tourism:

> The enclave is discrete yet de-differentiated and 'glocalized', and can be variously sold to high value tourists, locals, new investors and incoming key workers as a cultural attraction, a leisure facility, a lifestyle attribute, a good place to do business, and public good.[60]

In these tourist enclaves it is consumption that is promoted and not public participation. In these spaces one is a consumer and not a citizen.[61] In this way the spatial design of the city gives rise to particular forms of regulation, in particular the exclusion from such spaces of people who will not, or cannot be cast as consumers. Of course, it is not the practice of tourism which is blamed for the exclusion of certain groups. Rather those not welcome in such spaces are constructed as the 'threat', the 'others' who create a feeling of unease when they present themselves at these sites of consumption.

As a consequence the need to present a safe city for both the tourist who internalises these fears and city image makers who need to reinforce such sites as places of consumption has become a central objective. The increased concern about terrorist attacks has further strengthened that need. To 'see' the city as safe has thus become a matter of some importance. To that end security cameras have come to form part of the urban environment in many cities. The ability to capture inappropriate behaviour on camera has been accepted by the general public as a necessary tool against the local criminal element and the potential terrorist. Legislation which governs appropriate behaviour in public spaces has also been implemented to ensure the safety of persons to move about freely without being subjected to other persons being offensive and threatening in their behaviour.

Much of this legislation is vague and general as to what it proscribes in public places. In Queensland, Australia, for example, section 6 of the Summary Offences Act 2005 provides that a person commits a public-nuisance offence if they behave in a disorderly, offensive, threatening or violent way and their behaviour interferes, or is likely to interfere with the peaceful passage through, or enjoyment of, a public place by a member of the public. In the United Kingdom the anti-social behaviour order has become one of the major devices for controlling behaviour in public places. Such orders are available where a person has acted 'in an anti-social manner, that is to say, in a manner that caused or was likely to cause harassment, alarm or distress to one or more persons not of the same household as himself' and where 'such an order is necessary to protect persons in the local government area in which the harassment, alarm or distress was caused or was likely to be caused from further anti-social acts by him'.[62] Such laws deliberately use broad language to provide police and the courts with extensive discretion to deal with various situations. But the language also disguises the fact that in their application they often discriminate.

Tamara Walsh has recently completed a longitudinal study on the effect of public-space laws and the over representation of marginalised and homeless persons who have been charged under those laws in Australia. Her research indicates that indigenous people are the most significantly over-represented group of people who have been charged with offences under the Act followed by homeless and other marginalised persons.[63]

While the policing of public space is seen to be necessary for all members of the community whether they be citizens or tourists, it follows from our previous comments on the 'branding' of cities that it is for tourism that many of these safety initiatives take place. As Fainstein and Judd point out:

> Cities are sold just like any other consumer product. They have adapted image advertising, a development that can hardly escape any traveler who opens an airline magazine and reads its formulaic articles on the alleged culinary delights of Dallas, Frankfurt or Auckland. Each city tries to project itself as a uniquely wonderful place to visit where an unceasing flow of events constantly unfolds.[64]

An example of this is Newcastle upon Tyne, United Kingdom which has long had a reputation for being a 'hard' working-class city with consequent problems with public order. In more recent years it has begun to enjoy a renaissance as a tourist destination, a necessity as, like many formerly industrial cities, old industries (such as shipbuilding) have moved to other countries and new sources of employment have been required. The city developed a Safety Strategy to counter its earlier image with the explicit aim 'to reduce the harm caused by alcohol to individuals, children, families and communities in order that Newcastle is a healthy and safe place to live, work and visit'.[65] The strategy openly acknowledges the central role of the city centre in both safety issues and as the driver of tourism:

> The vast majority of crimes occur in the city centre which is regarded as a 'crime generator'. This issue is compounded by the fact that Newcastle is acknowledged as the regional capital and attracts large numbers of people – whether to live, visit, work, shop and socialise. The proportion of crimes which occur in the city centre has decreased over the last three years from 24.3 per cent in 2005–6 to 21.8 per cent in 2007–8.[66]

The Safe Newcastle project is interesting as it has included placing posters in the Tyne and Wear Metro asking people to stay safe in the community and commenting on how crime is being reduced in the city. Thus in recasting the image of the city the project has also been required to acknowledge the various social problems that exist in the community. Certainly, a poster in the metro advising that crime rates are 'improving' does not necessarily suggest a 'safe' city even if it is getting safer. Thus the critique that city image building is about exclusion is perhaps in need of some refinement. It is still argued that much of the 'branding' of cities sanitises and obscures social divisions in the city, as too much heritage preservation is about preserving a particular history of the city. But there are alternative discourses which focus on inclusion. Thus current trends in urban planning have a focus on the city being a place of inclusion. Duncan Grewcock surmises that urban planning today is largely about:

> the re-evaluation of the social and the spatial, the social and the physical nature of cities, underpinned by economy and environment: social in the sense of inclusion, participation, democracy and power, civil society, equality, identities, community and belonging; spatial in the sense of centre and periphery, movement, borders, boundaries, territory, region and the physical accommodation of social needs. The dialectical, multiple relationships between social and spatial are the key ingredients of place.[67]

Urban planners when designing cities as places of social inclusion create the space and place for all citizens to engage in that public space. Benches for seating, good lighting, gardens, public buildings are all part of the attraction of being in the city. Regulating the city is therefore bound to be about the contradiction of competing interests and outcomes and this is bound to be reflected in legislation and its application. And this is one of our central arguments in this book: that as tourism is regulated by legal discourse (or a discourse which utilises a juridical approach) this opens the possibility of contest and debate. This is the possibility of law. It is possible that tourism scholars have focused too heavily on the macro trends within the city that have cast the landscape for tourists. Law, on the other hand, while playing its role in constructing that outcome, nevertheless contains within its discourse the opportunity to argue for alternatives.

Keeping the poor, the homeless and the indigenous away from the tourist gaze in the well-ordered city is just one of the contradictions which emerge from the desire to see the city as safe while at the same time ensuring that the city remains an inclusive place. Of course, this can be partially resolved by removing from sight the 'unsavoury' aspects of the city. As Urry reminds us, the senses are the primary mode for the tourist experience:

> People encounter the city through the senses. In particular there is a fascination with the sense of sight as the apparent mirror of the world, and more generally with the "hegemony of vision" that has characterised Western social thought and culture of the past few centuries.[68]

Sightseeing has become fundamental to the tourist experience as are those memories captured through the lens of the camera. Of course 'the view' captured on film to take home is quite often one which is constructed to present the most favourable view of the tourist experience. The smiling faces of the happy tourists with the attractive city as backdrop is far more the likely scene recorded of the cityscape than one featuring homeless people dipping into rubbish bins for food or begging in the streets.

The 'problem' of having unsightly people so visible in the city cannot be divorced from larger social and economic issues which directly relate to the enforcement of conflicting legislation. Governments expend money to promote cities to entice tourists to visit cities for the economic benefits they bring. But government money is also spent on social welfare to support those citizens who are unable to survive at a basic level without that support. Whose needs take priority here?

Public space becomes by necessity the domain in which the marginalised – the homeless, the poor, displaced indigenous people – spend most of their time. This in turn proves to be a problem for the government also promoting a safe city as the same public spaces of the city are ironically where middle-class visitors also spend much of their time. In such spaces the marginalised are often perceived as a threat or unsightly in the city. Their behaviour can be too easily labelled as causing 'affront' to paraphrase anti-social behaviour legislation. In such situations should the state use the law to relocate homeless people to make the image of the safe city more enticing for tourists?

A case study – clearing space in Adelaide for tourists

In the 1990s Adelaide City Council in South Australia introduced legislation which effectively enabled the removal of one group of 'undesirable persons' from Victoria Square in the city by making the area a dry zone, that is prescribing certain areas within the city as being 'alcohol free' – meaning no alcohol can be consumed in public. This prohibition did not apply to licensed premises within the area. Victoria Square has long been one of several Aboriginal meeting places within the city area where people would gather together and sit under the trees for several hours. It is also in the geographical centre of the city, opposite the up-market Hilton Hotel and the Adelaide Central Market which is heavily promoted as a tourist attraction. Lee-Anne Hall's research critically examines 'contested Indigenous sociality and the use of urban space such as is apparent in Adelaide's City Squares, with particular reference to Victoria Square and the consumption of alcohol within'.[69] Hall's focus on Victoria Square provides a valuable example of the manner in which law can be used to implement change to enhance the tourist gaze through indirect means not overtly seen as relevant to the tourist trade. Hall suggests:

> The threat that indigenous populations might represent, particularly when gathered in a public space using alcohol, is perceived to require containment in order to achieve a compliant if not invisible population.

When drinking took place out of view, in the city black blocks of Whitmore or Hurtle Square, Aboriginal drinking in public was 'manageable' – a problem that most of the community did not have to face. The dynamics of sitting quietly in the less frequented Squares, and being 'looked after' by the Welfare agencies changes in the move to Victoria Square. In Victoria Square they were in 'everybody's face'. Here they risked giving offence that was eventually to become a political issue for the authorities.[70]

Not long after the introduction of 'dry zone' legislation the City Council removed a public toilet in the square late one Sunday night. This public toilet had been well known as a meeting place for indigenous people in the Square. It provided some shade, seating and of course the toilet facilities at no cost. It was also subject to popular press campaigns as an eyesore and 'dangerous' given the 'loitering' that took place around it. Its removal had an immediate effect in moving on many Aboriginal persons who had used it. In its place – for a number of years – the City Council erected some shade cloths (tents without walls) on the other side of the square. In time these also disappeared.

This action can be seen as repressive as it forced the Aboriginal people to move from Victoria Square to another meeting place in the city. The Council has never indicated that the reason for the removal of the public toilet and subsequent development was intended to ensure the removal of the unsightly view of some Aboriginal persons becoming inebriated in full view of the tourist gaze from the nearby international Hilton Hotel.[71] Yet this is one effect of the change. In recent years the Hilton Hotel has been described in tourist literature as follows:

> Hilton Adelaide is ideally located overlooking Victoria Square, just 100 metres from Adelaide's shopping, theatre and business centre. The hotel is adjacent to Adelaide's famous Central Market, the heart of the city's fresh food and dining precinct. Catch the tram from the hotel's doorstep ... [72]

Indeed, it would seem that this image of Victoria Square is exactly what the Adelaide City Council were aiming for. Hall quotes from the 2002 Report produced by the Adelaide City Council, *New Directions – Capacity, Vivacity, Audacity*:

> The square is under-utilised as a gathering venue for entertainment, cultural and artistic expression. The plan proposes the Square should be the cultural and artistic hub for Adelaide, attracting tourists and facilitating social and economic development opportunities in a positive, dynamic manner.[73]

The creation of the alcohol-free zone in Victoria Square was an effective force in disguising an efficient way to change the nature of the use of a particular public place to create greater possibilities for new and varied tourist use. International visitors can now sip their cocktails within the Hilton Hotel bar and overlook a square without fear of being affronted! The visible evidence of an indigenous presence is now formally left to a large flag pole which flies the Aboriginal flag daily alongside the national flag and the State flag.

Special laws, special events and public order

One evolution of the notion of the city as tourist destination is the role that special events now play in city marketing for visitors. The Olympics, itself granted to cities and not countries, is perhaps the best-known example, but major sporting events such as motor racing, cricket and tennis would also qualify. Global sports events appear to provide all the ingredients which appear to justify action on the part of the state which ensures that such events occur without hindrance. For example, the Olympics have an international audience, are expensive, attract high numbers of visitors and also offer groups who want a world stage for their cause an almost unique opportunity to disrupt such events and attract huge publicity. In this context it is not difficult for the state to use this knowledge (and the experience of some Olympic games) to legitimate the passing of laws which provide power to policing agencies to prevent any terrorist acts through surveillance, arbitrary arrest and detention and search of people and premises.

Of course, terrorism is not the only concern in the case of global sports events such as the Olympics. Such events also form part of an ongoing marketing of cities, after all, as we have noted, it is the city that is awarded the Olympics and not a country. Thus the image of a safe and attractive city is central to the event's management. Katie Hyslop has commented on the extent to which the Olympics has been preceded by laws that seek to remove the homeless from the streets as part of the city's image management.[74] She notes that, prior to the Winter Olympics in Seoul in 1988:

> the Urban Redevelopment Law (Public Law #3646) was passed under the guise of city beautification, 48,000 buildings housing 720,000 people were destroyed between 1982 and 1988 for the purpose of building highrise apartments and commercial buildings. Ninety per cent of the dislocated people could not afford the new housing, and many were forced to live in shantytowns erected in church parking lots and other open spaces, which were often subjected to eviction by police. Closer to the Games, homeless people and street peddlers were also rounded up and removed from the city for 'beautification'.[75]

In 1996 prior to the Atlanta Summer Olympics a law was passed that criminalises homelessness, by way of prohibiting such behaviour as sleeping in a park, entering a car park without owning a car parked there, entering a vacant building without permission.[76] These attempts to sanitise the city did not go unchallenged, as Hyslop observes:

> The Metro Atlanta Task Force on Homelessness later uncovered pre-printed arrest citations that had "male, African American, homeless" typed on them, with the name and crime left blank. They later used these and the arrest warrants of the 9,000 homeless in a Federal Court suit they brought against the city. The court granted a temporary restraining order and a preliminary injunction against the city, ordering them to "cease and desist" arresting and harassing homeless people without probable cause.[77]

The Sydney Olympics in 2000 also was accompanied by similar laws[78] designed to ostensibly control behaviour in public places but clearly aimed at certain groups. A feature of these laws is that once passed for the special event, they remain in force due to the ongoing tourism in such spaces. Thus the regulations made under the Sydney Harbour Foreshore Authority Act 1998 (NSW) (which apply to the area that includes highly popular tourist areas including the Harbour Bridge and Darling Harbour) allow for the prohibition of alcohol consumption in public places within the area (which does not affect the consumption of alcohol in private licensed premises in the same area),[79] prohibit camping or using facilities for sleeping overnight,[80] prohibit the erection of 'any tent or other temporary structure',[81] and do not allow any public assembly without permission.[82] The regulations also allow for the removal of any person from the area who 'causes annoyance or inconvenience to other persons in a public area'.[83] Hyslop cites Helen Lenskyj:

> Sydney Harbour Bridge area has been successfully privatized, and there used to be about 70 homeless people living and sleeping in a park fairly close to the harbour near the Opera House, she says.
> Sydney Harbour Foreshore's legislation is the pertinent one that's empowering private security and police to get rid of what they see as undesirable people in their tourist area, particularly for New Year because that's when the big fire works display is happening on the Harbour Bridge.[84]

The removal of the homeless from tourist areas in Sydney continues. In 2009 at Bondi Beach a group of seven homeless men who had taken up residence at a pavilion owned by the local council were subjected to eviction proceedings in the Supreme Court. Bondi Beach is one of the most popular tourist destinations in Australia and in recent times has undergone significant re-development. As the homeless men in this case argued, a consequence of this development is the lack of affordable housing in the area for traditional residents, thus for the Council to seek their removal is at odds with their obligation to ensure there is such housing in the area.[85] Even though State Environmental Planning Policy (Affordable Rental Housing) 2009 places obligations on local governments to aim to ensure that affordable rental housing is retained in their areas, the local Mayor was quoted as saying that: 'The issue of social housing is a State Government issue; it's not a council issue. Social housing is for people who are in desperate need, and fulfil lots of criteria, but the desire to live specifically in Bondi is unrealistic.'[86] Yet the meaning of 'affordable housing' in the Policy is clearly not restricted to social housing as in publicly provided housing. The government's own literature identifies the aims of the policy to include partnerships between private and not-for-profit housing providers to increase the supply of affordable housing, and that such housing 'is not just about providing accommodation, it is about overcoming patterns of social disadvantage and fostering healthy, inclusive and diverse societies and communities'.[87]

In December 2009 the New South Wales Supreme Court removed the temporary injunction preventing the Council from removing the homeless men from the Bondi Beach pavilion although they intend to appeal.[88] Cases such as this test the capacity of the law to balance the needs of the marginalised with the desire to develop the urban landscape for more affluent tourists. Such laws are usually presented as justifiable attempts to make a city safe for tourists. But they can also be criticised for hiding social problems and cleaning up the streets to present a false image for visitors and possible investors in the city. They clearly deny diversity within the city.

While the Olympics may be the highest-profile example of the way in which the state uses the law to create space for tourism there are others. The World Cup soccer tournament also carries with it this approach (witness French police arresting suspected terrorists prior to the start of the 1998 competition) and the Grand Prix in Melbourne, Victoria is another example. This latter case is instructive for it shows how the issues revolve around matters of space: in the case of the Melbourne Grand Prix local protesters opposed the use of a public park for the holding of the Grand Prix and their protests led directly to laws which seek to protect the race from disruption emanating from such opposition.

The Victorian law which regulates the Grand Prix – the Australian Grands Prix Act 1994 (Vic) – demonstrates how the law can be used to create space for events. The Act creates the Australian Grand Prix Corporation, with the power, *inter alia*, 'to do all … things necessary for or in connection with the conduct and financial and commercial management of each Formula One event promoted by the Corporation'.[89] The Corporation can control admission into the declared area (the area within which the race is held and spectators watch).[90] Section 32 authorises the Corporation to fence the declared area, and the Corporation may also close any road within the declared area.[91] The Act also exempts any activity carried out by the Corporation within the declared area from being held to be a nuisance[92] and vehicle emissions and noise within the declared area are not subject to environment protection, health or local government legislation.[93] These provisions are noteworthy because the area in question is otherwise a public park. In effect the law privatises the park for the duration of the race.

The Act also empowers the government to make regulations for, *inter alia*, 'the prohibition or regulation of any activity in the declared area in respect of a year during the race period in respect of that year', 'the exclusion or expulsion from the declared area in respect of a year during the race period in respect of that year of persons found contravening the regulations' and 'the prohibition or regulation of any activity in an area fenced off or cordoned off in accordance with section 32'.[94]

The legislation supporting the Sydney Olympics[95] might be a point of comparison with the Victoria Act above. While the Act placed Olympic development outside the usual environment and development processes[96] it nevertheless provided a number of principles which any Olympic development must be measured against as well as processes of consultation which must be followed.[97] These included such matters as 'the arrangements made for persons with disabilities', 'the consistency of the proposed development with ecologically sustainable development' and 'the impact of the proposed development on heritage items, heritage conservation areas and potential archaeological sites'.[98]

The modern city as 'legilopolis'

But of course, the laws which regulate behaviour arising from and related to the Olympics will not be found in such a law. Greater surveillance powers by law enforcement are not uncommon for such events. Increased powers for ASIO[99] go hand in hand with major events such as the Olympics because of the concern for terrorist attacks which now form a part of ongoing considerations for all large tourist events. The real issue is thus the extent to which the law in seeking to provide a context within which global sporting events can take place (and the related tourism which occurs with such events) also changes the legal culture of the place with respect to how that state treats its citizens. It is often said that such laws, brought in to deal with the short-term security issues arising out of a particular event, are rarely repealed when the event is over. The important matter to consider is thus whether the needs of the tourism industry should be used to justify significant changes in the relationship between citizens and the state.

Yet the relationship between the citizen and the state in the modern city is not simply mediated by the law. What this examination of the manner in which cities are being recast to accommodate tourism indicates is that the city has become a 'legilopolis' – a patchwork of law, legal discourse and spatial regulation that utilises other disciplines where necessary to achieve a change in the manner in which cities control their urban spaces. This control is for the most part directed to the needs of those who have an interest in attracting global capital. While that aim is presented as benefitting everyone, it is clear that this does not always result in actions which are in everyone's interests. The displacement of indigenous people and the homeless from many city spaces is testament to that.

However, it must be conceded that the 'legilopolis' does offer an opportunity for those who are dispossessed. The recasting of the city for the purposes of tourism is not a monolith that cannot be breached. At various turns it does require law to support it, or the language of the law. And whenever that occurs there is the possibility of debate and argument about how that law sits with other legal discourse. A central ethos of the law is that there is usually an alternative discourse to consider. In the case of the dispossessed this may result in the application of human-rights norms or other legislative developments, such as the affordable housing policy in New South Wales. Thus, while the legal patchwork can present as overwhelming and all powerful, it is more akin to a labyrinth from which properly resourced and skilled advocates might be able to discover the means to challenge the final shape of the city to some extent. The question is whether in the modern 'legilopolis' there are even many spaces for such advocates.

Notes

1 J. Hannigan, *Fantasy City: Pleasure and Profit in the Postmodern Metropolis* (Routledge, London and New York, 1998), p. 91.
2 B. Holcomb, 'Marketing cities for tourism' in D.R. Judd and S.S. Fainstein (eds) *The Tourist City* (New Haven, Yale University Press, 1999), p. 54.
3 S. Zukin, *The Cultures of Cities* (Cambridge, Mass., Blackwell, 1995), p. 290.
4 Ibid., p. 291.
5 See below, pp. 78–81.
6 M. Abrahamson, *Global Cities* (New York and Oxford, Oxford University Press, 2004), p. 37.
7 Article VI.
8 Article X.
9 P. Boniface and P. J. Fowler, *Heritage and Tourism in 'the Global Village'* (London, Routledge, 1993), p. 61.
10 Ibid., p. 70.
11 Ibid.
12 Ibid., p. 71.
13 The 'Queenslander' house is an iconic style of architecture with the main living area raised above ground (as if on stilts) and allowing cool breezes to flow through the house as windows face in each direction. The houses of this design were thus perceived as being particularly suitable for a hot, but often wet climate.

14 G. Davison, 'The Meanings of Heritage' in G. Davison and C. McConville, *A Heritage Handbook* (Sydney, Allen and Unwin, 1991), p. 3.
15 See, e.g., *Historic Buildings Act 1974* (Vic), *Heritage Act 1977* (NSW) and *Heritage Act 1978* (SA).
16 C. Simpson, 'Heritage what's in a name?', *Alternative Law Journal* (1994) 19(4): 161.
17 R. Fisher, 'Nocturnal demolitions: the long march towards heritage legislation in Brisbane' in J. Rickard and P. Spearritt (eds) *Packing the Past?* (Melbourne, Melbourne University Press, 1991), p. 55.
18 Ibid., p. 55.
19 Ibid.
20 See, e.g., s4 and Schedule of the *Queensland Heritage Act* 1992 (Qld).
21 Fisher, 'Nocturnal demolitions', p. 58.
22 P. Mullins, 'The evolution of Australian tourism urbanisation' in S.S. Fainstein, L.M. Hoffman and D.R. Judd (eds) *Cities and Visitors* (Oxford, Blackwell Publishing, 2003), p. 126.
23 B. Holcomb, 'Marketing cities for tourism' in D.R. Judd and S.S. Fainstein (eds) *The Tourist City* (New Haven, Yale University Press, 1999), p. 56.
24 J.K. Walton, *Blackpool* (Edinburgh, Edinburgh University Press, 1998), p. 1.
25 *Stay Blackpool 2009* (Brochure) (www.stayblackpool.com).
26 Ibid., p. 5.
27 Boniface and Fowler, *Heritage and Tourism in 'the Global Village'*, pp. 76–77.
28 Environmental Protection and Biodiversity Conservation Act 1999 (Cth)., s.528.
29 Environment Protection and Biodiversity Conservation Regulations 2000, regn 10.03A(2). Regn 10.03A(3) provides that 'the *cultural* aspect of a criterion means the indigenous cultural aspect, the non-indigenous cultural aspect, or both'.
30 Australia Department of the Environment, Water, Heritage and the Arts, *The Australian Environment Act: Report of the Independent review of the Environment Protection and Biodiversity Conservation Act 1999* (The Hawke Report Final Report, Canberra, October 2009), para. 116.
31 Ibid., para. 115.
32 Australian Government, *Tourism White Paper: The Future View of Australian Tourism* (Commonwealth of Australia, Canberra, 2003).
33 Ibid., p. 42.
34 Ibid.
35 Ibid., p. 43.
36 B. Boer and G. Wiffen, *Heritage Law in Australia* (Victoria, Oxford University Press, 2006), p. 93.
37 Heritage Act 1977 (NSW), s. 4A. 'Local heritage significance' has a similar meaning but in relation to an area rather than the State.
38 Heritage Act 1995 (Vic), s. 3.
39 Queensland Heritage Act (Qld) 1992, s. 2.
40 Department for Culture, Media and Sport, *Heritage Protection for the 21st Century* (Cm 5057, London, March 2007).
41 Ibid., p. 30.
42 Ibid., p. 21.
43 Draft Heritage Protection Bill (UK), cl. 1.
44 Ibid., cl. 2(1).
45 UK Department for Communities and Local Government: Planning Policy Statement: *Consultation Paper on a New Planning Policy Statement 15: Planning for the Historic Environment* (London, July 2009).

46 English Heritage, *PPS Planning for the Historic Environment: Historic Environment Planning Practice Guide* (Living Draft, London, 24 July 2009).

47 UK Department for Communities and Local Government: Planning Policy Statement: *Consultation Paper on a New Planning Policy Statement 15*, para. 1.1.

48 Ibid., p. 14 (Annex A: Draft Planning Policy Statement)

49 Ibid., p. 15 (Policy HE2.2).

50 Ibid. (Policy HE2.3)

51 Ibid., p. 30.

52 English Heritage, *PPS Planning for the Historic Environment: Historic Environment Planning Practice Guide*, p. 6.

53 J.M. Conforti, 'Ghettos as tourist attractions', *Annals of Tourism Research* (1996), 23(4): 830–42.

54 'Racial or religious groups could be picked out for hi-tech airport checks', *Guardian* 1 January, 2010. Since then the United States government has announced that passengers departing for the United States from 14 specified countries will be searched more thoroughly.

55 Australian Government, *Counter-Terrorism White Paper Securing Australia: Protecting Our Community* (Canberra, Commonwealth of Australia, 2010).

56 'Rudd's new terror trap', *The Age* (Melbourne), 23 February 2010.

57 E.g. 'Australia declares "permanent" terror threat', *The Vancouver Sun*, 23 February 2010 (www.vancouversun.com).

58 T. Mordue, 'Tourism, urban governance and public space', *Leisure Studies* (2007) 26(4): 447–62, p. 448.

59 Ibid., p. 450 citing T. Edensor, 'Staging tourism: tourists as performers', *Annals of Tourism Research* (2000) 27: 322–44, p. 328.

60 Ibid., p. 450.

61 Ibid., p. 451.

62 *Crime and Disorder Act 1998* (UK), s. 1(1).

63 T. Walsh, *No Offence: The Enforcement of Offensive Language and Offensive Behaviour Offences in Queensland* (2006), p. 1.

64 S.S. Fainstein, L.M. Hoffman and D.R. Judd 'Introduction', in D.R. Judd and S.S. Fainstein (eds) *The Tourist City* (New Haven, Yale University Press, 1999), p. 35.

65 *Safe Newcastle Strategy 2009–2012*, p. 27.

66 Ibid., p. 38.

67 D. Grewcock, 'Museums of cities and urban futures: new approaches to urban planning and the opportunities for museums of cities', in *Museum International*, No. 231, September 2006 (Urban Life and Museums, Proceedings of the first conference of CAMOC. ICOM'S new International Committee for the collections and Activities of Museums and Cities), 32–41, p. 35.

68 J. Urry, 'Sensing the City' in D.R. Judd and S.S. Fainstein (eds) *The Tourist City* (New Haven, Yale University Press,1991), p. 71.

69 L. Hall, 'Sitting down in the square: indigenous presence in an Australian city', *Humanities Research: Cultural Politics and Iconography*, Vol. XL No. 2004 Humanities Research Centre and the Centre for Cross Cultural Research, Australian National University, ACT, Australia (2004), p. 56.

70 Ibid., p. 63.

71 A newspaper report did note that calls for a ban on alcohol consumption in Victoria Square included the statement that 'people, particularly tourists, did not feel safe in Victoria Square': 'Call for alcohol ban in city square', *The Advertiser*, 17 December 1997, p. 37.

72 http://www.holidaycity.com/adelaide-victoriasq/index.html, accessed 30.11.2006.

73 Hall, 2004, p. 69, citing Adelaide City Council, *New Directions – Capacity, Vivacity, Audacity* (2002), p. 20.
74 K. Hyslop, 'With Olympics came new laws to sweep up homeless', *The Tyee*, 14 October 2009, http://thetyee.ca.
75 Ibid.
76 Ibid.
77 Ibid. Hyslop also notes reports that similar laws have been drafted in British Columbia requiring the homeless to be taken to shelters, although it is noted that critics argue such a law would possibly violate the Canadian Charter of Rights and Freedoms: 'BC preparing new law to apprehend homeless', http://thetyee.ca, 21 September 2009. Press reports suggest that a similar process is occurring in New Delhi where beggars are being cleared from parts of the city in preparation for the Commonwealth Games later in the year: 'Beggars pay price for Delhi's beautification' *The Weekend Australian*, 27-28 February, 2010, p.19.
78 Ibid.
79 *Sydney Harbour Foreshore Authority Regulation 2006*, reg. 9.
80 *Sydney Harbour Foreshore Authority Regulation 2006*, reg. 4(1)(j).
81 *Sydney Harbour Foreshore Authority Regulation 2006*, reg. 4(1)(k).
82 *Sydney Harbour Foreshore Authority Regulation 2006*, reg. 5.
83 *Sydney Harbour Foreshore Authority Regulation 2006*, reg. 23.
84 Hyslop, 'With Olympics came new laws to sweep up homeless', citing H. Lenskyj, *Olympic Industry Resistance: Challenging Olympic Power and Propaganda*.
85 'Homeless men at Bondi pavilion claim roof with a view', *Sydney Morning Herald*, 6 September 2009. The appeal was unsuccessful.
86 Ibid.
87 New South Wales *Supporting Affordable Rental Housing: Community Guide* (July, 2009), p. 3.
88 'Homeless to be evicted from Bondi', *Sydney Morning Herald*, 15 December 2009.
89 Australian Grands Prix Act 1994 (Vic), s. 20.
90 Ibid., s. 21.
91 Ibid., s. 33.
92 Ibid., s. 36.
93 Ibid., s. 39.
94 Ibid., s.51.
95 Olympic Co-ordination Authority Act 1995 (NSW).
96 Ibid., s. 23.
97 Ibid., s. 24.
98 Ibid., s. 24 (3) (e), (f) and (g).
99 Australian Security Intelligence Organisation.

Chapter 4

The exalted cultural tourist

Gazing on culture

> ... it was the opening of the Museum of Slavery in the new Albert Dock tourism complex that had the greatest symbolic and spiritual impact. This award-winning museum shows how Liverpool was central to the slave trade. It graphically depicts the whole process of slavery, and names the many established Liverpool families who made their fortunes from slavery. Here is a case where the telling of a buried story provides some grounds for healing a divided city, and, in so doing, acts as a catalyst for regeneration and growth.
>
> (Leonie Sandercock, *Mongrel City*, London, Continuum, 2003, p. 213)

The point of the exalted tourist is to present tourism as a noble pursuit. A *Global Code of Ethics* outlines this construction of tourism and the redefining of tourism as 'sustainable' reinforces this view of the place of tourism. Indeed, tourism is not only eco-friendly, it is cast in terms which makes it essential if the environment is to be preserved. Within the urban landscape the tourist is exalted for all the benefits he or she brings to the city and its inhabitants. Tourists are seen as a necessity for the regeneration of cities. Tourism is likewise presented as the means by which heritage is preserved for future generations.

Of course, we question much of this framework. This discourse of tourism is often self-justifying and more particularly when cast in these terms can lead to a redefining of cities as sites of consumption which remove citizenship rights from local people and raise the consuming tourist to such an exalted status that their needs override all others. Law can also be harnessed to reinforce this process at various points, or even if not the formal law, then a discourse that borrows heavily from law in its style and language.

In the last chapter we discussed the material world of the city and how tourism has acted to recast the city. The patchwork of heritage, public order and special-event laws support this process, even though most of these laws rarely refer to tourism. However, many official documents and reports do explicitly connect the processes of these laws with tourism and together they construct the discourse to which we refer. In this chapter we examine the notion of culture within tourism particularly as it first applies to movable culture. This is spatial regulation of a different kind and illustrates the contradictory impulses within law to which we referred at the end of the last chapter. For example, are antiquities plundered from another time to be retained as the property of one country, or repatriated as stolen artefacts? Which stories of a city are to be kept in our museums, our memories?

The tourist that travels for cultural purposes is often exalted to a higher degree than the 'pleasure seeker' tourist. To travel to visit a museum is often presented as more worthy than travel for sport or sunbathing. The question we ask is whether the cultural tourist is actually more dangerous than the 'pleasure seeking' tourist, as the former's appetite for more and more 'culture' requires the commodification of new objects in museums around the globe. Does the cultural tourist sow the seeds of the destruction of culture rather than assist in its preservation? We also explore in this chapter some aspects of the connection between Indigenous culture and tourism. Again, is the respect for other cultures that is called for in the Global Code of Ethics the protector of Indigenous culture, or does it implicitly create an acceptance that Indigenous culture too is 'for sale'. In telling the story of Indigenous people, is it to be packaged for tourist consumption by those who control the museums and other urban theme parks, or do we allow Indigenous people to speak for themselves and let the past haunt the present?

Cultural property and tourism

The cultural tourist will gravitate to the city to embrace the opportunity to consume those major sites of culture which are heavily promoted as part of the 'must see' places on the tourism map. Art galleries and museums are the usual cultural venues which are high on the priority list of tourists, and to that end the museum has undergone radical change in the past decade or so to accommodate tourist expectations. One also has to bear in mind the extent to which museums are now, in effect, competing with other parts of the urban scene for customers. As we discussed in the previous chapter the city generally has remade itself to attract tourism. Museums, as the holders of key items of cultural heritage, are part of that landscape. As Shaw and Williams say of Las Vegas:

> The city is one large fantasy space, comprising a series of theme parks, each of which offers varying elements to the visitor, such as hotels, casinos, art galleries, museums, tourist attractions and shopping malls. These, in turn, are a complex series of overlapping symbolic spaces, which have different orders of meaning.[1]

The extent to which the museum has become a 'theme park' is also evident in the literature. New technology is now used in many museums to explain the past[2] and the location of local museums, as Shaw and Williams note, within shopping centres 'represent new forms of competition, and often involve significant public–private collaboration in the context of new forms of governance'.[3] Thus in defining which forms of heritage will be displayed in such spaces, one can see that cultural artefacts, which might tell stories that are contradictory to the centrality of capital to the way of life, could be marginalised or disposed of altogether.

Cultural institutions and the city: the museum and art gallery

The example of the blockbuster exhibition

Is the modern museum today thus saving cultural heritage or commodifying the past? The museum is now seen to be in competition with other fields of entertainment and leisure and accordingly we have seen a new type of museum emerge which focuses on the 'museum experience' where consumptive 'infotainment' is the primary focus. This shift in the role of the museum occurred as government funding declined in the 1990s and museums came under pressure to seek private funding and so to regard their role as a business in the market place. Pitman succinctly described the situation in Britain at the time:

> Anyone with a taste for commercial absurdity and kitsch pop culture will find much to admire in the more 'advanced' enclaves of the museum world today. A new breed of museum directors, curators and historians by name but more like management consultants by nature is revamping and refocusing museum collections and exhibitions to lure the ever-growing hordes of fee-paying, gift buying visitors required to make ends meet.[4]

Pitman's comments could equally apply to Australian museums as they underwent a similar transformation in the 1990s. For example, museums would sometimes appoint marketing managers to their boards, to participate directly in decision making about which exhibitions to run. As a result we now often see the 'blockbuster' exhibition being held as a means of attracting visitors. Such exhibitions may be seen to bring new visitors into museums and so assist in their ongoing commercial viability. But it is also this need for commercial viability that calls into question the manner in which decisions are made about which cultural heritage should be preserved and displayed.

The museum and the marketplace

With the dominant government ideology of economic rationalism the change in museum policy reflected this approach. The new corporate model was seen as the way forward in an increasingly financially strapped institution. Thus the fundamental role of the museum as a keeping place was challenged.[5] The result of this new policy direction saw a resulting tension between the traditional scholastic approach of the museum and the new-look museum which emphasises 'mega' exhibitions and other forms of entertainment which have the broadest popular 'market' appeal.

With an eye to the tourist consumer the Victoria and Albert Museum in London entered into a commercial arrangement whereby it would market an exclusive range of products, such as wallpaper and fabrics based on items in the Museum's collection. It has further been described by a leading British advertising firm as 'an ace café with a museum attached'.[6] It is no accident that the museum café and the gift shop have become an increasingly important part of the profit-making aspect of the museum 'business'.

There is now a generation of budding tourists who have only ever known the large state museums and galleries as places of consumption where you will find a specially created shopping area at the completion of your blockbuster tour. Not only will you find glossy catalogues of the exhibition but anything from erasures, pencils, silk scarves and mugs all featuring some identification with the blockbuster you have just been to see. These exhibition shops are usually created solely for the purpose of selling merchandise of the exhibition. The museum or gallery still has a permanent store for you to purchase other 'knick knacks' to take home from your tour.

The pressure for museums to compromise their role as educator in order to provide entertainment has become increasingly difficult with the business of museums being focused on tourist numbers. The tourist dollar is the benchmark for gauging success and with that the exhibition which will have the broadest appeal to the mass market. The 'safe exhibit' and 'infotainment' are sure ways of satisfying the largest possible number of consumers. It has also been argued that corporate sponsorship will ensure that radical exhibitions which challenge important social history themes will either be sufficiently tamed or overlooked all together in the chase for corporate sponsorship.[7]

An example of the pressure placed on museums to sway towards the 'safe exhibit' was witnessed with the closing of the Serrano exhibition at the National Gallery in Victoria. It was suggested at the time that the notorious Serrano painting *Piss Christ* was removed primarily because of its disruption to the blockbuster Rembrandt exhibition and not because of the perceived danger to staff and other works of art at the National Gallery. The demonstrations held at the Gallery of the Serrano exhibition led to a significant drop in attendance numbers for the Rembrandt exhibition. If these numbers continued to decline there would be serious financial implications for the Art Exhibitions Australia company who were responsible for bringing the exhibition to Australia. *The Australian* newspaper summarised the financial position of the company as follows:

> AEA has more riding on the Rembrandt exhibition show than any it has ever been involved in, having invested its entire reserves of around $5million in making up the short fall between the total budget of $7million and sponsorship of $2.78 million. To break even it needs 2500 plus visitors a day. If anything detracts from this target claimed by some gallery watchers as optimistic the organization would be in severe trouble.[8]

With the amount of money tied up in the 'business' of the Rembrandt exhibition the expectation is that there would be considerable pressure placed on Timothy Potts the Director of the National Gallery at the time to take whatever steps were necessary to ensure the success of the exhibition.

The enormous cost of mounting 'blockbuster' exhibitions ensures that the visitor must have the greatest number of enticements to spend, to enable the recouping of the initial cost of mounting the exhibition. This is not to suggest that the blockbuster exhibit is completely devoid of cultural importance but rather that the nature of the exhibit has as its simplistic aim the obtaining of the largest amount of paying visitors possible passing through the gallery doors. The whole exercise begins to be formulaic and has been succinctly summarised as follows:

> These frankly commercial exercises are potentially hugely profitable and they more-or-less follow the formula invented by Thomas Hoving at the Metropolitan Museum of Art, New York combining high-profile museum objects, glamorous design and ruthless marketing to attract the public in large numbers and sell them vast quantities of goods specially created for the purpose. The scholarly content can be minimal or non-existent, but a few of the objects must always seem exceptionally eye catching and carefully selected for systematic exploitation by those marketing the goods being sold alongside the exhibition as well as advertising the exhibit itself.[9]

The Rembrandt example

'Rembrandt: A Genius and His Impact' was staged in Melbourne at a cost of $7million, with the works insured for more than $1 billion dollars.[10] On the first day of the exhibition, 2000 people had viewed the exhibition by 3pm. At a cost of $18.00 per person and $44.00 for a family consisting of 2 children and 2 adults, it is to be assumed that it is aimed at the tourist, the families of the middle-class and the affluent. With the expected visitor rate at 350 persons per hour to view 28 paintings by Rembrandt, 44 paintings by his pupils and another 50 drawings and etchings on display,[11] one can only guess at what might have been effectively viewed. But to 'experience' the event would be another matter altogether. The promotion of the Rembrandt exhibition also made mention of a Rembrandt Family Day and Christmas party which would provide free entertainment such as Twister the clown, Artie mouse, Dutch dance groups in traditional costume and other musical entertainment with a Dutch flavour.[12] Whether you see much of the exhibition may be irrelevant in the final analysis as long as you can say you have 'been there', and have some mementos purchased on the day to savour the memory.

The blockbuster by and large relies on large collections of cultural property being collated on a theme and packaged in a glossy fashion. The preparation for such exhibitions can take years of careful planning and involves considerable negotiation between galleries as well as legal commitments to ensure safe travel and return of cultural property to its original destination. The cost of the process as we have seen is very great especially with changes in the economy today which sees the cultural tourist considering carefully where the tourist dollar will be spent. In recent times some blockbuster exhibitions are becoming too expensive for galleries to consider. Australia, for instance, has already indicated it is not in the position to host the travelling Egyptian exhibition *Tutankhamun and the Golden Age of the Pharaohs* which could have been shown in Australia from 2012. The Director of the Australian Museum, Frank Howarth, has indicated that Egypt had set a loan price of the collection at $10million for every six months the exhibition was on display.[13] In comparison with the large cost of the Rembrandt blockbuster in the early 1990s it is clear that the larger Australian galleries are re-thinking where and how to best capture the cultural tourist.

In contrast, Munro and Koutsoukis point out that in Los Angeles:

> Since the opening at the Los Angeles County Museum of Art in 2005 *Tutankamen and the Golden Age of the Pharaohs,* which is co-produced by the National Geographic Society, has attracted more than 6 million visitors and earned more than $US110 million in sales.[14]

The cultural tourist within Australia is offered package deals covering flights, accommodation, meal vouchers all as part of the consumption of the cultural event. Australia simply does not have the number of tourists or the density of population to carry the high cost of such an exhibition. What Australia does have, however, that is highly sought after as a tourist experience is the unique cultural heritage of the Indigenous population as well as a thriving art market for Indigenous art.

The exalted tourist and the Indigenous dollar

Australian governments have seen the tourist value of promoting Indigenous cultural heritage. Under the Keating Labor government in 1994 Australia received its first formal cultural policy which was detailed in the *Creative Nation* report.[15] In that document the report of a survey of international travellers to Australia revealed the following:

> Forty eight per cent of international tourists to Australia were interested in seeing and learning about Aboriginal and Torres Strait Islander Culture.
>
> Over a third of visitors to Australia undertook an activity related to Aboriginal and Torres Strait Islander culture; for example, visiting a gallery or museum, or taking a tour involving Aboriginal and Torres Strait Islander culture.
>
> The value of purchases of Aboriginal and Torres Strait Islander arts and souvenirs by international visitors was estimated at $446 million a year in 1991, and an increase from $30 million in 1990.[16]

It is not surprising that there would be considerable competition between various state museums in displaying their wealth of Aboriginal heritage as the interest of the cultural tourist has continued to remain high. The South Australian Museum, in recognition of this trend, decided in the late 1990s to redevelop the museum making a feature of a new Aboriginal Gallery. The South Australian Museum is reported to hold the largest collection of Aboriginal artefacts in Australia and, consistent with government policy, sought to raise the profile of Indigenous heritage by exhibiting as much of the collection as possible. At the time it was not a viable option due to lack of exhibition space. The museum also housed a large exhibit of Pacific cultures. The Pacific cultures exhibit dated back to the nineteenth century and was very popular with the local community. There was much discussion at the time with the community and the director of the museum over whether the Pacific Cultures exhibition should be dismantled to make way for an expanded new Aboriginal gallery.

One member of the community was so concerned that the Pacific gallery would be dismantled to make way for new displays, specifically more space for Aboriginal displays that he took the unusual step of seeking to have the exhibit nominated as a place to be protected. An application was lodged to the heritage committee under Heritage Act (SA) 1993. The Act aimed to preserve, protect and enhance the physical, social and cultural heritage of South Australia. The requirement for registration under the Act is that a 'place' should be of heritage value (s16) and had to satisfy one or more of the listed criteria. In the Morrow application for inclusion of the collection in the State Heritage Register, the exhibit was described as that which 'Comprises the built-in display cases of wood and glass and the displays of items from the Pacific Collection of the South Australian Museum placed upon and in front of a construction wire of corrugated metal.'[17] It was also stated that 'heritage significance of the exhibit met the criteria of aesthetic, historical and cultural interest'.[18]

The usual matters coming before the Heritage Committee would be dealing with built heritage such as public buildings thought to have historic importance to the people of South Australia. Advice at the time from the Crown Solicitor to the Heritage Committee suggested that an exhibit could not be considered a 'place' under the Act and as a result the application failed. The community concern about the intention to remove the exhibit was further demonstrated by correspondence to the *Adelaide Advertiser* newspaper as well as national daily *The Australian*. It had been reported at the time that the then Museum Director, Dr Chris Anderson, was committed to retaining the traditional values of the exhibit and to displaying Pacific culture in the museum and that this could still be achieved with a smaller-sized exhibit relocated elsewhere in the museum.[19] Those who wished the exhibit to be retained in its original manner had focused on the unique nature of the exhibit. The *Adelaide Advertiser* quoted the views of the local community who were concerned for the welfare of the exhibit:

> Mr Steve Ronayne of Adelaide's Aptos Cruz Galleries, said the Pacific Islands Gallery was of national and international significance. He supported increasing the exhibition space for the Museum's Aboriginal collection but not at the expense of the Pacific Island's Gallery. All the other Australian museums have removed their Victorian turn of the century exhibitions: they no longer exist he said ...

and

> Lecturer in Anthropology at the University of Adelaide, Dr Deane Fergie, said the State would be the loser if the Pacific Island Gallery was altered. That's the perfect thing about Adelaide in a general sense, we've changed so little that we've retained what other places haven't. Dr Fergie said 'the minute you pull it down you've lost a huge opportunity for making people reflect on how they think about Indigenous people'.[20]

The tension between the role of the museum operating in the traditional sense and the museum as business is clearly visible in this instance. All indicators at the time did point to the commercial viability of a greater display of Aboriginal culture and each state museum was looking to capture the tourist dollar through this form of attraction. Tim Lloyd, writing for the *Adelaide Advertiser*, had reported at the time: 'Multimillion-dollar developments in Aboriginal Art at museums in Sydney, Melbourne, Brisbane and particularly in Canberra's proposed National Museum of Australia, are threatening to overshadow Adelaide's considerable international reputation in this area.'[21] But importantly he went on to comment that the Pacific collection 'is the biggest Pacific display in Australia, rivalling similar collections in St Petersburg Russia, in the Smithsonian in Washington and in the Louvre in Paris, where a major upgrade has been announced'.[22]

The proposed new gallery was clearly the major focus for the government of the day. The Premier of the State at the time, John Olsen, left no doubt as to where he saw the value of an expanded Aboriginal gallery. He commented at the time:

> The gallery would build on the museum's extensive Aboriginal collection the largest in the world and would cover about 2000 square metres. It would draw people from around the world and push the museum visitor's numbers toward one million a year. The gallery would become 'a tourist icon' the State could build upon in the future.[23]

The Pacific Cultures Gallery remains today as an example of a Victorian museum display. The exhibition was closed for quite a while as work was undertaken to further enhance the exhibit. The 1960s ceiling was removed from the area where the exhibition was housed to finally reveal once again the original Victorian lantern ceiling. The Pacific Gallery was relaunched by the current Premier of South Australia, Mike Rann, in 2006. He then said: 'The Gallery is one of the finest examples of Victorian Museology and the display cases which have been heritage listed, have also been renovated.'[24]

Community concern over the retention of the Pacific Gallery held sway and the heritage listing that was denied in the early stages of concern for the exhibit have since been accepted. It could be argued that at the time concern for the tourist dollar was exalted over and above the traditional concern of the museum as a keeping place. Today the Pacific Gallery is proudly promoted for its heritage value and offers a well-rounded experience of the changing perceptions by society of Indigenous cultures. What was seen as an old, outdated exhibit has now become part of the cultural tourist experience. The use of legislative confirmation of the heritage value of the objects has also served to raise its status. It is now a part of 'our heritage'.

A more recent example of how museums deal with Indigenous heritage and the ensuing conflict occurred in Melbourne. This episode again demonstrates the use of law as a political tool in attempting to question the validity of promoting Indigenous heritage to benefit the cultural tourist.

In 2004 the Melbourne Museum held an exhibition *Etched on Bark 1854: Kulun Barks from Northern Victoria*. Three nineteenth-century bark items made by the Indigenous people of north Victoria formed part of the exhibition. The Dja Dja Wurrung bark etchings were obtained on loan from the British Museum and from the Royal Botanic Gardens in Kew. The loan was arranged through Museum Victoria and the usual contractual arrangement had been made. The Curator Emeritus for Museum Victoria, Elizabeth

Willis, also indicated that the usual consultation practice with Aboriginal groups had taken place.

The Museum's Aboriginal Cultural Heritage Advisory Council (ACHAC) was consulted before any approach was made to the lending organisations, and informal consultation occurred with members of Aboriginal Community Councils in the year before the exhibition opened. At his request, Gary Murray, then a member of ACHAC, read the exhibition text and suggested an additional display element.[25]

The contractual arrangements were standard in that the loan was temporary and the objects would be returned safely to the lending institutions. It was only after the exhibition had been open for six weeks that everything went awry for the Melbourne Museum. Gary Murray, who was a member of Dja Dja Wurrung, made a plea to the Australian Prime Minister to keep the bark etchings permanently in Australia.[26]

Indigenous heritage is protected under a range of legislation dealing with tangible heritage. The Protection of Movable Cultural Heritage Act 1986 (Cth) as the title suggests aims to protect certain movable cultural heritage. The object of the Act is not to prohibit the export of all cultural heritage beyond Australian shores but only that which is so significant that its loss would diminish Australia's cultural heritage. Under the Regulations of the Act a National Control List is established setting out categories of objects which may be subject to a permit or certificate under the Act. Part one of the list covers objects of Australian Aborigines and Torres Strait Islander heritage. The Regulations make it clear that an object is in this category if:

(a) it is an object
   (i) of cultural significance to Aboriginal or Torres Strait Islander people;
   (ii) made by Aboriginal or Torres Strait Islander people;

and

(b) it is not an item created specifically for sale; and
(c) for an object mentioned in item 1.4 it:
   (i) is at least 30 years old; and
   (ii) is not adequately represented in Aboriginal or Torres Strait Islander community collections, or public collections in Australia.[27]

The Regulations continue to specify the following objects of this category as Class A objects for the Act, that is objects which are not allowed to be exported from Australia, although where the object is located outside Australia and someone wishes to temporarily import (say, for a museum exhibition) then the Minister may grant a certificate allowing for its export afterwards:

(a) sacred and secret ritual objects;
(b) bark and log coffins used as traditional burial objects;
(c) human remains;
(d) rock art;
(e) denroglyphs.[28]

The objects listed as class A objects under the Act demonstrate the variety of cultural heritage that has elevated status under the legislation. Section 12 of the Act outlines the procedure required to obtain an import certificate:

12 (1) Where a person intends to import an Australian protected object:

(a) for temporary purposes; or
(b) in circumstances in which the person may wish subsequently to export the object;

the person may apply to the Minister for a certificate authorising the exportation of the object.

This section of the Act allows for museums and galleries to bring in cultural property from overseas on a temporary basis for exhibition thus ensuring that the return of the object/s to the overseas destination from whence they came. The objective of the Act is to keep limited cultural heritage within Australian shores. Many Aboriginal artists have an outstanding reputation as artists and their work sells very well in the international market.

There is no intention in the Act to restrict the livelihood of living artists and the representation of Aboriginal work overseas has enhanced the desire for the cultural tourist to visit Australia to learn more about Indigenous heritage. The aim of the Act is not to restrict the movement of cultural heritage except in the limited circumstances outlined in the legislation. The Act also ensures that those objects of significant Australian heritage can be brought into the country on a temporary basis for exhibition or sale confident in the knowledge that provided the procedure is carried out correctly according to the Act there is a safe passage of the loan guaranteed. This would have been the reasonable assumption held by the British Museum and the Royal Botanic Gardens, Kew.

The Aboriginal and Torres Strait Islander Heritage Protection Act 1984 (Cth) also contains provisions that protect and preserve areas and objects of particular significance to Aboriginal people. Section 12 of the Act provides for the making of declarations by the minister in response to an application from Aboriginal people that a place or object of particular significance to

Aboriginal people is under threat of injury or desecration. The declaration can state what has to happen to ensure the preservation of the place or object, but it cannot prevent the export of the item if there is a certificate in force under section 12 of the Protection of Movable Cultural Heritage Act 1986 (Cth), discussed above.[29] Under s. 21C of the Aboriginal and Torres Strait Islander Heritage Protection Act 1984 (Cth) emergency declarations can also be made with respect to places or objects of particular significance to Aboriginal people. Prott explains the effect of that provision in her summary of the case:

> … an amendment to the Commonwealth Aboriginal and Torres Strait Islander Heritage Protection Amendment Act in 1987 provided that Victorian Aboriginal people could apply to the Victorian Minister for Aboriginal Affairs for an emergency, temporary, or other declaration if they considered that Aboriginal objects or places were under threat of desecration … The minister was also empowered to compulsorily acquire any Aboriginal cultural property if the minister was satisfied that it was necessary to maintain the relationship between Aboriginals and that object. The Dja Dja Wurrung Group used this legislation to obtain temporary emergency declarations from an inspector under the Act, preventing the museum from returning borrowed etchings to England.[30]

This whole process proved to be very embarrassing for Museum Victoria as the initial declaration was followed by eight more emergency declarations.[31] The newspapers had a field day with the story and it quickly grew out of all proportion. Willis describes how after the first emergency declaration had taken place Gary Murray in his role as prominent member of the Dja Dja Wurrung group was using very emotive language by claiming that the objects were stolen.[32]

Willis was especially concerned with the way the issue took on a life of its own with very little accuracy being reported but much being made of the British Museum and its long history with the retention of the Elgin marbles. Willis points out that:

> It was an easy move from the Kulin barks to the Elgin marbles. Murray visited the offices of a Greek language newspaper in Melbourne and described how 'the cultural heritage of both Australia's Aboriginal people and the Greek people have been plundered and devastated by … a common enemy, the disreputable institution known as the British Museum.[33]

The Museum of Victoria then went to the Federal Court of Australia to obtain orders that the emergency declarations were not validly made.

The terms of the emergency declaration included the following terms and conditions:

a. That the three cultural objects will continue to be displayed and/or secured at Museum Victoria under the direction of the Inspector in consultation with the relevant Traditional Owners by the Manager Bunjilaka Aboriginal Centre.
b. That the State of Victoria and Museum Victoria will negotiate with Traditional Owners the Dja Dja Wurrung and Jupagalk Native Title Groups as to the future location of the three cultural heritage objects.
c. That the British and Australian Governments negotiate the final repatriation of all Indigenous Australian Ancestral Human Remains and Grave Goods held without consent by various British institutions and privately for recovery, return and reburial by Australian Traditional Owners.[34]

The Act allows for a process of emergency declarations followed by temporary declarations and then a permanent declaration. The initial declarations are time limited and are made, as in this case, by an inspector. Following that, the scheme is to allow for ministerial decision making presumably after negotiation with all interested parties. The making of successive emergency declarations was thus held to be invalid by the Court.[35] In response to an argument that the Act should be read beneficially, Ryan said, 'it is clear from a close reading of the Part as a whole that it is intended to strike a balance between the preservation of Aboriginal cultural property and the interests of persons likely to be affected by that preservation'.[36]

This requirement to negotiate a solution was central to the judge's approach. When it was argued that as soon as the declaration was removed the objects would be removed back to the United Kingdom the judge said:

> That result, if it occurs, will flow, not from a construction of Pt IIA, which limits the effective life of an emergency declaration, but from the failure of the Minister or the relevant local Aboriginal community to take the steps provided by s 21D or 21E including, if necessary, activating the arbitral review for which provision is made by ss 21D(7), 21E(6) and 21F.[37]

The items were then returned to the United Kingdom. While the case may appear to have been decided on a technical point, it nevertheless demonstrates the contested nature of heritage preservation in the context of the role of the museum. Writing a few years after the event Willis noted the British Museum's position with respect to the return of the objects:

The British Museum's position was clear: 'It is in the interests of everyone concerned that objects of cultural and artistic significance continue to be able to move around the world and be seen by many different peoples.' The Emergency Declaration 'puts at risk the very legal framework that allows such exhibitions to take place'.[38]

Not all Aboriginal people supported the declarations in this case as they were concerned that it would affect their relations with overseas institutions and place in jeopardy the return of other remains and objects.[39] The case thus also illustrates how the law, in seeking to allow for all parties to participate in the process of decision making, by virtue of that process allows for those interests to be weighed up in a manner that might permit the interests of marketers to outweigh the retention of an ancient culture. Not that this process is a straightforward one as myths and assumptions can operate on all sides. Willis recounts how the objects became enmeshed in the Dja Dja Wurrung people's story of past dispossession:

> For the Dja Dja Wurrung, and for many non-Indigenous commentators, the damage consequent upon colonization and dispossession was the strong story that shaped how the issue was presented. Consequently the barks became 'stolen', caught up as part of the whole colonial project, and thus a symbol of exploitation and loss. The issue became more about the wrongs wrought by colonization than about the barks *per se*.[40]

This can play on the mind of the cultural tourist too. Are they to be exalted for supporting the perspective of Aboriginal people who have decided that the object is significant? Or is the tourist's role to demand an objective assessment of any cultural artefact, if objectivity is even possible in such an area? The problem is, in seeking the virtue of being the 'cultural tourist' with all the connotations it carries for respect for other cultures, it may well be that this form of tourism also presents a risk to those cultures upon which the tourist gazes. As Wight observes:

> Indigenous people are frequently represented in brochures as having static cultures which are largely unchanged by western colonialism, economic development and the activity of tourism itself. Entire cultural facets of nations are almost always missing from brochures presenting images of Third World countries. Since the tourist expects to see primitive Indigenous cultures, industrialisation and politics are overlooked altogether, and instead a pastoral myth is presented via images and narrative. The simulation of the marketed culture is, therefore, easily realised as expectations are kept within a narrow focus, often excluding major cultural aspects of the country. These expectations are inherent in western discourse, and the images will almost always appeal to the

Eurocentric (for example, Silver discusses marketing literature depicting Tahiti in which 'exotic' women are photographed in 'primitive' dress, frequently barely clothed).[41]

This is the problem of respecting the cultural heritage of mankind as the Global Code of Ethics for Tourism[42] requires us to do. How do we decide which culture to respect? The one we see, or the one we wish to see?

Land rights, tourism and changing patterns of land usage

At the base of discussions about Indigenous culture and tourism also lies the issue of land rights. The *Mabo* decision[43] of the High Court recognised that Australian Aboriginal people were in possession of their land prior to the arrival of Europeans. But this decision does not necessarily address the issue of what prior ownership means in terms of present-day recognition of native title and its content particularly with respect to tourism and that land upon which few legal commentators appear to have turned their minds.

Trotter,[44] writing some time ago, made the following points with respect to land rights in the context of tourism: there is to a certain extent a competition between Aboriginal people and some pastoralists and mining interests over the control of some lands; the Courts have found that these competing claims can be reconciled to some extent where the uses to which the different parties wish to put the land are not incompatible; where the uses are not compatible then the courts have decided in favour of one claimant – e.g. in the case of pastoralists and Aboriginal people the High Court said in *Wik*[45] that the rights of pastoralists would prevail; the uses to which land are sought to be put are not frozen in time – as Trotter points out[46] there has been an increasing emphasis on diversifying the use of land to increase the economic returns from land rather than relying on a declining pastoral base in the case of land held under pastoral leases, and to improve the relative wealth of Aboriginal people where the land is held by Aboriginal communities; this changing use of land complicates how the question of land rights for Indigenous people is addressed – is native title to be recognised over land just for the purposes of allowing 'traditional' uses of the land to occur *or* do such rights include the right to exploit the tourist potential of the land?

Trotter demonstrates how both pastoralists and Aboriginal people have been encouraged to develop the tourist potential of their land and culture. Leaving aside the various issues which the exploitation of land and culture for tourism raises Trotter points out how the law inhibits any straightforward resolution of who should be granted the right to develop land for tourism where there is some competition for the land.

Even though the High Court said in *Wik* that the interests of pastoralists should prevail if there was a conflict with the use of the land by the Aboriginal owners, this rested on the particular facts in that case and the terms of the lease. Trotter notes that some leases in Queensland limit the nature of what is being granted in such a way that the use of the land for tourism purposes may not be permissible. Trotter concludes:

> The various acts covering leases are the legacy of a colonial past and colonial assumptions about land usage. But these legislative decisions are now proving inappropriate for contemporary Australia, where a plurality of rights are expected to be met whilst at the same time structural changes are reshaping rural economies so that strategies being proposed for rangelands discourage the current reliance on pastoralism and instead encourage greater diversity of economic activity.[47]

The concept of native title, and for that matter the nature of a pastoral lease, have the origins of their recognition in the common law and thus rely on centuries-old principles for their meaning. Thus when the High Court in *Mabo* went looking for native title in 1770 what they found did not relate to land usage which was centred around tourism. The matter has been compounded by the passage of the *Native Title Act 1993* (Cth) which after the decision in *Mabo* was enacted to provide a process for the determination of native title claims. In particular, section 223(1) provides that for native title to be recognised in relation to the claim of a particular group of Aboriginal or Torres Strait Islanders it must be shown that:

(A) The rights and interests are possessed under the traditional laws acknowledged and the traditional customs observed by the Aboriginal peoples or TSI; and

(B) The Aboriginal peoples or TSI, by those laws and customs, have a connection with the land or waters; and

(C) The rights and interests are recognised by the common law of Australia.[48]

The requirement for a 'connection' has been linked with the notion of 'continuity' which makes it difficult for a people who have been dispossessed from their lands and moved on to then prove. Thus when a native title claim was then lodged over much of what is now the Perth Metropolitan area, it was successful in the first instance[49] but on appeal this was overturned.[50] While it was never intended that the native-title claim would remove the property rights of residential and commercial landowners of Perth (and nor could it in law), the consequences for many public spaces in Perth where native title might then still exist could have been immense for tourism. This would *as a matter of law* require at least some negotiation with Aboriginal people, placing them in a position of some strength, as to how such spaces might accommodate various interests. In this way native title could deliver real changes to how tourism spaces are conceptualised if found to exist.

A footnote to this discussion is the decision, made in January 2010, not to prohibit tourists from climbing Uluru (Ayers Rock) in central Australia. Aboriginal traditional owners have for many years asked tourists not to climb the rock as it is a sacred site. In deciding not to ban it after a period of community consultation the Australian Minister for the Environment remarked:

> 'I know that there are differing views on whether or not the climb should be closed, said Mr Garrett, who told reporters last year he had never made the climb and never would.
>
> 'However, I believe the future for this internationally significant icon lies in visitor experiences that reflect its World Heritage values.
>
> 'It is one of the few places in the world renowned for its stunning natural environment, alongside living Aboriginal culture and these are great tourism drawcards we need to develop,' he said.[51]

The preservation of Indigenous culture and tourism

We have already touched upon the extent to which the promotion of a tourism industry can undermine Indigenous culture through destroying it to make way for tourist development or repackaging it for tourist consumption in such a way that the packaged product bears little resemblance to the authentic culture.

It is important to see the manner in which these issues connect to rights of ownership of land discussed above. Clearly, who controls the land will go a long way to determining who will decide how Indigenous culture is represented. This is the point that Trotter makes: both Aboriginal people and pastoralists have recognised the value of tourism in relation to the lands they occupy and Indigenous culture will always be a large part of that tourism. But who is in the best position to decide how Indigenous culture is represented to tourists? And what different emphases will there be if Indigenous culture is packaged by pastoralists as compared with Aboriginal people?

It is also the case that ownership of land is intertwined with Indigenous culture. It is upon land that religious and other ceremonies take place and the dominant form of land usage in a society often determines its cultural practices. For example, the experience of Bali shows how a society based on agriculture is being transformed by the development of mass tourism on the island. One critic of what is occurring there has referred to:

> Ibu Mas, an aristocratic Balinese whose small village guesthouse near Ubud has been recognised internationally for its holistic approach to tourism ... She believes the island is threatened as never before. The pace of change is unprecedented. Land speculation is so rampant that

parents and children now fight over what to do with their heritage. Do they sell their small holdings for tourist purposes or retain it for agriculture? "The balance has been tipped," she says. "It is creating a lot of conflict ... because the culture of jealousy is becoming stronger and working its way through families."[52]

The selling of land for tourist development not only shifts the pattern of land usage in that area it also disconnects people who have perhaps farmed that land for centuries. While the experience of Bali may be additionally affected by corruption and nepotism not so prevalent in Australia there is much to learn from this experience. Importantly, it once again raises the question – especially important for cultural tourism – that if one simply markets a locality for the purposes of maximising profit from mass tourism without limits then does one risk destroying what makes that locality unique or different and so attractive to visitors?

The Balinese experience is also illustrative of how one cannot treat protection of the environment as separate from protection of culture. There may be more widespread acceptance of preservation of the environment from the harmful impact of tourism but it is important to recognise that destruction of the environment can also destroy Indigenous culture. Put simply, polluted beaches do not just turn away visitors because of the smell – they also turn away local people from engaging in activities which enrich a locality. Thus inappropriate land usage is not just an environmental issue – it can also lead to the loss of cultural practices which can provide visitors with an insight into the history and nature of a society.

Beneath the superficial

Boniface and Fowler also examine the connection between how Indigenous culture is represented and deeper understandings of a society and its history. In the case of Hawaii there are popular stereotypes which abound. Boniface and Fowler note that there is more to Hawaii than meets the eye of the average visitor:

> Essentially, large areas of the Hawaiian islands, and particularly their leeward sides, were formerly under intensive cultivation. Remains of 'ancient fields', sometimes part of extensive organized landscapes complete with rectilinear frameworks, sophisticated irrigation systems, settlements, temples, burial sites and tracks, survive across swathes of countryside, on west-facing slopes, along river valleys and around estuaries in particular. Current research is dedicated to locating and mapping them, to elucidating their deep chronology and typologies, and to modelling their uses. The whole may be pure archaeology, of global significance in an academic sense; in another perspective, it is authentic

> Hawaiian heritage, marvellously if fortuitously preserved in a way which puts it on a par with any of the very best of analogous survivals that I have so far seen anywhere in the world.[53]

This is, of course, another example of the manner in which 'heritage' can be constructed in different ways. But it would be too simplistic to argue that the 'heritage' represented by Waikiki Beach in Hawaii is no more or less 'real' than that depicted above. This is the argument that there is no 'real' heritage – just many competing versions or claims on that notion.

While the judgement of what constitutes heritage is certainly subjective to a degree there must be some basis for making such judgements, otherwise it is merely Alice in Wonderland – 'it is heritage because I say it is heritage'. And once a person begins to articulate the basis upon which they make their decisions about heritage value it is possible to evaluate whether those judgements are well based.

For example, if a person states that certain areas of Hawaii are to be preserved because they represent important aspects of Indigenous life it might be shown by careful research that this is not the case. Or conversely it could be said that certain areas have significance for Indigenous people – but upon closer inspection there may be no evidence that this is the case. Of course, the process that determines whether such judgements have been well made must itself be open to scrutiny. But that is a separate matter. The point is that if a person wishes to argue that a place has heritage significance – or no heritage significance – then there must be reasons for so doing which can be examined and possibly shown to be ill-informed, ignorant of certain facts or otherwise lacking in validity.

The above example is useful in this regard. By looking beyond the accepted wisdom one can discover new meanings for a locality and see the place in a different way. So too in Bali a more informed understanding of the process of tourist development and its consequences enables quite different judgements to be made about the impact of tourist development on Indigenous culture.

Meaningful tourism and Indigenous culture

Perhaps one of the greatest problems in relation to Indigenous culture is deciding which representation of Indigenous culture to present to tourists. From the above it might be said in summary that a proper understanding of Indigenous culture begins with an appreciation of the manner in which land usage flows into a culture; in the case of Indigenous people there are often groups competing with them (e.g. pastoralists) for the use of the same land for tourism; whoever wins the right to use the land will likely affect how Indigenous culture is presented in that area; and while judgements about what constitutes Indigenous heritage and what is significant are somewhat subjective there is considerable scope for ensuring such judgements are soundly based.

But to the above must be added the role of the tourist in 'forcing' certain constructions of Indigenous heritage. If the market for tourism is thought to desire a particular representation of tourism then in order to profit from tourism whoever controls the definitions will be under considerable pressure to ensure that the representations conform to those expectations no matter how unauthentic such representations may actually be.

Krippendorf refers to this tension between the tourist and the natives of a locale. In his view tourism leads to greater misunderstanding or at least confirmation of the stereotypes held by tourists and their hosts. Krippendorf regards travel as promoting 'mutual misunderstanding'.[54]

An anecdotal example might be a visitor who 'really wants to purchase some Aboriginal art' to take home with them. Do they really understand the art? Is it popular with them because it is simply fashionable? Or because it is 'different'? In the latter case, is this the case – or is it that they simply believe this to be so? Are they taking home a greater appreciation of Aboriginal art or simply a token which has little meaning for them beyond some understanding of what the image might represent?

It might be asked, does this matter? Of course, to the extent that we can survive without understanding very much at all the answer might be no. But if we accept that the more understanding we have of our world the more we 'see' then of course it does matter. How can one ever judge the value of anything – for heritage or its cultural importance – without knowledge of the thing?

Indigenous culture, competing meanings and rights

In the end the role of law may be to provide a process through which these competing considerations can be assessed and protected. Krippendorf provides some advice which seems particularly apt in relation to Indigenous culture and tourism. He says that more tourism does not automatically mean more well-being.[55] In the context of the promotion of Aboriginal culture by Aboriginal people as tourism this has some importance. It is simply about not investing in tourism alone as the way forward for any group – if there is a downturn in tourism then what? For this reason other activities, cultural practices, should be preserved to either provide alternative sources of revenue or, just as importantly, mechanisms for coping with such downturns.

Second, he argues that the marketing of tourism should be honest and responsible: it is not acceptable to engage in the tourism business on the basis that one's actions can be justified as providing the customer with what he or she wants: a code should set down what is acceptable; travel marketing should be honest; destinations should be presented realistically and not as an escape to Paradise.[56] The problem is, in a post-modern age of uncertainty, what is 'reality'?

Notes

1 G. Shaw and A.M. Williams, *Tourism and Tourism Spaces* (London, Sage, 2004), p. 249.
2 Ibid., p. 256.
3 Ibid.
4 J. Pitman, *The Exhibitionists in the Directory* 1997 5–11 April 1997.
5 A.J. Beeho and R.C. Prentice, 'Evaluating the experiences and benefits gained by tourists visiting a socio-industrial heritage museum: an application of ASEB grid analysis to Blists Hill Open-Air Museum, the Ironbridge Gorge Musuem, United Kingdom', *Museum Management and Curatorship* (1995) 15(4): 371–86.
6 Editorial, *Museum Management and Curatorship* (1996) 15(4): 345.
7 R. Russell, 'The politics of interpretation: interest groups, sponsors and exhibitions', *Museum National* (1996) 5(2): 17.
8 *The Australian*, 1997: October 18–19.
9 Editorial, *Management and Curatorship* (1996a) 15(4).
10 *The Age* (Melbourne) 1997: 1 October.
11 *The Age* (Melbourne) 1997: 2 October.
12 *The Age* (Melbourne) 1997: 1 October.
13 *Sydney Morning Herald*, 5 December 2009.
14 Ibid.
15 Australian Government, *Creative Nation: Commonwealth Cultural Policy* (Canberra, October 1994).
16 Ibid., p. 100.
17 Original documentation cited courtesy of Mr Morrow the applicant.
18 Ibid.
19 *The Australian,* 1997: 11 April.
20 *The Advertiser.* 1997: 1 March.
21 *The Advertiser,* 1997: 8 March.
22 *The Advertiser,* 1997: 8 March.
23 *The Advertiser*, 1997: 9 September.
24 South Australian Museum Newsletter, December, 2006
25 E. Willis, 'The Law Politics and "Historical Wounds": The Dja Dja Wurrung Bark Etchings Case in Australia', *International Journal of Cultural Property* (2008) 15: 49–63, p. 53.
26 Ibid.
27 Protection of Movable Cultural Heritage Regulations 198 (Cth), Schedule 1, para. 1.2.
28 Ibid.
29 Aboriginal and Torres Strait Islander Heritage Protection Act 1984, s.12(3A).
30 L.V. Prott, 'The Dja Dja Wurrung Bark Etchings Case', *International Journal of Cultural Property* (2006) 13: 242–46, p. 243.
31 Ibid.
32 Willis, 'The Law Politics and "Historical Wounds"', p. 53.
33 Ibid., p. 54. Of course, the use of law to avoid issues related to the desire to recover lost objects for their tourist potential may also be an issue. The curator of a Greek museum spoke of the Elgin Marbles around the same time as this case but spoke of the legality of original transaction as justification for their

return: 'The Greek position is that this transaction [between Lord Elgin and the Ottoman authority he dealt with] was not official,' Vlizos says. 'It was just between two men, not between the governments of that time.' ('Beautiful to look at, and then to return', *Sydney Morning Herald*, 4 May 2005).

34 *Museums Board of Victoria v Rodney Carter* [2005] FCA 645 (20 May 2005), para. 2.
35 Ibid., para.25.
36 Ibid., para.34.
37 Ibid., para.36.
38 E. Willis, 'History, strong stories and new traditions: the case of "Etched on Bark 1854"', *History Australia* (2007) 4(1): 13.1–13.10 (Monash University Express), p. 13.4.
39 Ibid., pp. 13.4 – 13.5.
40 Ibid., p. 13.6.
41 Craig Wight, 'Contested national tragedies: an ethical dimension' in R. Sharpley and P.R. Stone (eds) *The Darker Side of Travel* (Bristol, Channel View Publications, 2009), pp. 129–44, p. 134.
42 Art. 4(2).
43 *Mabo v Queensland* (No. 2) (1992) 175 CLR 1.
44 R. Trotter, 'Land rights, tourist rights: whose rights?', *Media and Culture Review* (1997) 1: 1–10.
45 *Wik Peoples v Queensland* (1996) 187 CLR 1.
46 Trotter, 'Land rights, tourist rights'.
47 Ibid.
48 *Native Title Act 1993* (Cth)., s. 223(1).
49 *Bennell v State of Western Australia* (2006) 153 FCR 120.
50 *Bodney v Bennell* [2008] FCAFC 63.
51 'Tourists still free to climb Uluru', 9 January 2010, www.abc.net.au.
52 'Farewell my lovely', *Good Weekend*, 3 May 1997, p. 18.
53 P. Boniface and P.J. Fowler, *Heritage and Tourism in the 'Global Village'* (London, Routedge, 1993), pp. 57–58.
54 J. Krippendorf, *The Holiday Makers* (Oxford, Butterworth-Heinemann, 1987).
55 Ibid.
56 Ibid.

Part III

Tourism as transgression

The targeted tourist

The legal construction of fear

As of this moment we cannot predict the future of tourism. It is an industry especially sensitive to social disorder, because it relies on the unimpeded movement of large numbers of people who cluster in vulnerable places (airports, public spaces) and stand out in many circumstances, making them obvious targets.
(S.S. Fainstein, L.M. Hoffman and D.R. Judd, 'Making Theoretical Sense of Tourism' in S.S. Fainstein *et al.* (eds) *Cities and Visitors* (Malden. Blackwell, 2003, p. 250)

To deliver a safe and secure Games, in keeping with the Olympic culture and spirit.
(Home Office, UK, *London 2012 Olympic and Paralympic Safety and Security Strategy*, July 2009)

In the first half of the book we investigated tourism as a just cause. In this half of the book we consider the possibility of tourism as transgression. As we have suggested, the notion of tourism as a noble pursuit was in part a response to the extent to which tourists did not consider the consequences of their behaviour on host communities, spaces and environments. Tourism as an aspect of leisure is, as Urry suggests,[1] the opposite to work. Pleasure and not ethical or responsible behaviour is the goal that many tourists pursue. We have discussed in the first part of the book the degree to which that purpose of tourism has now been reconstructed.

Here, however, we wish to pursue the extent to which tourism *is* about transgression. In a sense, we ask the question whether transgression rather than any noble or just cause is the essence of tourism. 'Escape', 'do what you want to do', 'explore and indulge' are all terms that one connects with tourism marketing. These words seem to fit with a view of tourism that constructs it in terms of its excitement rather than its ethical behaviour. In understanding how legal discourse constructs tourism it appears to be of central importance to ourselves to explore the manner in which transgression defines the tourist and tourism.

In an age of uncertainty we are led to believe that we confront acts of transgression more frequently in the context of travel and tourism. Yet terrorism, as perhaps one of the most extreme forms of transgression, is hardly a new phenomenon in this context. What we have to consider is whether it is the *fear* of transgression that has increased, rather than the incidence. A related aspect of this discussion is the extent to which transgression – and therefore fear also – is a more central aspect of the tourist experience than we are prepared to accept. Legal discourse of course provides us with the notion of 'risk' and the extent to which modern society seems unprepared to accept risk might have more to do with the fears we construct around tourism than the reality of transgression. This may be the uncomfortable reality then – that transgression is the essence of tourism more than any notion of justice or ethical behaviour may be.

Tourism and injustice

The sense of documents such as the Global Code of Ethics discussed in earlier pages is that in some way tourism stands outside poverty, oppression and injustice. Thus, the notion that tourism can lead to tolerance, greater equity between the developed and underdeveloped nations and even world peace gains currency. In this understanding, tourism is a vehicle that can somehow be harnessed for good. It is not tourism *per* se that is often the problem, but rather how it is practised. Hence ethical codes will regulate that style of tourism away.

But there is another view of tourism that places it at the centre of the problem of injustice, instead of being its solution. This constructs tourism as part of the system of injustice and oppression. While tourism discourse – such as in the Global Code of Ethics – often speaks of the right to be a tourist, an alternative discourse poses the question of whether the act of being a tourist can be interpreted in itself as a political statement. The difference between the two discourses may be seen in the example of a country that commits breaches of international human-rights standards. In that instance the Global Code of Ethics might suggest that visiting that country is not ethical. But the alternative discourse would suggest that engaging in tourism in a country that is flouting human-rights standards is itself an act which lends support to that regime. The issue, then, is one of determining whether tourism is constructed as being in some circumstances an act that can support repression (tourism *and* repression) or whether it is essentially a repressive practice (tourism *as* repression).

Tourism and repression

One example of a 'good tourist's charter' states: 'Don't go somewhere if you think that being a tourist there supports a repressive regime.'[2] There are, of course, difficulties with this statement. One view of tourism is that its essence

is one of escape – hence the concern that tourists will often engage in behaviour they would not engage in within their home country. Thus tourists may
claim that the nature of a country's political system has nothing to do with
them. They are there to indulge in their fantasies, not embroil themselves in
the politics of the host nation. In addition tourist behaviour that does not
conform to local norms is often excused because the tourist does not
understand the subtleties of local customs. In this approach it does not seem
to make sense to hold a tourist from, say, the United States, responsible for
supporting a repressive government through the mere act of visiting that
country, when the tourist may know little about the policies of the country's
government.

But, on the other hand, we know that tourism brings important economic
benefits to a country and that governments actively promote tourism as a
consequence. These perceived economic gains also reap political rewards for
governments as a healthy economy is usually linked to competent government. It is also the case that international tourism can bring legitimacy to a
regime on the basis that a country which is attractive as a tourist destination
can portray itself as generally desirable. Richter makes this point well in
relation to the Philippines under the Marcos' dictatorship:

> Tourism which had fallen off dramatically in the period immediately
> before and after martial law, was quickly seized upon as a means to
> refurbish the Philippines' and Marcos's image. Tourism had not been a
> priority industry prior to martial law and had in fact done very poorly
> during the premartial law period of Marcos's administration. That was
> not to be the only irony: the country, which only eight months earlier
> was reputedly seething with subversion and violence, declared tourism to
> be a priority industry eligible for a variety of tax incentives and customs
> concessions and had set up its first Department of Tourism [DOT] by
> 11 May 1973.[3]

In this context the tourists become mere pawns in the world of power politics. The aim is to profit from tourism – not just economically but also
politically:

> Tourists per se mattered less in the early years of martial law than did
> the publicity about tourism. The DOT launched an ambitious series of
> invitational visits to the Philippines for travel writers and tour operators,
> groups which could be depended upon not to bite the hand that fed
> them and who were not likely to be preoccupied with civil libertarian
> issues. In a friendly, beautiful country it was enough that the gun sling-
> ers were gone and no tanks patrolled the streets. To further the image of
> a peaceful, contented society, the DOT built a promotional campaign
> around the Philippine's most important asset – a cheerful, hospitable

people. The slogan "Where Asia Wears a Smile" was a particularly adroit choice for defusing criticism of life under the New Society.[4]

In more recent years there have been campaigns to discourage tourism to Burma in protest at their human-rights policies and ongoing house arrest of Opposition Leader Aung San Suu Kyi. When the Burmese Government designated 1996 as Visit Burma year, some campaigners asked tourists to not travel there.[5] This carried with it the warning of a direct link between the act of being a tourist and consequences for people's lives:

> Derek Fatchett MP, Shadow Foreign Affairs Minister, said: "Burma stands condemned by the United Nations for its human rights abuses. The regime is clearly one of the worst in the world. The development of the tourist industry has been at a price to the local community which every decent person would regard as unacceptable. I would strongly urge tourists to think carefully before booking a holiday in Burma. The price of an exotic holiday could be someone else's life."[6]

Similarly, in 1999 Aung San Suu Kyi was quoted as having said:

> I still think that people should not come to Burma because the bulk of the money from tourism goes straight into the pockets of the generals. And not only that, it is a form of moral support for them because it makes the military authorities think the international community is not opposed to the human rights violations they are committing all the time.[7]

Others argue that tourist visas to Burma maintain outside links and that provided it is done responsibly it can be a positive force in effecting change in the country.[8] The move to encouraging tourism includes claims that Aung San Suu Kyi now supports travel and tourism to Burma, 'should the result of the visit draw attention to the oppression of the people by the military junta'.[9] In this context 'responsibly' means avoiding doing acts which enrich the ruling elite, for example through using banks for currency exchange where fees paid end up in the hands of the country's rulers. One group suggests that to be a responsible tourist there is a need to offset the 'social deficit' created by the unavoidable fees paid to the government as a consequence of arriving there. As they note:

> Remember that before you've set foot in Burma, your visa fees and airline taxes have already generated some revenue for the regime. All entrance fees at popular tourist sites will do the same. A responsible tourist should recognize this and always be thinking of ways to bring positive impacts to the communities they visit. Giving a donation to a local or international NGO will help further the efforts of people working

to better the lives of the people of Burma. Volunteering time with such a group would be better yet, it would allow you to interact directly with people and the struggles they face. Giving money to beggars, especially children, isn't a great idea. Better to buy them a meal or donate to a charity group involved with the homeless.

There are infinite ways to offset your "social deficit". Be creative![10]

One of the problems in making the decision to travel to places such as Burma is that the arguments in favour of such travel will be used to justify the visit, just as those who oppose travel will rely on the contrary arguments. Thus Simon Hudson found that the result of his survey of a group who had actually visited Burma indicated that 'the majority seemed in favor of citizen diplomacy as a means of fighting against the repressive regime versus a tourism boycott'.[11] He acknowledged that surveying only those who had visited was a limitation of the study, but he also noted that this might also be explained 'because they are unconcerned or ill informed about the socio-cultural impacts of tourism.'[12] As he was surveying students Hudson also suggested that this might be explained by reference to the greater focus given to environmental issues in tourism literature and the resultant awareness of those matters amongst students as compared with the lesser focus placed on the social impacts of tourism.[13] His conclusion on this point is that '[p]erhaps, there is a need for curriculums to integrate more social and economic ethical dilemmas'.[14] What this might also suggest is that more generally amongst the tourist population there is an acceptance that environmental impacts will affect both rich and poor alike, and so threaten directly the income earning capacity of the tourism industry. The social impacts of tourism – particularly when the consequences will fall on residents of another country that one will be leaving – do not directly affect the tourist. This may explain why tourism studies curricula and its literature place the emphasis on the former area rather than the social impacts of tourism. This then creates a discourse that guides us towards certain areas of concern and away from others. In this way behaviour is affected with respect to the extent to which tourism is regarded as being supportive of repression.

Tourism as repression

Whether or not particular boycotts of destinations are justified, the example of Burma illustrates a particular construction of tourism which takes it beyond that as simply being an act which may or may not support repression. There is also the view here that the act of tourism is essentially political and automatically plays a part in either repression or liberation. Thus the tourist that travels to Burma and does not act responsibly may well pay the price of somebody's life. 'Being a truly responsible tourist means exercising great discretion at all times. The visitor must be vigilant to avoid creating negative impacts whenever possible and engage in activities that will have a positive impact.'[15]

Some may argue that a tourist who visits a country with a repressive government is quite a different character from a tourist who visits a country in order to engage in repression. In the case of the former, the tourist may claim ignorance as far as local politics are concerned. The latter has less legitimacy with respect to the claim of being 'only a tourist'. But this distinction is not necessarily so clear when one considers the construction of tourism as repression. Underlying this approach to understanding tourism is the question whether tourism is of its essence repressive in various ways and the extent to which human rights are so universally recognised that it is difficult for tourists to claim ignorance with respect to their tacit support for repressive governments. And beyond this, is ignorance relevant at all? If the tourist who acts without regard to the consequences of their behaviour affects negatively the lives of others, then have not their actions been repressive?

Crick maps at length the connection between international tourism and repression in a way that indicates a patchwork of connected acts:

> In the West Indies, as in other areas, national tourism authorities launched "courtesy campaigns" in which citizens were instructed how to be civil to tourists, and beggars were swept out of sight. International tourism requires, above all, peace and stability. Governments may therefore crack down on the local people in order not to upset a growing tourism industry, suppressing signs of civil disorder and of animosity towards tourists themselves. The argument is sometimes put that the tourism industry tends to support right-wing regimes. Conrad Hilton is famous for his remark that "each of our hotels is a little America." He added: "We are doing our bit to spread world peace, and to fight socialism." For the Philippines, L. Richter has shown how the rapid development of tourism facilities after the imposition of martial law by President Marcos in 1972 acted as a message to the international community that life was normal in that country. The World Bank Conference of 1978 was held in Manila. In 1976 12% of the funds of the Philippines Development Bank was devoted to financing hotel room construction, resulting in windfall commissions for those with political influence. This level of expenditure on hotels was 40 times that on public housing. At that time crimes against tourists carried more severe punishments than those against locals, and journalists criticizing tourism risked dismissal. Fortunes were made by Marcos supporters in charge of the implementation of tourism policy. Governments sometimes use rough tactics against their own people to safeguard tourism. In Indonesia, for instance, when the government decided to create tourist facilities around the Borobodur Temple, there was much local protest at the sacrilege this involved. Local people were simply moved away and

rehoused: then land values skyrocketed. In countries like Australia and the United States, tourism has become a force for internal colonialism as peoples of the so-called Fourth World (e.g. Australian Aboriginal groups and American Indian communities) are represented as tourist attractions. In 1962, for instance, an Australian tourist advisor suggested the removal of a group of Aborigines to a reserve half a day's drive from Adelaide to function as a tourist spectacle.[16]

The notion of 'internal colonialism' is most pertinent to our discussion as it helps to explain the process by which those who might be defined as repressed themselves fail to see the nature of their repression. Thus in the case of indigenous peoples the idea that their culture can be packaged for tourism seems to be appropriate for many indigenous people themselves – of course the economic benefits can sweeten this process. But the danger is that as with most forms of colonisation what occurs is the division of the colonised. On the one side are those who 'go along' with the oppressor and adopt the colonising power's values and perspectives. On the other side are those who resist the colonial power and refuse to give up their culture into a different value system.

If tourism does inevitably involve a degree of repression *as part of the nature of tourism* then we must question whether the tourist can simply 'opt out' of responsibility when governments harness tourism for its benefits. In this context the nature of government may have little to do with the manner in which being a tourist becomes political. Debates surrounding the manner in which 'seedy' activities can be tourist attractions – for example, the local sex industry – show how government direction can be ambiguous. On the one hand, governments license, regulate and tax such activities. But it is also the case that government policy can be ostensibly opposed or indifferent to the promotion of such activities as part of the image of the country, states, or cities.

It is then the act of being a tourist which becomes the political statement, not the manner in which being a tourist directly or indirectly supports repressive regimes. Of course, there will be instances where tourism is incorporated in to government policy and repressive government occurs as a consequence. This is Crick's argument. In such cases tourism as repression leads to repressive government when government institutionalises the values and norms of those who might be described as the 'profit-makers' from tourism. Perhaps this is simply a convergence of the repressive essence of tourism with government that supports that understanding of tourism.

The role of international law

In many cases particularly repressive regimes will be identified in the media and so many tourists will have some sense of countries to which visiting might be considered to be a political act. Of course, such categorisation of countries is itself political. Thus allies of the tourist's host country might be represented as appropriate destinations and any human-rights violations played down while tourism to enemy countries might be discouraged through greater emphasis on their human-rights record.

The evaluation of a country's policy or behaviour with respect to human rights does rely heavily on accepted international standards. The universal acceptance of these standards does make it somewhat difficult for tourists to claim that a simple act of tourism cannot easily be defined to be supporting acts of repression at least inasmuch as repression can be said to be culturally defined.

Thus acts which infringe the Universal Declaration of Human Rights, International Convention on the Elimination of all Forms of Discrimination Against Women, International Convention on the Elimination of Racial Discrimination and the United Nations Convention on the Rights of the Child are so widely accepted that once facts are known to a tourist which indicate that a country does not comply with these international laws then such a person who travels to that country must have some trouble in justifying their tourism in terms of ambiguity as to what is acceptable around the world.

Of course, what is more difficult is to determine at what point breaches of these international norms renders tourism 'inappropriate' and thus turns any form of tourism into a political statement of support for that government's regime.

A simple example to illustrate the point is the case of apartheid in South Africa. During the time when that was official policy in that country the international community was so widely opposed to apartheid that it was made very clear that dealing with South Africa for trade or sporting purposes would always raise the question as to whether this amounted to tacit support for the regime. Thus the International Convention on Apartheid in Sport sought to prohibit sporting contact with any country which practised apartheid.[17] Countries which subscribed to this Convention also agreed not to finance sporting bodies or individuals which had sporting contact with countries which practised apartheid[18] and to penalise teams and individuals which did.[19] Parties to the Convention also agreed to refuse visas to persons who had participated in sporting events in South Africa.[20]

Clearly this limits the potential for 'sport tourism' but it also conveys a sense that a regime which is based on apartheid does not have the support of the international community and should be shunned. Of course, this Convention did not prevent tourism to South Africa. But it is clearly more difficult for a tourist to say that he or she was not aware of the human-rights position in such cases and so the potential for the act to be seen as some form of political support for the regime. More difficult is the situation where the act of tourism occurs in a country which breaches human rights but where that knowledge is not widely circulated. For example, if one considers the full range of rights expressed in the various human-rights instruments noted above and if one considers these to be fundamental (as they are), then there will be many countries which might be considered to be in breach of at least some of them. Should tourists visit such countries? Or should governments limit travel to such countries by its nationals?

This last question is problematic as it is also a fundamental human right that persons have free movement.[21] Thus it is difficult for a government to prevent travel without also breaching human rights. However, this may not prevent a country deterring travel to certain countries by, for example, prohibiting direct flights. But this leaves the issue of the individual responsibility of the tourist. One might thus have to question the responsibility of the state to inform tourists of the human-rights situations in other countries and to suggest that such matters form part of their decision-making process when deciding on a tourist destination.

That legal discourse often lets the matter rest with 'individual choice' should come as no surprise when so much of the law is grounded in support of a free market. Even the Global Code of Ethics has been identified as rooted in that ideology.[22] The more important point is that the law tends to construct the matter around notions that whether or not a tourist supports a repressive regime by travelling to a country will be ultimately a matter of judgement for the traveller. What is entirely missing from this discourse is the notion that the act of being a tourist can be in itself repressive.

The notion of tourism as repression usually involves issues of travellers importing into the host country their worldview. Thus, it is an entirely different question to whether one should travel to a country with a poor human-rights record. This construction of tourism is the reverse, as it asks whether a person should travel to another country and impose their culture, politics or ideologies on the hosts. It is difficult for a legal system to regard its own country as based on unsound ideological principles. Thus one can see how this notion of tourism will have little legal discourse surrounding it from the 'sending' nation.

Tourists as targets and the 'war against terror'

But one can see in this understanding of tourism how tourists can become targets for those in host countries who resent the values and ideas that tourists from elsewhere bring with them. Frey Higgins-Desbiolles explains it in the context of the 'wretched and the rich' meeting in now 'hostile meeting grounds':[23]

> Are the marginalised and the poor realising the hollowness of the promises of development that emanate from both tourism and globalisation as they jostle with the privileged on the playgrounds of tourism and the battlegrounds of terrorism?[24]

Higgins-Desbiolles, recognises the manner in which the attacks on the World Trade Center in 2001 and then more particularly the Bali bombing in 2002 led to the war on terrorism being recast as a war on tourism.[25] She also refers to the evolution of the principle of the 'right to travel' and it becoming embedded in various international documents on tourism together with a corresponding responsibility to engage in ethical tourism.[26] These are points that we have already canvassed in preceding chapters and represent the divide between the pleasure-seeking tourist, on the one hand, and the 'exalted tourist' – as we have styled it – on the other. The latter notion of tourism suggests that it can be practised in a manner which reduces poverty and injustice and contributes to development in a sustainable manner. Higgins-Desbiolles is ultimately optimistic about the direction tourism can take, albeit there is a choice to be made:

> Resorting to the language of the 'war on terror', tourism has a choice to make. It can either encamp itself with the market fundamentalists and secure itself a world that is increasingly dangerous and fragmented, or it can encamp itself with humanity and take up the reins that it has as such a powerful force. ... Tourism must serve the 'wretched' as well as the 'rich' if it is to continue to enjoy the open access it has been given to the world's resources and the faith that has been instilled into it to improve the lives of people.[27]

She is also critical of the Global Code of Ethics, for example, for clinging to a market-based approach to wealth distribution from tourism rather than advocating for development more broadly.[28]

The problem we see in this approach is that it assumes that tourism can be done in a responsible manner. This must be predicated on a view that tourism is fundamentally neutral, and that it is the manner of its practice that impacts on people. This is a view embedded in the various World Tourism Organization documents to which we have already referred. But tourism can never be understood outside its social reality. There is no 'abstract' notion of tourism. What we suggest is that tourism is of its essence an act loaded with meaning by the social circumstances in which it is performed. In the present circumstances, most global tourism is performed in a manner which makes it automatically repressive and transgressive. Higgins-Desbiolles herself makes this point in her work:

> The concern is that the act of enjoying the right to travel is an ideological act which is predicated on a system of inequity and therefore may invite another ideological act, terrorism, as a response. This is not sympathising with terrorism but saying that the hubris of First World tourists asserting their rights to travel freely, with maximum comfort and guaranteed safety is 'sinister' when others cannot even ensure the means

of survival for themselves, their families and their ways of life. We stubbornly refuse to consider that our free movement may be related somehow to the asylum seekers imprisonment at Baxter Detention Centre in Australia, our silence in the illegal invasion of Iraq in 2003 might be a catalyst to the bombs in Madrid and London and the others that are to follow, our tourist hedonism might be implicated in the poverty of the destitute and our consumerist lifestyle might contribute to the loss of biological diversity and ecological integrity and so threaten our very long-term existence.[29]

But while Higgins-Desbiolles refers positively to the literature on 'alternative' views of tourism as embodied in the notions of social tourism, responsible tourism and sustainable tourism,[30] we think it is timely to ask whether 'tourism' as a concept has become so tainted by the powerful forces in society that have co-opted its social function for economic gain that it has become impossible to divorce tourism from its performance as an economically and culturally colonising social force. In effect, the arguments for responsible and ethical tourism assume their opposite, and in the context of these forms of tourism being posited as the alternative discourse, this suggests that the mainstream form of tourism is both unethical and irresponsible. This is the conceptual barrier that is increasingly difficult to bridge for those who regard tourists as 'legitimate' targets.

At one level the notion of tourists as targets has been recognised by rich nations. In 2004 an Australian Government paper on international terrorism summarised the terrorist threat as:

> Australia and Australians are directly threatened by transnational extremist-Muslim terrorism. We have been named as a target. This has been verified by our policing and intelligence work and through our cooperation with our regional and international partners.
>
> We know some of the reasons. We are now well familiar with the uncompromising rhetoric of Al Qaida, Jemaah Islamiyah and the like. Those who do not support their cause are deemed obstacles to their objectives and legitimate targets. They extend their contempt for moderate, tolerant Muslim society to their hostility towards the West.
>
> They feel threatened by our values and the place we take in the world. Our international alliances and our robust foreign policy are opportunistically invoked in the name of their 'war'. Our conspicuous example of economic and social prosperity is deemed a threat to their cause. We hear our values and social fabric attacked.[31]

But this is not to suggest that this acknowledged any unethical or irresponsible acts on the part of international tourists. The reference to attacks on 'our values and social fabric' appears to be in the sense of illustrating how extreme and unreasonable is the position of the terrorist. As Higgins-Desbiolles suggests, the 'Bush Doctrine' following the September 11, 2001 attack on the World Trade Center in New York City established the position that there was no middle ground. One either was with the United States, or on the side of the terrorists.[32] Clearly, this offers little scope to consider that perhaps 'our values and social fabric' might be contributing to at least some of the ill feeling on the part of the globally marginalised which in turn might provide some succour for terrorist attacks.

When tourism is regarded as inherently transgressive this shifts fundamentally the manner in which tourism discourse is constructed. Instead of constructing tourism as something that can be harnessed in order to produce a social good, it instead encounters the problem of whether such an outcome would be contradictory to the manner in which tourism is now practised. The problem is that even in attempting to connect tourism with responsible and ethical behaviour there is a tacit acceptance that tourism is more than the simple act of visiting. As Higgins-Desbiolles notes the 'right to travel' that is entrenched in various international documents emanates from a particular ideology based on the primacy of free-market economies.[33] And this connection between tourism and capitalist free-market ideology is not simply in terms of tourism being regarded as an industry and a business. As Patricia Goldstone argues, companies whose business is interwoven with tourism such as American Express have used the 'democratizing potential of tourism ... to advance their own interests'.[34] As she explains:

> One company has almost single-handedly promoted the idea of tourism as democracy onto the policy map and into the public view. From the end of World War II, American Express sold foreign travel as en extension of the Marshall Plan, a way in which ordinary Americans could help the economy of the Western world. Through creating, funding, and placing its executives on the boards of such organizations as the WTTC, MEMTA, the World Monuments Fund and the World Monuments Watch, Rebuild Dubrovnik, and Businesses for Sustainable Tourism, the company has continued to maintain that travel is a 'social, political and economic force ... a powerful instrument of helping foreign nations gain much needed dollars.' Through these not-for-profit organizations and its foreign exchange dealings, the company has nurtured strong affiliations with the World Bank and the United Nations. Former executives are now statesmen. Even if former CEO James Robinson III still wanted to form a government agency to deal with Third World debt problems he wouldn't have to: it exists in the form of American Express.[35]

Tourism is not so much *regulated* by the state as it is *represented* by the state. The OECD review of Australia's national tourism policy in 2003 could only refer to terrorism in the context of its impact on the business of tourism:

In 2001–2 international visitor numbers declined with the impact from the terrorism attacks of 11 September 2001 and the demise of a domestic airline carrier. ... [36]

Domestic tourism (visitor nights) is expected to continue to show relatively low growth over the forecast period to 2012. In the short term, the continuing effects of SARS and heightened international travel concerns due to terrorism are likely to negatively impact on outbound travel, with some switching to domestic travel. Australian domestic holiday travel is expected to be one of the main beneficiaries of the current concern over SARS. ... [37]

The National Tourism Issues Response Plan was developed by the Federal, State and Territory governments, in consultation with industry, and represents a nationally coordinated approach to dealing with unanticipated shocks or events. The Plan provides a response mechanism to events such as acts of terrorism or war that may impact on the Australian tourism industry. ... [38]

Like environmental and social sustainability, economic sustainability of the tourism sector is critical to its longevity. Solid global economic growth and the strong domestic macroeconomic prospects are the best preconditions for tourism growth over the medium to long term. However, the most recent assessment from the World Tourism Organization indicated that the situation had not become favourable for international travel with continuing uncertainties caused by SARS and concerns about new acts of terrorism. ... [39]

This approach to analysing the connection between tourism and terrorism reinforces the discourse which constructs tourism as a business that places economic interests above the social impacts of both tourism and terrorism. This discourse is reiterated constantly in official policy documents in both Australia and the United Kingdom. The Australian tourism White Paper in 2004 also only discussed terrorism in terms of the challenge it brought to the economic viability of the tourism industry:

The environment for tourism is changing and, to grow and prosper, the tourism industry will need to be more flexible and responsive to challenges. These range from catering to a better informed, more discerning, culturally and linguistically diverse consumer, to effectively using the Internet in motivating long-haul travel in the face of fears of terrorism and events like the outbreak of SARS. For Australia to maintain and grow market share as an attractive long-haul destination in the years to come, it is crucial to revitalise our marketing and promotion strategy to ensure that we continue to grow both visitor numbers and yield.[40]

Likewise the United Kingdom *Tourism Strategy for the 2012 Games* consultation clearly placed social considerations to one side in preparing for the Olympics. Thus while 'local structural issues and social inclusion' were not to be 'downplayed' the view in the consultation was that 'it is important that the tourism sector's work towards 2012 should be identified and prioritised separately'.[41] It is clear from the final report on the strategy for the 2012 games that the priority is to utilise the Olympics for the benefit of the tourism *industry*. The value to the United Kingdom economy is stressed and the potential for growth is emphasised with the claim that it could increase revenue from tourism by £2.1 billion.[42] It also stresses the value of the business visitor who spends 'almost twice as much as the average holidaymaker'.[43] In addition the business visitor becomes the 'exalted tourist':

> The business sector also helps to sustain the wider tourist infrastructure, filling seaside hotel rooms for conferences out of season. It supports urban regeneration through the provision of new conference facilities in cities like Manchester, Glasgow and Cardiff. Business tourism is resilient during economic downturns, and business tourists who enjoy their visit can be excellent ambassadors for a destination to colleagues and friends.[44]

This is an area marked for significant investment in the strategy. But of interest here is that there has been a subtle redefinition of 'tourism' to connect it with 'business' visitors. Thus, it is no longer that tourism is the business of leisure, but that business is now a central part of actual tourism. This cannot be over-emphasised. The effect of the manner in which tourism is being now constructed, and its concern with economic matters even when discussing the impact of terrorism all goes to suggest that tourism is now centrally concerned with the generation of profit and the rebranding of cities to attract that business – a business which is now itself focussed very much on the business tourist. There is, for example, no discussion of the social impacts of regenerating cities to attract business tourists along with their capital in the 2012 Strategy. Just as the homeless were displaced in previous Olympic cities, the failure to discuss such matters in the 2012 document do little to dispel fears that this will continue to happen.

The loss of innocence: tourists as political targets

Such strategies and constructions of tourism appear silent on the social impacts of tourism. The consequence is that it appears that for the rich the right to travel is real, while for the world's poor the only promise of tourism is the possibility of employment in the tourist industry although often at low rates of pay.[45] Thus to 'be' a tourist often implies wealth and status. To be a non-tourist implies exclusion from the lifestyle that practising tourism usually entails.

In this sense tourism cannot only be constructed as repression, but can also be constructed as *symbolic* of repression. In this context, it may be that there are no 'innocent' tourists. Yet the imagery of the innocent tourist is strong in the case of acts of terrorism as news reports indicate following various terror incidents:

> The attack happened just after dark as people were gathering around coffee shops to watch a televised soccer match, a witness, who did not give his name, told Reuters.
>
> "There was a big noise but at first we thought it could be people celebrating," he said. "But then some people running away started screaming and fell on the ground. There was a lot of screaming."
>
> Egyptian television showed spots of blood on the paved square as police officers combed the area, which was quickly cordoned off as ambulances and police cars poured in.
>
> "We heard a huge sound but we didn't know what it was," a witness told state television. "These are just innocent tourists who are not involved in politics coming to visit our country."[46]

Of course, it could be argued that the targeted tourist is merely a convenient way to undermine governments through affecting the capacity of the tourism industry to generate revenue. This narrow view of the relationship between tourism and terrorism has much support in the literature. The focus in that work is on the manner in which terrorism seeks to deprive government of revenue, making the tourist victims almost incidental.[47] The result is a simple equation that as more tourists visit a location and so attract greater investment, the location and the tourists become a more attractive target for terrorism. This work relegates the political purpose of terrorism to the background, presenting it as a phenomenon around which the industry has to be accommodated.[48] What this fails to do is consider the changing nature of the current times and how tourism discourse has evolved to operate at various levels to suggest that the notion of the tourist is more centrally located in the problem of terrorism and its causes.

In 1997, 60 foreign tourists and four Egyptians were gunned down and killed outside Hatsheput Temple. Afterwards the Islamic Group or al-Gama'a al-Islamiya claimed responsibility and said their aim was to take hostages in order to secure the release of their leader from a United States prison who was jailed for his role in the 1993 World Trade Center bombing.[49] On the day after the incident it was reported that tour operators were cancelling tours to Egypt.[50] The Egyptian Government was keen to indicate that it was taking measures to improve security, although this was tempered with the reality that a risk-free environment was almost impossible to create, not only in Egypt but anywhere in the world. The President of Egypt was quoted as saying: 'We are going to take many new measures to secure everybody here',

Mr Mubarak said. 'But nobody can guarantee security 100 per cent, not in the United States, not in London, nowhere.'[51] Statements that no place is completely safe have become more commonplace when tourists are targeted in recent years. Certainly, to remove the perception that the risk of travelling is located in particular parts of the world might remove some of the impact to the tourism industry in particular locations from terrorist attacks. Soon after the attack in Luxor one Australian commentator offered the analysis that:

> Murdering innocent tourists is clearly not an acceptable tactic, not even in an undemocratic polity such as Egypt where political freedoms are strictly curtailed. Without hesitation, those responsible should be brought to justice. But justice in contemporary Egypt is not the same as it is in Australia. In part this is one of the issues that Al-Gama'a al-Islamiya and others, most notably the Muslim Brotherhood, are struggling to change.
>
> Detention without trial, torture, military rather than civilian trials dispensing the death penalty without adequate legal representation for those accused by the Government all are part of the problem.
>
> The discrepancy between the rich and the vast majority of the poor, the visibility of this discrepancy in the media and in urban centres and a rise in expectations among Egyptians over the past two decades, complete the picture of the range of problems facing Egypt. ...
>
> It is therefore not surprising to find that frustration with the regime leads to political violence, especially in southern Egypt where economic conditions are the worst and poverty is rampant. It is there that support for Al-Gama'a al-Islamiya is the highest. It is there where most of the atrocities, including the latest one, have been committed.[52]

Here again the starting point is the innocent tourist, which is the basis for the condemnation of the particular act. But the underlying message is one that seeks to understand that act in the context of a political cause. The question is whether following the creation of the Global Code of Ethics for Tourism and a heightened awareness of the need for responsible tourism, tourists to countries which methodically practice repression can truly be called 'innocent'. While tourists will be targeted by terrorists for the publicity it will bring and because they are moving about in spaces that present the opportunity for attacks, it would also be folly to ignore the extent to which the tourist is more directly implicated.

It is in this context that the question of the responsibility of the state to protect tourists arises. In some jurisdictions, such as Thailand and Rio de Janeiro, there are tourist police – special units designed to assist foreign tourists. Goa, which is heavily dependent on tourism revenue, is in the process of establishing a tourist police force.[53] This appears to have been hastened by a number of attacks on female foreign tourists.[54] But even in this instance the response from those states is often balanced against the individual tourist's responsibility for their fate. The Chief Minister of Goa was quoted as saying:

> Goa Chief Minister Digamber Kamat Thursday asked tourists to adhere to certain "code and responsibilities" while on holiday in the state. "There is no restraint on tourists moving out at night but they should follow certain code and responsibilities," Kamat said, without quantifying what he meant by "code and responsibilities".[55]

Thus it is important to distinguish between different ways in which tourists can be targets because they affect how the state is likely to respond. Tourists might be targeted as persons with cash and items of value by pickpockets and thieves; persons who represent a foreign culture intruding into the territory of those who target them; persons who because they represent economic value to the government of the host country may become the targets of those who oppose the government; or persons who have themselves committed crimes arising from the opportunities which tourism present.

The response of the state will be influenced by the way tourists are targeted and the motives for such behaviour. While there may be some consensus to protect tourists from crime, such protection might be resented by local people if tourists were given greater protection than those who permanently reside in a locality. For example, when Victoria Square, Adelaide was cleared for the benefit of tourists[56] the need to act was also presented as making the city safe for local residents too.

Special laws to protect tourists from crime are also a device that can be used to provide greater protection for tourists. For example, providing higher penalties if the tourist is a victim may also be resented by local people as it appears to place greater value on tourists than it does on locals. So too might the allocation of additional police to tourist areas result in fewer police for other duties and/or additional costs (especially if such policing requires overtime due to the nature of tourist activities and related events and the time of day they are held). This could easily cause local resentment. Likewise where tourists are targeted because they are seen as intruders or importers of foreign culture it may appear to be unduly oppressive for the state to enforce 'good manners' amongst the host population. There are also tensions when targeting tourists who engage in crime due to the opportunities which travelling present. Such targeting carries with it the potential to deter tourists to the country. For example, travel-insurance fraud or minor customs violations if targeted may lead to extra convictions but does such policing create the wrong image of the country as a hospitable tourist destination?

Thus the manner in which the state responds will be heavily influenced by how the targeting is perceived locally, nationally and internationally. It is not a simple matter of identifying the need to protect tourists as the context within which they have become targets is of prime importance.

The politics and moral panic of travel advisories

These considerations and tensions are most prevalent in relation to government-issued travel advisories. These advisories are designed to alert travellers to various risks when going abroad. In Australia they are issued by the Department of Foreign Affairs. They generally include warnings about passport requirements, personal security, driving and traffic accidents, drugs, medical insurance, illness and injury, scams practised in various locations. The 1997 travel advisory for Bali warned Australians about the following gambling scam:

> Young men are being targeted for gambling scams. The usual scenario is that they are befriended and driven by a round-about route to a house in Denpasar. The unsuspecting victim is shown how to cheat at cards. Initially they think they are winning but then the stakes are raised and they suddenly lose vast amounts of money. (The Consulate has had reports of $2,000–$40,000 being demanded.) The perpetrators have been known to threaten the victim physically in order to obtain the money from a credit card or by bank draft.
> Gambling is illegal in Indonesia and you should not get involved in such activities.
> There are regular incidents of tourists being drugged before being robbed and/or sexually assaulted. Take care, especially at the bars along Kuta Beach, as well as at the discos and open air "clubs" along Jalan Legian.
> Don't accept drinks or food from people you don't know well![57]

The content of the travel advisory is an important means by which the image of a country is cast and fear in relation to travel is constructed. Compared with the most recent travel advisory for Indonesia the 1997 advisory seems almost quaint with respect to the level of fear it engenders. The current advisory for Indonesia is prefaced:

> We advise you to reconsider your need to travel to Indonesia, including Bali, at this time due to the very high threat of terrorist attack.
> On 17 July 2009, terrorists detonated bombs at the Ritz-Carlton Hotel and the JW Marriott Hotel in Jakarta. Australians were among those killed and injured.

There is a possibility of further terrorist attacks in Jakarta and elsewhere in Indonesia, including Bali.

Terrorists have previously attacked or planned to attack places where Westerners gather including nightclubs, bars, restaurants, hotels and airports in Bali, Jakarta and elsewhere in Indonesia. Analysts judge that these types of venues could be targeted again.

In past years, we have received information about possible terrorist attacks in Indonesia in the Christmas and New Year period. Analysts consider that gatherings of Westerners over the Christmas and New Year holiday season may again be appealing targets for terrorists.

We continue to receive credible information that terrorists could be planning attacks in Indonesia and that Bali remains an attractive target for terrorists.

If you do decide to travel to Indonesia, you should exercise great care, particularly around locations that have a low level of protective security and avoid places known to be possible terrorist targets. ... [58]

The fear of terrorism has clearly altered the perception of danger when travelling. But there are choices that have to be made about how the risk is presented to travellers. Indonesia has been critical of the manner in which Australia has presented the risk of harm when travelling to that country, as a negative advisory, or one that overstates the danger, could have dramatic consequences for its image and hence the potential loss of tourist revenue. By way of comparison, the Canadian government at the same date has advised a 'high degree of caution' in relation to travel to Bali, a lower level of warning than 'avoid non-essential travel' and 'avoid all travel'. It advises:

You are advised to maintain a high level of security awareness when travelling in Indonesia.

There have been a number of terrorist attacks in recent years in Jakarta and on Bali, resulting in significant loss of life to both foreigners and Indonesians. While effective counterterrorism measures by Indonesian authorities have reduced the risk of terrorist attacks, terrorist cells are believed to still exist and could have the capacity to carry out attacks anywhere in the country. There is a heightened risk of attacks during holidays and celebrations.

On July 17, 2009, two bombings occurred at the JW Marriott and Ritz-Carlton Mega Kuningan hotels in Jakarta, resulting in death and injuries. Security forces throughout Indonesia, including Bali, are on heightened alert as a result of these incidents. Travellers should exercise extreme caution as further attacks in Indonesia are possible, and Bali remains an attractive target for such attacks. Canadians in or travelling to Indonesia, including Bali, should remain alert and maintain a high level of security awareness.

High-profile Western facilities or businesses and places frequented by foreigners may be considered potential terrorist targets. Canadian travelers should assess their own safety and security and exercise caution in choosing accommodations, places of worship, shopping venues, restaurants, clubs, and other tourist facilities. They should opt for accommodation facilities with adequate security arrangements in place.[59]

The US State Department also does not list Indonesia as a place to avoid travelling although it does describe ways in which citizens should take precautions with respect to terrorism:

Safety and security

Indonesian police and security forces take active measures against both ongoing threats posed by terrorist cells, including Jemaah Islamiyah (JI), a US-government-designated terrorist organisation that carried out several bombings at various times from 2002 to 2009 and outbreaks of violence elsewhere. While Indonesia's counter-terrorism efforts have been ongoing and partly successful, violent elements have demonstrated a willingness and ability to carry out deadly attacks with little or no warning. Most recently, in November 2009, unknown assailants shot at foreigners in Banda Aceh, North Sumatra, an area that was devastated by the 2004 tsunami and the scene of a long-running separatist conflict that ended in 2005. The gunfire wounded a European development worker. A house occupied by US citizen teachers was targeted and hit by gunfire, but there were no US citizen casualties. In July 2009, attacks by armed assailants in Papua resulted in several deaths, including security personnel and one Australian national. Also in July, suspected JI elements bombed two Western hotels in Jakarta, killing nine Indonesians and foreigners and injuring over 50, including six US citizens. US citizens in Indonesia must be physically and mentally prepared to cope with future attacks even as they go about their normal daily routines.[60]

The United Kingdom travel advice for Indonesia begins:

There is a high threat from terrorism throughout Indonesia. Terrorist groups continue to plan attacks and have the capacity and intent to carry out these attacks at any time and anywhere in the country. Attacks could be indiscriminate, including in places frequented by expatriates and foreign travellers.

Terrorists have shown that they have the means and motivation to carry out successful attacks in Indonesia. On 17 July 2009 suicide bombers carried out attacks against the Ritz Carlton and Marriott Hotels in Jakarta. Seven people were killed and 55 injured. JI is believed to have been responsible for the Bali bombings in October 2002, which killed 202 people (including a number of British nationals), the Marriott Hotel bombing in Jakarta which killed 12 people in August 2003, and the Australian Embassy bombing in September 2004, which killed 11 people; and the Bali suicide bombings of 1 October 2005 which killed 20 people and injured a further 90.

These attacks underscore the ongoing terrorist threat in Indonesia. Venues known to be frequented by foreign visitors and expatriates, including beach resorts, bars and restaurants, hotels and shopping malls hosting major international brand outlets are potentially targets for such groups ... [61]

The United Kingdom levels of warning for terrorist threats are: high threat from terrorism (a high level of known terrorist activity), general threat from terrorism (some level of known terrorist activity), underlying threat from terrorism (a low level of known terrorist activity), low threat from terrorism (no or limited known terrorist activity).[62] Of course, while such levels suggest a scale of risk, the intelligence upon which it is assessed must be interpreted and judgements made. The United Kingdom Foreign Office also warns that 'we do not warn against travel to every country where there is a risk of terrorists operating'.[63] But as even the slight variations (whether as to level of threat or substantive emphasis) in the above advices about the same country might indicate, there are no doubt many matters that have to be weighed up. For example, the United Kingdom Government states in its strategy on international terrorism that:

The FCO issues travel advice notices for 217 countries and overseas territories. Each travel advice notice includes a section on the threat of terrorism. This allows British travellers and expatriates to have up to date information on which to base their decisions about travel. Travel advice needs to strike a balance between danger and disruption: making public safety its prime concern whilst seeking to minimise the disruption that terrorists seek to cause. In cases where the terrorist threat is sufficiently specific, large-scale or endemic to affect British nationals severely, the FCO will advise against travel.[64]

While seeking 'to minimise disruption' could be read to mean 'not letting the terrorists win', it can also be construed as a need to balance the risk from terrorist attack with the effects on the tourism industry of responding to every possible risk at the highest level. Most of the concern about the impact of terrorism on tourism is about the effect on revenue, and as we have already noted this is itself utilised by some terrorist organisations as a reason for targeting tourists. But what this balancing act also introduces into the process of constructing a travel advisory is a significant amount of discretion as to how the particular agency will construct fear. This must be so, for advice not to travel to a particular destination will almost definitely result in many travellers changing their travel plans to avoid visiting that location.

In this process other considerations of global politics will enter into the equation. Indonesia has disputed Australia's travel advice for travel to that country for some time.[65] Part of this disagreement has noted the disparities between Australia's advisory and that of the United Kingdom with respect to travel to Indonesia.[66] In January 2010 following a number of attacks (including a murder) on Indian students in Melbourne the Indian Government issued a travel advisory for Australia. This advisory warned of the potential dangers in Melbourne carefully avoiding describing the attacks as racially motivated. The Australian Government reacted defensively, stating that Australia was 'a welcoming place for all international students'.[67] It was also reported that:

> The Australian Tourism Forecasting Committee (TFC) found that Australia's reputation had been damaged by the attacks and forecast that the number of Indians studying in Australia would fall by about 4,000 at a cost of around $78 million to the economy.[68]

In defending Australia as a safe place by world standards, the Australian Deputy Prime Minister said that, 'In big cities around the world we do see acts of violence from time to time; that happens in Melbourne, it happens in Mumbai, it happens in New York, it happens in London'.[69] The references to Mumbai, London and New York were obviously carefully chosen, for although there has been no suggestion that the Melbourne attacks are acts of terrorism, the cities she referred to have all experienced terrorist attacks in recent times. In the uncertain times we live in, travel to a destination where the fear of harm does not arise from terrorism may well be portrayed as less threatening than where it does. And of course as the New Delhi Commonwealth Games approach with security concerns causing reports that the English team – although denied by officials – could pull out of the competition, the Indian Government has nothing to gain from other governments emphasising the risks posed to personal security in their own country.[70] On that point, the travel advisory issued by Australia for India warns of 'possible threats against prominent business and tourist locations, including in Mumbai and New Delhi' and for travellers 'to exercise a high degree of caution in India at this time because of the high risk of terrorist activity by militant groups'.[71] In the context of global diplomacy and risks to the economic benefits from staging major events such as the Commonwealth Games, one wonders to what extent criticism of the safety of one country by another in constructing travel advisories is tempered by considerations other than the simple assessment of travellers' personal security.[72]

Tourism and the construction of fear

While the tourism industry continues to assess the impact of terrorism on tourism in terms of lost revenue there will be a failure to fully appreciate its impact on the very manner in which tourism is conceptualised. If tourism is supposed to be about leisure and escape, then the fear created by terrorism risks changing the very sense of what tourism is supposed to be. How can one relax and enjoy the experience of travel if one is constantly placing everyone else under suspicion in case they are about to attack? To some extent there is a process of normalisaton taking place where the limits of the law and law-enforcement agencies are presented as successful within practical limits:

> The UK has achieved some significant successes in dealing with potential attacks by Islamist terrorists, since before 2001. A number of credible plans to cause loss of life have been disrupted; in many cases the individuals involved have either been successfully prosecuted and imprisoned or are awaiting trial. However, as the tragic attacks of 7 July 2005 have shown, it is not possible to eliminate completely the threat of terrorist attacks in this country. The rest of this paper describes what is being done to minimise that risk.[73]

Thus 'minimisation' of risk is presented as the best possible result in the context of terrorism. But to accept that a normal part of travel is the risk of terrorist attack is potentially to ask a lot of tourists. It also changes the notion of the tourist, where one is expected to accept that the person in the next seat might be travelling for a much more sinister purpose than his or her appearance suggests. The age of terrorism leads inexorably to the age of suspicion.

There is also an irony about the effects of terrorism on tourism. For many years it was the transgressive practices of 'ordinary' tourists that led to a rethinking of what tourism should be. The Global Code of Ethics, to a great extent, is about a concern with the injustices that tourism itself has created, and a desire to create a more responsible form of tourism. It could be said that the increased fear of terrorism works against that outcome as tourists, instead of acting tolerantly towards others are suspicious of difference for fear of what it conceals. Thus new forms of transgression by 'terror-tourists' have caused 'ordinary' tourists to look inwards. Yet this may come full circle as the United Kingdom Government has recognised in its counter-terrorism strategy the need also to address the causes of radicalisation of individuals which can lead to such people using terrorism. This includes addressing disadvantage:

> The first area of action to counter radicalisation lies in addressing structural problems in the UK and elsewhere that may contribute to

radicalisation. In the UK, this forms part of the Government's broader equality agenda and we are working with communities and the public and private sectors to address these wider issues. Many Government programmes that are not specifically directed at tackling radicalism nevertheless help to build cohesion in communities across the country – for example, Sure Start.[74]

Thus the answer to the terrorist threat may lie more in the principles embedded in the Global Code of Ethics than is realised. It would indeed be ironic if the effect of international terrorism was to examine the structures that cause inequality and poverty in society and so often lead to the affluence for which tourists have been criticised for often flaunting when they travel. Out of fear perhaps, the examination of the causes of resentment may yet occur.

Notes

1 See above p. 3.
2 The Good Tourist's Charter, *New Internationalist* Issue 245, July 1993, available online at http://www.newint.org/issue245/simply.htm.
3 L. Richter 'The political use of tourism: a Philippine case study', *Journal of Developing Areas* (1980) 14: 237–57, p. 242.
4 Ibid., p. 243.
5 See, e.g., *DON'T Visit Burma Year 1996* (Burma Campaign UK) http://www. burmacampaign.org.uk/index.php/news-and-reports/news-stories/DONT-Visit-Burma-Year-1996 (accessed 8 January 2010).
6 Ibid.
7 'Letter: don't visit Burma', *Independent*, 5 December 1999 (http://www.independent. co.uk/opinion/letter-dont-visit-burma-1130495.html).
8 See, e.g., Free Burma Coalition: http://www.freeburmacoalition.org/; Voices of Burma http://www.voicesforburma.org/.
9 Voices of Burma, ibid.
10 Ibid.
11 S. Hudson, 'To go or not to go? ethical perspectives on tourism in an "outpost of tyranny"', *Journal of Business Ethics* (2007) 76: 385–96, p. 394.
12 Ibid.
13 Ibid.
14 Ibid.
15 Voices of Burma, http://www.voicesforburma.org/responsible-tourism/responsible-tourism/.
16 M. Crick, 'Representations of international tourism in the social sciences: sun, sex, sights, savings, and servility", *Annual Review of Anthropology* (1989) 18: pp. 307–44, p. 325.
17 International Convention on Apartheid in Sport, article 3.
18 Ibid., article 5.
19 Ibid., article 6.
20 Ibid., article 10.
21 UDHR, article 13; ICCPR, article 12.
22 See above p. 16.

23 F. Higgins-Desbiolles, 'Hostile meeting grounds: encounters between the wretched of the earth and the tourist through tourism and terrorism in the 21st century', in P. Burns and M. Novelli (eds) *Tourism and Politics: Global Frameworks and Local Realities* (Amsterdam, Elsevier, 2007), pp. 309–32, p. 309.
24 Ibid.
25 Ibid., p. 310.
26 Ibid., p. 317.
27 Ibid., p. 330.
28 Ibid., p. 318.
29 Ibid., p. 324.
30 Ibid., p. 328.
31 Australia, *Transnational Terrorism: The Threat to Australia* (Commonwealth of Australia, 2004), p. xi.
32 Higgins-Desbiolles, 'Hostile meeting grounds', p. 311.
33 Ibid., pp. 317–19.
34 P. Goldstone, *Making the World Safe for Tourism* (New Haven and London, Yale University Press, 2001), p. 257.
35 Ibid., p. 257.
36 OECD Directorate for Science, Technology and Industry, *National Tourism Policy Review of Australia* (July 2003), p. 6.
37 Ibid., p. 11.
38 Ibid., p. 23.
39 Ibid., p. 43.
40 Australian Government, *Tourism White Paper: A Medium to Long Term Strategy for Tourism: The Future View of Australian Tourism* (Commonwealth of Australia, Canberra, 2003), p. ix.
41 United Kingdom Department for Culture, Media and Sport, *Welcome Legacy: Tourism Strategy for the 2012 Games – A Consultation* (London, 2006), p. 5.
42 United Kingdom Department for Culture, Media and Sport *Winning: A Tourism Strategy for 2012 and Beyond* (London, 2007), p. 6.
43 Ibid., p. 8.
44 Ibid., p. 10.
45 See below, Chapter 7.
46 'French tourist killed, 20 wounded in Egypt attack', Reuters, 22 February, 2009 (http://www.reuters.com/article/idUSTRE51L23S20090222).
47 See, e.g., G. Feichtinger, R.F. Hartl, P.M. Kort and A.J. Novak, 'Terrorism control in the tourism industry', *Journal of Optimization Theory and Applications* (2001) 108(2): 283–96.
48 Ibid., esp. pp.2 84, 295.
49 'Massacre a failed grab for hostages', *Adelaide Advertiser*, 20 November 1997, p. 39; 'Shock waves hit Egypt's tour industry', *Adelaide Advertiser*, 20 November 1997, p. 39.
50 Ibid.
51 Ibid.
52 R. Lisner, 'Long Road to Luxor paved with injustice', *The Age* (Melbourne) 20 November, 1997, p. 17.
53 'Goa's special force to combat crimes against tourists', MSN News, 17 December 2009 (http://news.in.msn.com/national/article.aspx?cp-documentid=3486785).
54 Ibid.
55 Ibid.
56 See above p. 76.
57 http://www.dfat.gov.au/consular/hints/bali_advice_97.html

58 Australia Department of Foreign Affairs and Trade, *Travel Advice: Indonesia* (http://www.smartraveller.gov.au/zw-cgi/view/Advice/Indonesia), visited 10 January 2010.

59 Foreign Affairs and International Trade Canada *Travel Report Indonesia* 10 January 2010 (http://www.voyage.gc.ca/countries_pays/report_rapport-eng.asp?id=130000).

60 US Department of State *Indonesia Country Specific Information* January 10, 2010 (http://travel.state.gov/travel/cis_pa_tw/cis/cis_2052.html#safety).

61 UK Foreign and Commonwealth Office, *Indonesia Travel Advice*, January 10 2010 (http://www.fco.gov.uk/en/travel-and-living-abroad/travel-advice-by-country/asia-oceania/indonesia1).

62 UK Foreign and Commonwealth Office, *Terrorism* (http://www.fco.gov.uk/en/travel-and-living-abroad/staying-safe/terrorism).

63 Ibid.

64 HM Government, *Countering International Terrorism: The United Kingdom's Strategy* (Cm 6888, July 2006), p. 24.

65 'Indonesia irked at fresh travel warning', *The Australian*, 10 July 2007; 'Indonesia complains about travel advice', *The Age*, 19 February 2009.

66 'Indonesia irked at fresh travel warning', *The Australian*, 10 July 2007.

67 'India issues travel advisory for Australia', *Times Online*, 6 January 2010.

68 Ibid.

69 'Gillard dismisses Indian travel warning', *ABC News*, 6 January 2010 (http://www.abc.net.au/news/stories/2010/01/06/2786504.htm).

70 'No move for Delhi Games pull-out', *The Age (Melbourne)*, 31 December 2009.

71 Australian Government Department of Foreign Affairs and Trade, *Travel Advice: India*, 11 January 2010 (http://www.smartraveller.gov.au/zw-cgi/view/Advice/India).

72 This has arisen most recently in relation to the Australian Government's White Paper on counter-terrorism in February 2010 (see above p. 72) and its subsequent announcement that travellers from ten countries would be subjected to greater visa scrutiny. While some countries were immediately suggested as being on the yet-to-be-announced list (such as Somalia and Yemen), the possible inclusion of India and Indonesia has been regarded as diplomatically much more sensitive (see, e.g., 'Curious case of the white paper', ABC Online: http://www.abc.net.au/unleashed/stories/s2828825.htm, 24 February 2010).

73 HM Government, *Countering International Terrorism: The United Kingdom's Strategy* (Cm 6888, July 2006), p. 8.

74 Ibid., p. 11.

Chapter 6

The pleasure tourist
Sex tourism as a legal dilemma

Another familiar image of the Red Light District is of packs of men, young and old, couples holding hands and pointing in shock of it all, giggling groups of women celebrating a hen night, and busloads of Japanese tourists toting cameras (except not in the direction of the female entertainers! Strictly banned!). This is proof enough that the RLD deserves a visit, if not a little look in.

(www.amsterdam.info)

Sex, pleasure and tourism

While the impact of terrorism on tourism may have been to remove from the experience of being a tourist some elements of pleasure more usually associated with escaping everyday existence, the connection between sex and tourism appears to be a more obvious match. Indeed, much has been made of the use of sexual imagery in tourism advertising,[1] and the extent to which tourism leads directly to a concern with sex. That is to say, does the phenomenon of so-called 'sex tourism' qualify a particular form of tourism, or is it an aspect of what tourism *is*.

As a consequence, much of the literature on sex tourism spends a great deal of time on its definition. Martin Oppermann, for example, begins his analysis of the phenomenon by noting that it is 'everywhere'.[2] However, he also notes that it conjures up different images in different parts of the world, from 'the image of men, often older and in less than perfect shape, traveling to developing countries (in Asia, Africa, Latin America, or the Caribbean), for sexual pleasures generally not available, at least not for the same price, in their home country',[3] to certain African countries where female sex tourists are more prominent.[4] He notes that the literature until that point produced a very narrow definition of sex tourism – travelling to engage in sexual relations.[5] He regards this as too narrow and introduces other variables into an understanding of sex tourism – purpose of travel, length of time, relationship, sexual encounter and who falls into this category of travel.[6] What this produces is a far broader approach that suggests sex tourism may not necessarily be a practice with that aim alone, as he notes many tourists who have sex while travelling are not travelling primarily for that purpose, such as the business tourist.[7]

Oppermann also discusses the manner in which sex tourism is too often equated with what occurs in South East Asian destinations, such as Thailand. In this understanding it is also assumed that the sex tourist is from the developed world and is male. But as he suggests:

> Sex tourism within developing and developed destinations has also received very little attention, perhaps partly because it is difficult to place it in a dependency perspective. However, several authors have noted that domestic demand for sex in developing countries, including Thailand, is of similar if not greater importance than highly publicized international sex tourism. In Thailand many international sex tourists reputedly also come from neighboring countries in Southeast Asia … furthermore, many Western women can be seen in Gogo-bars and other establishments in Thailand, apparently in a voyeuristic role observing male sex tourist behaviour … female tourists are [also] to be found in massage parlours, perhaps testing out their lesbian nature. Clearly, many red light districts around the world constitute major attractions for tourists who do not pay for sexual services, but rather visit those places for voyeuristic purposes.[8]

Ryan and Hall discuss sex tourism within the context of the liminal nature of tourism and sex work as:

> being a tourist is to occupy a liminal role within a temporal marginality. It will subsequently be argued that this is important in our understanding of sex tourism as in the western world the prostitute is also marginalised. The act of sex tourism can therefore be explained as an interaction between two sets of liminal people – but with a difference. The one, the tourist, is enacting a socially sanctioned and economically empowered marginality, while the second, the prostitute, is stigmatised as a whore, a woman of the night, as the scarlet woman.[9]

They do acknowledge that within this description it would be wrong to assume that the prostitute and 'homosexual and lesbian holiday markets utilising sex for reasons of relaxation and self-identification are also of growing importance'.[10] The other aspects of their analysis which are most useful for our purposes is that they also regard the holiday as a 'source of self-identification'[11] and that sex tourism challenges dominant norms:

both tourism and prostitution possess dangerous forces; forces that, while subordinate to the mainstream of society, by their very presence challenge the norms of the dominant. Their existence continues to represent alternative lifestyles.[12]

They also recognise that while it can be claimed that the (female) prostitute can be seen as a woman who has taken control of her sexuality to earn an income, others will see this as exploitative of women.[13] Their rejoinder is that 'ambiguity is inherent in the very nature of liminality'.[14]

Here then is the notion of tourism as transgression, in the form of sex tourism. But even more importantly Ryan and Hall seem to be suggesting it is in the idea of tourism that one discovers sex tourism. They see the tourist and the prostitute as existing in the same liminal spaces:

> it is not surprising, given the hedonistic nature of tourism, that in many places the spatial areas of both tourist and sex worker overlap, and many hotel managers can bear witness to the fact that their premises might be regarded as both holiday accommodation and brothel. In some parts of the world the overlap becomes obvious and explicit. Amsterdam's red light district and the soi of Patpong are tourist attractions for clients and on-lookers alike.[15]

They thus write of sex tourism being located 'within the wider discourse of tourism'.[16] They connect sex work and tourism through broader social and economic forces and discuss the role of the law in marginalising sex work. For what purpose? According to Ryan and Hall this has much to do with the process of industrialisation and the need for a disciplined workforce which was potentially undermined by how leisure time was used:

> Industrialisation separated these two worlds, but it went further. It emasculated the latent challenge of non-work lives as an alternative life-style. It commoditised periods of consumption of leisure in places other than home, and made safe such periods by the processes of consumption associated with the forms of capitalism common from the start of the twentieth century. The period of holidays, being a consumer product, no longer represents embryonic alternative lifestyles. Rather, the worker consumer needs to continue to work in order to afford the holiday period, and remnants of the Puritan work ethic continue as we declare that 'we have earned our holiday'.[17]

This has created sex tourism as an interaction between two groups of liminal people that escape other roles, doing so on the margins of society, a marginal status which is reinforced by legal rules and discourse.

Sex work and tourism

Ryan and Hall, while constructing the sex tourist and prostitute relationship as symbiotic, do recognise the potential for exploitation within sex tourism.[18] In particular there is the exploitation of children and women from poor backgrounds which organisations such as *End Child Prostitution, Child Pornography and Trafficking of Children for Sexual Purposes* (ECPAT) highlight.[19] They also refer to the literature which argues that the relationship is not simply exploitative, but that it can provide income to otherwise poor families.[20] This is clearly problematic and creates a dilemma for those attempting to eradicate the sex trade.

Of course, the status of tourist might also be used to justify engaging in acts which are exploitative. Tourists might seek to rationalise such acts as part of the tourism experience rather than simple acts of oppression. As Ennew notes:

> Whether it is the *Spartacus* guide catering for the paedophile tourist, or the many advertisements appearing in the press in developed countries encouraging heterosexual males to enjoy the delights of submissive Asian girls, tourists and agencies alike often use the myth that there is no harm involved because the culture of the host country entails a greater sexual freedom than that enjoyed in the tourist's homeland. The actual sexual morality of the host countries is ignored. What is conveniently viewed instead is an apparent freedom created by the demands of the tourist customers. In a mutual exchange of dreams, the tourist finds the exotic promiscuity of Sri Lanka, Seoul or Bangkok, while the prostitutes come into contact with the bountiful, prosperous developed world.[21]

The view that the tourist is aiding the prostitute by handing over 'hard currency' is, as we suggested above, often used as a justification for such acts. It may be true that the prostitute will earn more from the act of prostitution than he or she could earn in their village or in a local factory. But this fact ignores the question of why such alternative sources of income are so poorly paid. It is a very real question whether the use of cheap labour in certain countries by transnational corporations (and their resistance to increasing wages in those countries) contributes to prostitution being taken up by some people in those countries as a more financially beneficial occupation.

Of course, this connection cannot explain all acts of prostitution – simply because not all poorly paid workers resort to sex work to make more money. But to the extent that some tourists might seek to justify their use of prostitutes in places they visit in these terms then that explanation or justification must be scrutinised. Seabrook analyses the manner in which a number of factors contribute to the rise of the sex industry in Thailand – a mixture of economic and social laissez-faire, social inequality and little official concern with remedying such disparities in wealth.[22]

The point here is of course that the sex industry – including sex tourism – flourishes in an environment of social inequality. This raises the question of the extent to which that industry depends on such inequality and thus whether it needs to maintain the status quo. Where, for example, would the pool of prostitutes come from if wages were high for all workers? In those circumstances those who control the industry might have to pay prostitutes more (or allow them to retain a greater share of their earnings) if they are to attract people to that form of work. In other words, they would have to compete in the marketplace for a workforce. In such circumstances would prostitution hold out the same level of attraction for those who run the industry or would they shift their attention to more profitable forms of business?

In part this is the argument of Leheny.[23] Although he focuses mainly on the changes in consumer demand it nevertheless suggests that the degree to which a sex industry flourishes is not a given. If new markets open which are more profitable one might well witness a flight of capital from brothels and bars and towards those other activities. It is instructive to note that it seems to be the case that countries which have limited means to earn foreign exchange often depend on tourism for such earnings and that prostitution can become an important part of this. For example, consider Cuba where prostitution was 'wiped out' after the revolution in 1959 but where it is claimed that it is now increasing as the nation deals with boycotts and hard economic times.[24]

Prostitution as a tourist attraction

It is problematic to discuss sex tourism as exploitative when we consider the extent to which many cultures have internalised the notion that prostitution is 'the oldest profession' incapable of being wiped out presumably because of the insatiable market for the services of prostitutes. There are of course long traditions, particularly in Western nations, which debate acts of prostitution as victimless crimes (where the activity is illegal) or matters which would be left between the parties where both are adult and consenting. This approach logically leads to talk of 'regulation' of prostitution rather than 'prohibition'.

There is also a tradition of regarding prostitution as a possible tourist attraction in its own right. The red-light district of Amsterdam is notorious in this regard. King's Cross in Sydney may be another example of the manner in which prostitution – or at least the sites where it occurs – can be portrayed as a cultural experience to be viewed by tourists. In this regard there is no doubt an element of 'sociological voyeurism' in this phenomenon. One only has to cite the popularity of guided tours of the red-light district in Amsterdam to illustrate this point. There have also been successful organised tours of legal brothels in Melbourne. Once again this supports the notion that 'sex sells'.

Clearly there is always going to be interest in the 'taboo' areas of life and the opportunity to participate in such areas is often going to be facilitated when one is a tourist for the reasons outlined above. This is after all the essence of Ryan and Hall's thesis with respect to the same liminal spaces that tourist and sex worker share. The notion that tourism contains within it the *raison d'être* for sex tourism rather than it being the 'dark side' of an otherwise noble pastime is confrontational to many. It is in sex tourism that we see tourism as transgression in a very clear form.

The problem for the state is how to address sex tourism as a legal problem. While some may see it as a 'natural' part of the tourism experience, it also has to be recognised that many in society regard prostitution as an exploitative practice – as well as the sex industry in general. For such members of the community the notion that prostitution should be seen as a tourist attraction is repugnant. To some extent this is resolved by tourism discourse rather than the law. Tourist promoters, when marketing places as tourist attractions based on their 'sex appeal' will avoid direct references to sex. Often tourist brochures will make vague references to this aspect of the place (e.g. Hindley Street as 'something for everyone' or 'cosmopolitan King's Cross') rather than make clear reference to the availability of sexual matter or activity. On the other hand as Ryan and Hall point out, one must not forget that there exist publications for those who do wish to seek out sexual activity when travelling. One cannot simply analyse the mainstream tourist literature.[25]

Alternatively, certain areas of cities may be so well known that their connection with the sex industry becomes part of the fabric of the city and a tourist attraction in itself. For example, La Pigalle in Paris, the red-light district in Amsterdam and perhaps even the bars in Bangkok might well find they become part of tours directed at the 'general' tourist market. But of course, such tours also point out such locations for any of these tourists who might wish to return later. And they may even provide a certain degree of respectability to such places and for those who visit them – not as tourist attractions but as sites of sexual trade.

As the preceding discussion indicates the notion that sex tourism – in its broadest sense – is part of tourism may be accepted by many, but this does not make it an easy matter to make this connection when selling destinations or packaging what they have to offer. Factors which influence this area appear to include the extent to which sex is still taboo in may parts of the community and cultures making it a sensitive area to discuss and thus 'sell'; the extent to which much of the attraction of the sex industry and sex tourism lies in the fact that it is a taboo area in many quarters; that to make such matters as prostitution into a tourist attraction means that one has to address issues connected to the human rights of those who work in the industry, questions of exploitation and whether the industry depends on social inequality to thrive; the extent to which sex tourism and the issues it raises in relation to exploitation and inequality particularly impact on women and children; whether being a destination for sex tourism is the image that the inhabitants of a location wish to portray for their city or town; whether sex tourism might attract the 'wrong' type of tourist; the extent to which sex tourism and any adverse impacts it has on a locality might be diluted by ensuring that sex tourism is not the only form of tourism which exists in the locality; and considering whether there is a need to draw a distinction between organised sex tours and individuals who travel and participate in acts of prostitution. This distinction might be valid on the basis that organised sex tours are too blatant a form of sex tourism, whereas a more discreet form of sex tourism does not provide inappropriate role models or present negative imagery. Of course, this leads to the question of whether 'disguising' the activity in some way addresses the many questions surrounding it.

This means that the role of the state in sex tourism is often going to be contradictory. In one sense sex tourism caters for a market which might demand protection in the name of the need to protect legitimate economic activity. But on the other hand, the moral issues surrounding sex tourism can raise the question of whether such activity is indeed legitimate economic activity. This is often the dilemma for those on the political Right – while they profess to be supportive of the free market when matters of morality arise the Right can be split between those who insist that the market alone should determine whether the activity occurs while others demand state intervention to prevent such 'immoral' activity.

Sex tourism vs child-sex tourism

It may well be that the dilemma of how to regulate sex tourism, for all the complex reasons described above, is resolved to some extent by a focus instead on child-sex tourism. Child-sex tourism can be seen as a 'safe' target because the view that children should not be involved in prostitution is almost universally shared and so it is not difficult to mount a case that this form of tourism is exploitative and should be wiped out. Of course, a concern with child-sex tourism does not deal with the many questions which sex tourism generally gives rise to. And a failure to understand the matters discussed above when considering how one might respond to child-sex tourism might also mean that one misses the mark. One must ask the question of whether child-sex tourism is a case apart from sex tourism in general or whether it is part of a more general social concern.

One might also consider whether governments legislate on child-sex tourism as an 'easy option' – that is, instead of tackling the larger matter of sex tourism and the powerful interests that would entail it is perhaps easier to deal with a part of the area for which there will be few opponents. This is not to say that governments lack sincerity in dealing with child-sex tourism – but an appreciation of the wider context might suggest a broader agenda is required.

For example, the very notion of 'child-sex tourism' is problematic. On the one hand is the problem of the 'child'. Such laws which seek to protect children in relation to decision making about their bodies will always create issues around the margins about the capacity of the child to consent. For example, the law in many countries prescribes 16 as the age at which consent to sexual conduct may be given. But in the context of child-sex tourism is a 15-year-old (to which the laws apply) any less able than a 16-year-old to decide about sexual behaviour? One could equally ask of course why a 16-year-old is less deserving of protection than a 15-year-old. Of course, in part the answer is that there is a need to draw a line somewhere, but there is also the dilemma that if one carries the protection agenda to its (possibly) logical extension then one might prevent even adults from engaging in prostitution. Thus is the question really one which relates to child protection or is it to do with the preservation of the liminal spaces of tourism?

Tourism discourse and child-sex tourism

It is in the area of child-sex tourism that we return for the moment to the notion of the exalted tourist. The Global Code of Ethics contains a provision directed to sex tourism generally, but child-sex tourism in particular. Article 2(3) states:

> The exploitation of human beings in any form, particularly sexual, especially when applied to children, conflicts with the fundamental aims of tourism and is the negation of tourism; as such, in accordance with international law, it should be energetically combated with the cooperation of all the States concerned and penalized without concession by the national legislation of both the countries visited and the countries of the perpetrators of these acts, even when they are carried out abroad.[26]

This article embodies a fascinating discussion of how tourism is to be conceptualised. In effect it could be seen to construct 'sex tourism' as *not* tourism at all. Of course this would depend on seeing sex tourism as exploitative. Indeed, it is broader as it regards any exploitation, albeit particularly sexual, as the 'negation of tourism'. In placing sexual exploitation as a 'special case' it also creates a hierarchy of 'bad practice' in tourism. Exploitation of human beings in any form is not tourism, but sexual exploitation even more so.

As the earlier discussion in the chapter has outlined, the boundary between tourism and sex tourism is at best blurred and possibly the latter is subsumed in the former. This appears to be the practice of tourism globally.

As has been noted above the form of sex tourism is that it is practised by the rich 'against' the poor with the consequence that it then recasts the very nature of tourism:

> The flow of sex tourists is mainly from the economically developed world (Western Europe, Scandinavian countries, North America, Australasia, the Gulf States) to poorer countries of South-East Asia, Africa, Latin America and the Caribbean. However, some wealthy individuals from less economically developed countries such as Mexico, Argentina and India, are also known to practise sex tourism and there are a small number of sex tourist destinations (for example Amsterdam, New Orleans, Las Vegas) in affluent countries. Some countries in Eastern Europe are also now beginning to attract sex tourists and export child prostitution to other countries. There is enormous variation between the receiving countries in terms of the degree of national level involvement in organising sex tourism. Many receiving countries are under economic and political pressures to promote tourism as a means of generating foreign exchange revenue. In some cases, there is what amounts to official acceptance of the fact that tourism means sex tourism, some government officials have spoken of 'sacrificing a generation of women' in pursuit of economic development.[27]

The notion that in some locations at least 'tourism means sex tourism' creates a dilemma for the regulation of tourism. Is it possible to actually regulate the ugly side of tourism when the problem of sex tourism goes to the core of the tourism experience:

> By treating the child as a commodity which can be purchased, hired, sold or thrown away the issue is no longer just a question of poverty but rather one of values – and in particular the values of consumerism.
> This is a subtle distinction but of considerable importance for the way in which tourism is marketed. When tourism advertising promotes the values of consumerism and hedonism as the central goal of the tourism experience it is affirming the same values which make the prostitution of children possible.[28]

The importance of this statement for the manner in which sex tourism is addressed cannot be over-emphasised. On the one hand, the argument is that the current core values and encouraged experiences of being a tourist support the commodificaton of places and people. Yet, as the Global Code of Ethics states, the exploitation of people is the 'negation of tourism'. Sex tourism is the logical consequence of the consumerism which is at the centre of tourism as currently practised. The argument then is that only a fundamental change in the values upon which tourism is based will properly resolve the problem of sex tourism. What was the response of some affluent nations? The passage of child-sex-tourism laws.

Laws on child-sex tourism

A number of countries have now passed laws to criminalise the sexual exploitation of children overseas. That is, the offender can be prosecuted in that country for an offence involving a child even though the offence occurred overseas. In Australia the Crimes (Child Sex Tourism) Amendment Act 1994 (Cth) in effect makes it an offence punishable by courts in Australia for Australian citizens or residents to engage in acts of sexual intercourse and other sexual acts with children under 16 overseas.[29] In the United Kingdom the Sexual Offences Act 2003 makes it an offence for a British citizen or resident to commit sexual offences against children under 16 while overseas.[30] Canadian legislation also extends various sexual offences to acts committed overseas by Canadian citizens or residents that would be offences in Canada.[31] The legislation actually goes beyond sexual offences involving children under 16 to include some offences involving children under 18 and in some cases certain general sexual offences.[32] United States legislation also provides for the prosecution in the United States of American citizens or residents who 'travel with intent to engage in illicit sexual conduct' with persons under 18 years of age.[33]

Such legislation gives rise to a number of issues of both legal and practical relevance. For example, such a law requires the collection of evidence overseas which usually means that the co-operation of the police force of the country within which the alleged offence occurred is necessary. It also means that the resources of the police force of the country seeking to prosecute the offender must be sufficient to enable them to investigate such offences in other countries. This alone can cause many difficulties. As has already been noted one has to consider the extent to which some governments in some countries may unofficially condone (child) sex tourism. This could mean that the police forces in such countries may be reluctant to fully co-operate. It also could mean that the police forces of the country from which sex tourists originate may not follow up all such cases for fear of harming the interests of a friendly country. And then, of course, how does one investigate acts of child-sex tourism in a country where relations between that country and the country from where the sex tourists originate are not friendly?

The legislation in a technical sense attempts to address some of these problems of enforcement, For example, there are also provisions in the Australian legislation which permit the giving of evidence via video link.[34] But these do not overcome the practical difficulty in locating a victim and ensuring that they are available to give evidence. Nor does it consider the extent to which a child victim in another country might feel reluctant to provide evidence in such a formal setting, due to cultural or language reasons.[35]

One consequence of some of these practical difficulties in enforcement has been reports that the legislation has not been enforced adequately. One report suggested that the Canadian law had resulted in 146 prosecutions but only one conviction between its enactment in 1994 and 2007.[36] The same report also commented on the lack of resources for Canadian police to pursue the cases in overseas locations.[37] In Australia it has been commented in 2002 that, 'Australia has prosecuted ten people for offences relating to child-sex tourism in countries such as Cambodia and the Philippines, more than many other countries with similar extra-territorial legislation.'[38] At that time the Australian law was criticised for not achieving its 'potential':[39]

> To permanently decrease demand for prostituted children, the CST Act [Child Sex Tourism Act] needs to ensure continued accountability for offences under the Act. Unfortunately, procedural and evidentiary deficiencies in the operation of the CST Act have constrained its performance. First, the CST Act as originally drafted lacked child-friendly procedures that allow child witnesses to give accurate and convincing evidence. Second, the impact upon the child is generally not considered in sentencing. Finally, limited resources and inadequate recognition of investigatory difficulties have restricted the operation of the Act. These flaws are primarily due to the inadequate conversion of the Act's ideals into practical procedures.[40]

Part of the apparent difficulty in achieving the aims of the Act has also been said to be the manner in which the power disparity between the affluent tourist and the child victim is perceived. As Brungs says in relation to the reasoning of a judge in sentencing one offender in 1999:

> In his judgment, Kennedy J did not recognise the considerable personal impact upon the children, categorising them as 'Asian children in poverty', rather than individual victims of child sexual abuse, and so accordingly reduced the sentence. In addition, despite acknowledging the economic and power disparities between the offender and the victim, Kennedy J still found that the sexual activities could have been consensual.[41]

It is in such remarks that one can see how the court's approach to child-sex tourism appears disconnected from the manner in which tourism is practised, as well as sex tourism in particular. Clearly, as the Global Code of Ethics for Tourism stressed, global inequalities lie behind the causes of child-sex tourism in the first place. To regard such inequality as a mitigating factor in sentencing appears to fail to protect the child such laws are designed to protect.

However, such comments also say something about the law's understanding of tourism. Arguably, the above comments also indicate the manner in which the law does not need to refer to tourism discourse or knowledge in determining how it will construct tourism and its consequences. This point is even more explicit in a recent Australian prosecution for an offence under child-sex tourism laws. On appeal against sentence the appellant argued that the court had failed to take into account the purpose of the laws to prevent 'child-sex tourism' as opposed to in his case where he had happened to engage in sexual activity with a child while overseas on business. One appeal judge commented:

> Counsel for the Crown conceded that appellant's counsel had probably been correct in arguing that the 'worst case' would be that where a person had gone overseas for the purpose of engaging in sexual activity with a child or children. Such a circumstance, counsel submitted, ought be viewed as a matter of aggravation.
>
> In my opinion, notwithstanding the applicability of the relevant sections to the appellant's conduct, the concession made by counsel for the Crown was properly made. If a person was to travel overseas for the purpose of engaging in sexual activity with a child or children (or if that was one of the purposes for which the person travelled overseas) it would suggest a level of premeditation different in kind to an incident in which a person, whilst overseas, opportunistically took part in sexual activity with a child. So a purpose such as I have identified might properly be regarded as a circumstance of aggravation. It does not follow, of course, that the sentence in the one case would necessarily be greater than the sentence in the other. A person might go overseas for a purpose of engaging in child sex yet desist after one instance of offending conduct. Another person, whilst overseas, might engage in opportunistic child sex with different features of aggravation – as in the present case, where a particular breach of trust was involved.[42]

The judge did not think the trial judge had failed to consider this when sentencing the accused so there was to be no change in the sentence imposed according to this appeal judge. While this judge clearly stated that the offences were still serious even though it was not a part of a 'sex tour' or as the judge said 'the appellant did not go overseas "for the express purpose of engaging in sexual activity with children"'[43] it still indicates a preparedness to read into the legislation a stereotype about how 'sex tourism' occurs and indeed what is the very notion of tourism. Thus while the London Olympic Strategy 2012 now speaks of the 'business tourist' as being the principal focus of their tourism strategy, in the case of child-sex tourism, offenders who happen to be travelling for business and not for leisure can presumably claim that not being a 'tourist' they can hardly be placed in the same category as 'child-sex tourist' when being sentenced for an offence. It must be added that the other two appeal-court judges did not agree with the interpretation of Ashley, JA and took the view that the provisions 'apply equally to those who go overseas for the specific purpose of engaging in sexual activities with children and those who form that intention after they have arrived in a foreign country'.[44] Nevertheless, this case still illustrates the shifting notion of the 'tourist ' at work and how the law can, as expressed in Ashley, JA's judgment operate without reference to other disciplinary insights. It is the autopoietic nature of the law which permits it to conclude that for this purpose a tourist might not be someone who is primarily travelling for business.

It seems that in more recent years there has also been a shift in policing away from child-sex tourism and towards the sexual exploitation of children online. In the United Kingdom the Child Exploitation and Online Protection Centre (CEOP) is responsible for policing child-sex tourism laws but it also deals with online child-sex offences as well as other child-sex matters. CEOP's annual reviews for the past two years have no mention of child-sex tourism and indicate a far greater focus on online sexual exploitation of children.[45] The Australian Federal Police Force also provide little detail about the extent of matters investigated under child-sex tourism provisions other than to state that '[i]n collaboration with its international partners, the AFP successfully identified and charged numerous offenders for child sexual exploitation and child sex tourism offences'.[46]

The concern about child-sex tourism follows from the international commitment to protecting children from sexual exploitation pursuant to the United Nations Convention on the Rights of the Child[47] and also from the Optional Protocol to the Convention on the Rights of the Child on the Sale of Children, Child Prostitution and Child Pornography which actually connects the causes of child-sex tourism with global inequality as it requires 'States Parties [to] promote the strengthening of international cooperation in order to address the root causes, such as poverty and underdevelopment, contributing to the vulnerability of children to the sale of children, child prostitution, child pornography and child sex tourism'.[48] But as we have noted the area of sex tourism transcends child-protection issues. However, to seek to regulate sex tourism more broadly also requires an engagement with matters that go more centrally to the nature of tourism – the notion of escape, self identity and as Ryan and Hall describe it those liminal spaces inhabited by both tourist and sex worker. The effect is that the 'problem' of sex tourism has been transformed into a problem of child protection, as if support for doing so would bring more certainty in a field where uncertainty tends to prevail.

Codes of conduct as regulation

The shortcomings of legislation in the field of child-sex tourism are apparent. While prosecutions occur it is almost impossible to assess the actual incidence of this form of exploitation. As a result much greater store has been invested by organisations such as ECPAT in codes of conduct or practice for various parts of the tourism industry. These are important to examine for they say much not just about concern with children's protection, but also how the role of the tourist and the tourism industry in the social impacts of tourism is constructed.

The Code of Conduct for the Protection of Children from Sexual Exploitation in Travel and Tourism is a tourism-industry-initiated Code formulated with ECPAT International,[49] funded by UNICEF and with the support of the World Tourism Organization.[50] Adoption of the Code requires tourism services to commit to the following:

1. To establish an ethical policy regarding commercial sexual exploitation of children.
2. To train the personnel in the country of origin and travel destinations.
3. To introduce a clause in contracts with suppliers, stating a common repudiation of commercial sexual exploitation of children.
4. To provide information to travellers by means of catalogues, brochures, in-flight films, ticket-slips, home pages, etc.
5. To provide information to local "key persons" at the destinations.
6. To report annually.[51]

The foreword to the Code itself places the social impacts of tourism as a 'lesser' by-product of tourism:

> The rapid growth of international tourism represents most of the times an economic boom for tourism destinations. However, it may sometimes also lead to negative socio-cultural impacts which become evident, in particular in the exploitation of human beings through sex tourism.[52]

Note here that the reference is to 'sex tourism' and not 'child-sex tourism'. It is the next paragraph in the foreword that makes that slippage:

> Although research has shown that tourists involvement in this practice represents only a tiny minority of the persons sexually exploiting children, the UN World Tourism Organization (UNWTO), along with other international stakeholders such as ECPAT and the tourism private sector have mobilized and joined forces to prevent and combat this phenomenon.[53]

The words 'this practice' follows directly from the previous paragraph and so is referring to 'sex tourism'. The foreword then proceeds to refer to the Global Code of Ethics for Tourism as 'allowing tourism stakeholders the possibility of addressing the issue of child exploitation within an internationally agreed framework for the responsible and sustainable development of tourism'.[54] While this is not untrue, it does fail to acknowledge that the Global Code of Ethics in fact covers the broad exploitation of all human beings, although particularly sexual, and especially children. It refers to the manner in which the Code then links with the European Union's desire to address child-sex tourism and claims that it 'is recognized by UNICEF and the World Tourism Organization as the primary international tool for the prevention and combating of child-sex tourism by the travel and tourism private sector'.[55]

The Code notes that '[t]he commercial sexual exploitation of children often occurs openly without government reaction or with governments preferring to "look the other way"'.[56] It also states that in 1988 UNICEF estimated that there were two million children forced into commercial sexual practices and that in 1990 there were estimated to be 250 million child-pornographic films available in the world, with the Internet fuelling demand as well as providing a medium to advertise children for commercial sexual practices.[57] The Code also speaks to the responsibility of the tourism industry with respect to child-sex tourism. In doing so it describes those within the industry as having 'direct responsibility' when 'those in the tourism sector ... knowingly publicize, promote, and receive sex tours ... as well as ... the operators of establishments and premises where abusers can actually meet and sexually exploit children'.[58] In addition the tourism sector has 'indirect responsibility' when 'tour operators, travel agents, and carriers, especially airlines, ... become aware that they are used as vehicles to carry declared or potential sex offenders to the destinations'.[59]

The document also outlines the action that hotels can take with respect to the eradication of child-sex tourism. These are:

1. The hotel's policy shall clearly state the hotel's position with regard to the trade in child sex. The hotel shall also make this understood among its staff and provide them with knowledge on how to handle problems should they arise.
2. Hotel management shall provide information to its personnel and guests regarding national laws and the penalties imposed for the sexual abuse of children.
3. The hotel's security staff shall be trained to handle guests or personnel who sexually abuse a child, particularly on the hotel's premises.
4. Co-operate with the relevant labour unions.
5. Prevent children from entering the hotel via bars, restaurants, lobby or reception.
6. Work actively. As a precautionary measure, build up links with police, social authorities and other organizations that may be involved with an encroachment.

7. Personnel, who observe anything that suggests that the commercial sexual exploitation of children may be taking place, must report immediately to the police or some other authority with the right to intervene.[60]

There is also reference to the European Commission's desire to establish norms of conduct based on ethical tourism standards.[61]

While there is no objection to the principle of creating a process which seeks to eliminate the sexual exploitation of children, that objective should not make immune from critique the manner and motivations for pursuing that goal. In effect the Code is an example of industry self regulation, which is a strong feature of the modern state. Self-regulation of media and other industries is, on the one hand, thought to ensure higher levels of compliance as the norms are 'owned' by the industry. On the other hand, they may be criticised on the basis that the very creation of the norms or standards expected of the industry are created by the same industry. In the instant case of child-sex tourism, it can be argued that the industry has achieved a narrowing of the focus away from exploitation in general, as well as the sexual exploitation of adults and in effect redefined 'sex tourism' as a child protection issue. The Global Code of Ethics for Tourism does not cast the area that narrowly, nor did the Tourism Bill of Rights and Tourist Code 1985 which simply stated that tourists must 'refrain from exploiting others for prostitution purposes'.[62]

In part this narrower emphasis is due no doubt to the capture of the area by child-advocacy groups. But it also meets the objectives of an industry that has little to gain from a wholesale examination of the extent to which exploitation occurs with tourism and the tourism industry.[63] There is also the dilemma of defining adult prostitution as a private matter where, provided both parties consent, then the state is often disinterested. Of course, in some parts of the world prostitution is either legal or officially accepted, but even where it is illegal it is often overlooked as a matter of public importance. But in the case of constructing responsible tourist practice, there is an opportunity to define expectations that might not be in simple conformity with the law or its enforcement as a practical matter. In particular, the extent to which tourism generally, and sex tourism in particular, promotes a gendered global labour force that commodifies women's bodies would suggest that ethical tourism might be concerned not solely with child-sex tourism but with the manner in which adult-sex tourism ties in with the whole tourism sector. Mary Mills comments in relation to Zhang's work[64] on this point:

Zhang examines male-peer culture among new entrepreneurs and state officials in Beijing. This is characterized by ritualized outings to nightclubs where men negotiate globally inflected norms of masculinity through the consumption of imported alcohol and the commodified bodies of women. Such ties between expanding business circuits and the heightened demand for women's labor as sex workers also suggest interesting parallels with the ways women's sexual labor supports similar relations of masculinized power linked to global tourism or military expansion.[65]

This work suggests that sex tourism is, as Nancy Wonders and Raymond Michalowski argue, 'a form of global commerce that is transforming sex work, cities, and human relationships'.[66] In their analysis sex tourism occurs as a result of broader inequalities in the world, bringing together migrants and tourists who have something in common, a desire for something 'better than what their current home has to offer'.[67] They observe:

> The intersection of tourism and migration in the globalized world system facilitates the production of sex tourism by bringing together mobile sex workers with mobile sex consumers. This increased mobility has two vectors. On the one hand, increased concentrations of wealth within industrialized nations means that more people–mostly men, but also some women–can afford to travel as tourists in foreign lands where they can enjoy "exotic" sights, sounds, and in some cases, "otherly" bodies. On the other hand, as global capital disrupts established patterns of economic survival in less developed nations, unemployment, urban migration, and national out-migration rise. This push toward migration was clearly visible in the International Labor Organization's (ILO) estimate that around thirty percent of the world's labor force is "unemployed and unable to sustain a minimum standard of living".[68]

The size of the global sex industry is difficult to estimate given the nature of the phenomenon, but it is thought to be growing and worth at least $US20 billion a year.[69] The problem this poses for the tourism industry is that to confront this area of exploitation is to confront the very dynamics of the world order and the forces of globalisation. Leaving aside the extent to which the global sex industry meshes with the global tourism industry and is dependent on it, to attack sexual exploitation on the broader scale would mean to question the manner in which global business takes place.

In this context it makes sense to reconstruct sex tourism as a child-protection problem. Other international treaties (such as the United Nations Convention on the Rights of the Child) can readily be referred to as support for this recasting of the agenda. And the child-protection lobby are always waiting in the wings to defend the needs of the child. It also makes good business sense. Marilyn Carlson Nelson has spoken of her engagement with the Code of Conduct.[70] Nelson is Chairperson of Carlson Companies which operates a hotel, restaurant and travel business. It claims to be one of the largest privately held companies in the United States. It lists its businesses as

'Carlson Hotels – with Regent Hotels & Resorts, Radisson Hotels & Resorts, Park Plaza Hotels & Resorts, Country Inns & Suites By Carlson^S, and Park Inn hotels; Carlson Restaurants – with T.G.I. Friday's and Pick Up Stix; and Carlson Wagonlit Travel, a global leader in business travel management'.[71] It operates in 150 countries with over 150,000 employees.[72] It has a record of good employee work conditions.[73] Nelson is also on the board of Exxon Mobil, one of the largest public companies in the world and which has been the subject of criticism of environmentalists and human-rights activists. Whatever the fairness or otherwise of those criticisms, her membership of this Board shows some of the interconnectedness between the tourism industry and other global interests that benefit from globalisation and the current economic order. While we would not question the sincerity of Nelson and others in similar positions as to their concern for the welfare of children, nor do we suggest that those same business leaders are responsible for the particular construction of sex tourism being discussed here, nevertheless there must be a question as to whether the casting of child-sex tourism as *the* sex-tourism problem runs with their broader economic interests. Support for codes of conduct against child sexual exploitation also sits well with 'family-friendly' marketing campaigns. In August 2009 Carlson Companies announced a 'See My Country' programme that 'feature a variety of attractions of interest to families'.[74] The itineraries include a 'new "Mom's Choice" designation for top attractions in each itinerary' 'based on factors such as family fun, price and mom approval'.[75] Clearly, such marketing pitches to a particular market segment and in creating a 'family friendly' image the philanthropic causes the organisation will support must have some synthesis with that image.

Tourism and legal discourse in sex tourism

In some countries the norms expressed in the codes have found their way in to formal law. For example, in Goa the Children's Act 2003:

> proscribes *commercial sex exploitation, barring* children from hotels or other similar facilities unless registered with a person related by blood. It further mandates the State to design a *Child Friendly Tourism Code* and to appoint *"under cover agents to pose as prospective clients for child prostitutes or as employers of child labour"* with a view to arresting perpetrators.[76]

This Act has been described as unique because:

> it does not merely recommend punitive measures against offenders, but suggests ways and means of dealing with the larger issues of protecting, promoting and preserving the best interest of children in Goa and to

create a society that is proud to be child friendly. It attempts to place responsibility on different sections of the society and its institutions to play a role in protecting all children and in preventing the abuse of any child. The hotel owners, the photo studios, cyber care operators, the police, the tourism department, the travel and tourism trade industry are each expected to keep their eyes and ears open as well as perform particular roles to achieve this.[77]

To some extent the child-sex tourism laws in countries such as the United Kingdom, Canada and Australia are other examples of this incorporation of international expectations into domestic law, although on a much narrower level than the Goa example purports to be. That is the first criticism of legal discourse in this area – it for the most part leaves most of the legal standards at the international level where there is little ability to directly enforce them. Of course, the deeper criticism is that the discourse tends to focus on children and sex tourism, rather than the broader issues raised by sexual exploitation (and even exploitation of other kinds) for adult women and men.

In constructing the discourse around child-sex tourism a larger area of concern has been completely overlooked. As Ryan and Hall comment in relation to the passage of the Australian law:

> Little concern was expressed in discussion of the legislation about the sexual activities of international visitors to Australia and the various campaigns of the Australian Tourist Commission which sought to display bikini-clad women in order to create a favourable and attractive image to certain market segments. In this situation, it may therefore be argued that while something has been seen to be done in the solution of 'sex tourism' issues, in reality, very little fundamental change has occurred.[78]

As they also suggest, this legislation, and the construction of the problem of sex tourism as one which is primarily about children, avoids addressing issues arising from the commodification of the body and its connection with tourism.[79] While Ryan and Hall appear optimistic about that debate being engaged, given the powerful economic interests behind the current arrangements we would doubt that it will be an easy road. But there is another reason for being perhaps pessimistic that is to do with the wider matter of how this discussion constructs the 'tourist'. As the Global Code of Ethics for Tourism states, the exploitation of people is the very negation of tourism. Thus, in transgressive tourist practice we are told what tourism is, or perhaps can be. For how can we know who is the exalted tourist without knowing what it is to fail in being noble? In that sense, the sex tourist is possibly a necessary part of tourism, to be pilloried and prosecuted perhaps, but nevertheless sitting at the centre of the tourism experience.

Notes

1 This area is reviewed in C. Ryan and C.M. Hall, *Sex Tourism: Marginal People and Liminalities* (London and New York, Routledge, 2001), pp. 28–35.
2 M. Oppermann, 'Sex Tourism', *Annals of Tourism Research* (1999) 26(2): 251–66, p. 251.
3 Ibid.
4 Ibid.
5 Ibid., p. 252.
6 Ibid.
7 Ibid.
8 Ibid., p. 254 (references omitted).
9 Ryan and Hall, *Sex Tourism*, p. 1.
10 Ibid.
11 Ibid.
12 Ibid., p. 2.
13 Ibid.
14 Ibid.
15 Ibid., p. 6.
16 Ibid., p. 8.
17 Ibid., p. 19.
18 Ibid., pp. 22–23.
19 Ibid., p. 23.
20 Ibid.
21 J. Ennew, *The Sexual Exploitation of Children* (New York, St. Martin's Press, 1986), p. 111.
22 J. Seabrook, *Travels in the Skin Trade* (London, Pluto Press, 1996), p. 128ff.
23 D. Leheny, 'A political economy of Asian sex tourism', *Annals of Tourism Research* (1995) 22(2): 367–84.
24 See, e.g., 'Youth prostitution feeding Cuba's tourist industry', National Society for Hispanic Professionals Network (http://network.nshp. org/profiles/blogs/youth-prostitution-feeding).
25 Ryan and Hall, *Sex Tourism*, p. 28.
26 Global Code of Ethics for Tourism, art. 2(3).
27 World Congress Against Commercial Sexual Exploitation of Children, 1996, 'Tourism and children in prostitution' (http://www.usis.usemb.se/children/csec/216a.htm).
28 Ibid.
29 Crimes Act 1914 (Cth), ss.50AD, 50BA-BD (as amended by Crimes (Child Sex Tourism) Amendment Act 1994).
30 Sexual Offences Act 2003 (UK), s. 72, Sch. 2. The relevant offences have a wider application for Northern Ireland, but in relation to England and Wales only child-sex offences are covered.
31 Criminal Code (R.S., 1985, c. C-46) (Canada), s. 7(4.1).
32 Ibid., the Act applies the extra-territorial provisions to offences under ss.151, 152, 153, 155, 159, 160(2) and (3), 163, 170, 171, 173 and 212(4) of the Code.
33 Prosecutorial Remedies and Other Tools to end the Exploitation of Children Today Act of 2003 (PROTECT Act), Pub. L. 108–21, 117 Stat. 650, S. 151, s. 105.
34 Crimes Act 1914 (Cth), s. 50EA.
35 M. Brungs, 'Abolishing child sex tourism: Australia's contribution' [2002] *Australian Journal of Human Rights*, 17.
36 'Child-sex tourism law not enforced', *The Vancouver Sun*, 3 April 2008 (www.canada.com).

37 Ibid.
38 Brungs, 'Abolishing child sex tourism'.
39 Ibid.
40 Ibid.
41 Ibid.
42 *R v O N A* [2009] VSCA 146 (18 June 2009), per Ashley, JA, paras. 9–10.
43 Ibid., para.12.
44 Ibid., para. 54 per Neave, JA, Mandie, JA concurring.
45 See *CEOP Annual Review 2008–2009*, *CEOP Annual Review 2007–2008*.
46 Australian Federal Police, *Annual Report 2008–09* (Commonwealth of Australia, 2009), p. 97.
47 See article 34:

> States Parties undertake to protect the child from all forms of sexual exploi-
> tation and sexual abuse. For these purposes, States Parties shall in particular
> take all appropriate national, bilateral and multilateral measures to prevent:
>
> (a) The inducement or coercion of a child to engage in any unlawful
>   sexual activity;
> (b) The exploitative use of children in prostitution or other unlawful
>   sexual practices;
> (c) The exploitative use of children in pornographic performances and
>   materials.

48 Article 10.
49 ECPAT is the abbreviation for End Child Prostitution, Child Pornography and Trafficking of Children for Sexual Purposes.
50 See http://www.thecode.org/.
51 Ibid.
52 Code of Conduct for the Protection of Children from Sexual Exploitation in Travel and Tourism, foreword, p. 3.
53 Ibid.
54 Ibid.
55 Ibid.
56 Ibid.
57 Ibid., p. 7.
58 Ibid., p. 10.
59 Ibid.
60 Ibid., pp. 10–11.
61 Ibid., citing the European Commission KOM (96) 547 final, p. 3. 199.
62 Tourism Bill of Rights and Tourist Code1985, art. XI.
63 See the following chapter for a discussion of employment practices in tourism.
64 L. Zhang, *Strangers in the City: Reconfigurations of Space, Power, and Social Networks Within China's Floating Population* (Stanford, CA: Stanford University Press, 2001).
65 M.B. Mills, 'Gender and inequality in the global labor force', *Annual Review of Anthropology* (2003) 32: 41–62, p. 54.
66 N. A. Wonders and R. Michalowski, 'Bodies, borders, and sex tourism in a glo-balized world: a tale of two cities – Amsterdam and Havana', *Social Problems*, Special Issue on Globalization and Social Problems (2001) 48(4): 545–71, p. 546.
67 Ibid., p. 549.
68 Ibid. (references omitted).

69 Ibid.
70 See http://www.thecode.org/.
71 http://www.carlson.com/overview/index.cfm.
72 Ibid.
73 See e.g. 'Carlson recognized as one of the 100 Best Companies for Working Mothers' (http://www.carlson.com/media/article.cfm?id=822&group=corporate& subhilite=1& terhilite=0); 'Carlson is one of the 'Best Adoption-Friendly' Workplaces in America, According to Dave Thomas Foundation' (http://www.carlson. com/media/article.cfm?id=749&group=corporate& subhilite=1& terhilite=0).
74 http://www.carlson.com/media/article.cfm?id=796&group=hotels.
75 Ibid.
76 UNICEF Global Perspectives on Consolidated Children's Rights Statutes Legislative Reform Initiative Paper Series (Gender, Rights and Civic Engagement Section, Division of Policy and Practice, New York, 2008), p. 84.
77 'Responsibility in tourism and the Goa Children's Act in the context of tourism', *Equations* December 2006, p. 1. (www.equitabletourism.org).
78 Ryan and Hall, *Sex Tourism*, p. 144.
79 Ibid., p. 149, One could stress here that this particularly is about women's bodies.

Chapter 7

Work and death in tourism

From darkness to voyeurism

Despite the seductive impression created by Hollywood films, television, and popular periodicals, working in the tourist economy usually means earning low wages, receiving few benefits, and tolerating unpredictable work schedules and stressful working conditions.

(Robert Parker 'Las Vegas: Casino Gambling and Local Culture', in D.R. Judd and S.S. Fainstein, *The Tourist City* (New Haven, Yale University Press, 1999), p. 119)

What happens in Vegas, stays in Vegas.

(www.visitlasvegas.com)

Arbeit Macht Frei ('Work makes one free')
(Sign over gate to Auschwitz former concentration camp)

In the previous chapter we examined sex tourism as an aspect of tourism as transgression. What is discovered is a form of tourism which appears to be driven by the same dynamic as tourism in general and which has become interwoven as a consequence with what might be said to be the 'mainstream'. This also reinforces the point that a significant part of tourism exists in the margins, or in those liminal spaces as Ryan and Hall would describe them. The dilemma this creates for state regulation is manifold. To the extent that such forms of tourism constitute the 'negation' of tourism and offend certain values they cannot be allowed to flourish unchecked. On the other hand, as they are driven by the same forces that have allowed global capital to thrive, over-regulation may create other forms of discomfort for those with economic power. The solution has been in reconstructing the problem of sex tourism around child protection, a less contested concern. The consequence has thus also been to leave a considerable amount of sex tourism in the darkness of quasi-regulation.

In this chapter we pursue this theme of how tourism deals with transgression around two areas that may not immediately seem related: work and death. While those that work in the tourism industry occupy a central role (perhaps leaving aside the role of the sex worker) in terms of supporting tourism, it is often in their working conditions, wages and status that one can find issues of liminality. It is also as a consequence of some other marginal status that people come to work in tourism, such as being a migrant worker or a refugee. Thus issues of regulation and justice are often to the fore for those that work in tourism. In the case of death tourism (and we include for present purposes illness in this category) the liminal space is one suggested by either travel for medical intervention or suicide, or a fascination with the macabre, as sites where death has occurred. To some extent the death or medical tourist exists in a darkness for the notion of what tourism might be for such pursuits conflicts with the idea that tourism is about leisure and relaxation. For those who travel to see 'sites of death', it is in this form of voyeurism that one finds a darkness that also potentially negates what tourism might be in a more exalted state. For the state and the law, the issue of how to regulate these areas presents many dilemmas and challenges.

Regulating tourism work

Tourism is often presented as a significant contributor not only to national economies but also to employment. In this way it is promoted by governments as one means to address unemployment, poverty and inequality. Thus article 5(1) and (2) of the Global Code of Ethics for Tourism proclaims:

(1) Local populations should be associated with tourism activities and share equitably in the economic, social and cultural benefits they generate, and particularly in the creation of direct and indirect jobs resulting from them.

(2) Tourism policies should be applied in such a way as to help to raise the standard of living of the populations of the regions visited and meet their needs: the planning and architectural approach to and operation of tourism resorts and accommodation should aim to integrate them, to the extent possible, in the local economic and social fabric; where skills are equal, priority should be given to local manpower.

Clearly, national governments are often at pains to stress the employment-generating potential of tourism. The United Kingdom's government tourist strategy for the 2012 Olympics and beyond begins with a reference to the tourism industry 'being directly responsible for 1.4 million jobs, or one in every 20 people in work'.[1] That same document makes the following comment on the nature of employment in tourism:

Across the UK the tourism industry sustains about 1.4 million jobs directly and more indirectly – 5 per cent of all employment in the UK. There is great variety of job type and employment levels across the UK.

The restaurant industry is the largest in terms of employment, followed by pubs, bars, night clubs and hotels. It is predicted that by 2014 there will be a decrease of 19,000 in the number of those working in 'elementary occupations' and an increase of 41,000 in the number of managers. In London, tourism directly supports 280,000 jobs.[2]

The document than presents charts that indicate the number of workers in each occupation within tourism. This data indicates that approximately 880,000 people are engaged in the 'elementary occupations' (kitchen and catering assistants, bar staff and waiting staff), approximately 275,000 people in skilled trades (chefs and cooks) and 300,000 people in managerial roles.[3] Thus a shift of 19,000 jobs out of the elementary group and a rise of 42,000 in managerial positions would have a small overall effect on the relative proportions of each group. In effect the vast majority of jobs in the sector are unskilled.

The other important data arising from the UK Tourism Strategy document is that the overall split between part-time workers and full-time workers is almost even, with the qualification that in the pubs, bars and nightclub sector part-time work is higher at 60 per cent of all positions.[4] While full-time positions dominate in visitor attractions the work is seasonal.[5] There are also high staff turnover rates, with over 600,000 people lost to the industry.[6] Thus the overall picture is that employment in tourism is predominately in the lower-paid unskilled jobs, and is either seasonal or unstable. The UK Tourism Strategy then emphasised the need to improve managerial and customer-service skills in order to improve the prospects of retaining staff and improving the country's attractiveness as a tourist destination:

> The 2012 Games will showcase the skills of people working in these industries. We must also see the Games as an opportunity to improve the skills, retain more staff and develop a better career structure, helping those industries contribute to the UK ambition of becoming a world leader in skills by 2020.[7]

There is no mention here of wages or working conditions for workers in the tourism industry. Instead it is, in a similar vein to Tourism Australia's campaign to be a domestic tourist for what was tantamount to patriotic reasons,[8] a strategy which presents the employee's role in improving her or his skill and making Britain a world leader as a national duty. It is only in the document's discussion of how to improve the sustainability of tourism that one encounters reference to the working conditions of employees:

> Improve the quality of tourism jobs – how the sector is perceived as a career choice revolves around the quality of jobs, salary levels, the

pattern, length and consistency of working hours (while recognising that these match the pattern of customer demand), the ability to offer full-time, year-round jobs and long term contracts, and career opportunities.[9]

The Australian Government's White Paper on tourism made similar comments. It stated that in 2001–2 there were 550,000 people or 6 per cent of the workforce employed directly in tourism.[10] It then noted:

> Tourism employment in Australia is characterised by a high degree of diversity, both in terms of the skills and training needed and the hours worked. The occupational profile of jobs in the tourism industry consists of a higher proportion of part-time, casual and seasonal jobs, and a higher rate of female participation than in the overall labour force. The tourism industry is dominated by small business operators and characterised by a strong seasonal component to the market, especially in alpine or beach resorts.[11]

The nature of the work and the needs of the tourism industry were considered to be met by the workplace laws then in place:

> The Workplace Relations Act 1996 allows for more flexible workplace arrangements to facilitate Australia's growing international competitiveness. There is considerable potential for greater use and uptake of these flexible arrangements by the tourism industry.[12]

The centrepiece of this legislation was individual workplace agreements which were negotiated between employer and employee, with a limited role for unions. The legislation was campaigned against by trade unions and the Australian Labor Party and was a highly unpopular law. It has now been replaced by the Fair Work Act 2009 which provides for the possibility of representation of employees by trade unions. The problem in the context of the tourism industry is whether seasonal, part-time and low-skilled workers will assert their right to representation to the fullest extent.

The official discourse thus constructs the tourism industry as an industry that generates significant amounts of employment for the population, albeit mainly in low-paid and unskilled roles. This does not lead to any real discussion of workers' rights and conditions but creates a need for 'flexibility' in hours and conditions of employment.

Shaw and Williams, however, question the statistics on jobs created by tourism. They argue that there is a tendency to overestimation, particularly as what constitutes employment in the leisure industry can be blurred at times.[13] They also caution against the stereotype that work in tourism is low paid and unskilled, arguing that it is as complex and heterogeneous as the rest of the industry.[14] They do, however, note that there are gender divisions in the tourism industry, with women tending to be peripheral (tending to be part time) rather than core workers and performing tasks such as cleaning, serving meals and making beds.[15] This, they claim, is because 'women workers carry into the workplace their subordinate status in society at large'.[16]

They also mention the role of international migration in the tourism industry, noting that (at the time they wrote) there were approximately 16 million international migrants and in countries such as Luxembourg and Switzerland they made up one-third of the labour force.[17] They comment that:

> Most research shows that unskilled migrants tend to occupy poorly paid, insecure, unpleasant and/or boring jobs. Tourism and leisure often figure large as potential employers. The weak organization of internal labour markets in these industries tend to make them easy to enter. ... Such migrants invariably tend to occupy peripheral jobs, and sometimes their illegal status serves to reinforce their insecurity. The importance of this reserve army of low-cost, unorganized industry is immense, and underpins the tourist industries of many areas, including several of the world's major capital cities, such as London, Paris, Sydney and New York.[18]

While this suggests a number of inequalities, Shaw and Williams present this as nevertheless a complex area as many migrants move on to better-paid jobs or establish their own businesses, as well as providing employment and a source of income that can be sent back to their countries of origin.[19]

In relation to the example of Las Vegas, Parker describes it as a place where jobs in the tourism industry require little formal education and so leads to 'underemployment' and lower wages as a consequence.[20] As a consequence tourism workers in that city have difficulty in accessing home ownership in a city where most homes are built for the upper end of the market while most jobs exist at the lower end.[21] In addition most general tax revenue in Nevada is directed towards promoting and supporting tourism and tourism taxes themselves (such as the hotel-room tax) must be spent on tourism.[22] Thus the state has difficulty in paying for public education. The state also has few 'wealth' taxes (such as inheritance, estate or gift taxes) as well as no corporate or income taxes and the low-income earners there do not tend to join unions. Nevada has a union membership of 7 per cent compared to a national average of 15 per cent.[23]

What all of this suggests is that workers in the tourist industry exist on the margins of the labour market to a great extent. This can be exacerbated by such factors as their gender, age or immigration status. While aspects of this marginal status may facilitate initial entry into the workforce, this does little for addressing long-term inequality. As Wonders and Michalowski suggest, the globalisation of the workforce has created particular inequalities. They cite a 1996 International Labour Organization (ILO) report which stated that 'the feminization' of international labour migration is 'one of the most striking economic and social phenomena of recent times'.[24] Their concern is with how this leads many women to take up sex work as their best (or only) chance of survival.[25] But no doubt for other women the option will be to undertake work in the tourism industry for long hours and low rates of pay.

A recent paper produced for the ILO concerned with the connection between poverty reduction and tourism remarks that for every job created within the tourism sector, one and a half jobs are created indirectly in the economy.[26] They estimate the number of tourism-related jobs as a consequence globally as 230 million, or 8 per cent of the global workforce.[27] But of importance is the gender division in the industry:

> Women make up between 60 and 70 per cent of the labour force in the industry. This gender dimension can be especially important: according to the United Nations Development Programme (UNDP), empirical evidence suggests that developing countries with less gender inequality tend to have lower poverty rates. Paid work by women reduces overall poverty and inequality. In fact, eliminating barriers to women's participation in paid work (as is typical of the tourism industry) has a much stronger effect on poverty and economic growth than ending wage discrimination.[28]

The various inequalities generated by the nature of work in tourism is no doubt a motivating factor in the concern expressed in the Global Code of Ethics for Tourism article concerned with the rights of workers (and entrepreneurs) in the tourism industry.[29] That article provides that the 'fundamental rights of salaried and self-employed workers in the tourism industry' are to be 'guaranteed' under national and local laws, 'given the specific constraints linked in particular to the seasonality of their activity, the global dimension of their industry and the flexibility often required of them by the nature of their work'.[30] There is here no definition of 'fundamental rights' nor is it clear how the constraints and need for flexibility will operate to qualify these rights. It is of note that 'flexibility' appears to be the new mantra in workplace relations. The Australian legislation passed in 2009 to replace an unpopular workplace law has as its object this need for 'balance' and flexibility, that is, the law aims to provide a 'balanced framework for cooperative and productive workplace relations that promotes national economic prosperity and social inclusion for all Australians by' (amongst other matters) 'providing workplace relations laws that are fair to working Australians, are flexible for businesses, promote productivity and economic growth for Australia's future economic prosperity'.[31] The concern for workers in jobs such as many in tourism where there are little skills required and minimal security due to the nature of the industry is that 'flexibility' will often transform into the need to accept poor working conditions.

Uncertainty and the global financial crisis

Regulating for a fairer workplace for tourism workers becomes more difficult in times of economic downturn. This may be a current example of how the need for 'flexibility' can have dire consequences for workers. To that end the International Labour Organization and the World Tourism Organization issued a statement on tourism and employment on 18 September 2009. This statement emphasises the economic importance of tourism for sustainability as well as dealing with economic downturn. The statement declares: 'tourism can and should be used by governments and international financial institutions to reactivate the economies of countries affected by the current recession, especially by offering fresh, green and decent job opportunities'.[32] This reflected the aims in an ILO Resolution in 2009, 'Recovering from the Crisis: A Global Jobs Pact', which called for 'a fair globalization, a greener economy and development that more effectively creates jobs and sustainable enterprises, respects workers' rights, promotes gender equality, protects vulnerable people'.[33] This represents once again the promise of the exalted form of tourism, where it is not 'jobs' that are created 'but decent and productive work in sustainable enterprises through national and local tourism development strategies, new tourism products and services, with a high labour content, a high labour multiplying impact and a high level of sustainability'. The statement also speaks to providing adequate levels of remuneration.[34]

In declaring what should be provided the statement suggests what might be either currently absent or in danger for workers in tourism. It provides an alternative discourse to that so often seen in national 'tourism strategies' that proclaim the bountiful benefits to the economy and employment without discussion of the negative aspects. Such strategies also usually refer to levels of employment that, according to Shaw and Williams, may be questionable. On this point the ILO/UNWTO statement also referred to the need for better data:

> Tourism has been recognised as one of the largest generators of employment, especially for those segments of the population with less access to the labour market, such as women, young people, immigrants and rural populations. There is a need for accurate, timely and comprehensive data on employment in the tourism industries. To this end, governments and the private sector should cooperate to ensure the proper measurement of employment in the tourism industries including: the number of jobs directly generated by tourism, hours of work, compensation and the seasonality of employment. This data should also be disaggregated by gender, age, occupation, business type and size.[35]

This statement is part of an alternative discourse about the manner in which tourism is constructed in relation to work. While governments have an interest in stating the benefits of tourism, the labour practices in tourism cannot be regarded as immune from the effects of globalisaton any less than how it has impacted on the marketing of cities, the notion of what heritage is of value or the targeting of tourists for political purposes. Nor do tourism strategies say much about the impact of gender on participation in the tourism workforce. Julie Scott has written about the employment of Russian and Rumanian women to work in gambling venues in Northern Cyprus as the work is deemed 'unsuitable' for Turkish Cypriot women.[36] Her work maps how some female migrant workers, identified as being almost prostitutes by some people from the host nation, were recruited as croupiers in casinos. The women are subject to strict border controls because of associations between women from the former Eastern bloc and prostitution. This increases their status as transgressors. As Scott concludes:

> Russian and Rumanian women … .are constituted both as 'outsiders' and as a sexual/sexualized category by the formal border controls regulating their entry; by the informal mechanisms of 'community standards'; and by the manner in which they are placed into the tourism workforce, where they perform those jobs not socially and culturally acceptable for Turkish Cypriot women to perform.[37]

The various discourses which exist in this example of tourism work seem to be much more powerful than any international convention or national law that seeks to regulate the tourism workplace. Even the message of the formal law in the above instance is not that for which it is designed – to control the movement of prostitutes – but in its application how it defines the sexuality of women from certain countries generally.

Hidden work and the law

The sheer scale of areas of work within tourism which involve illegal labour (such as children and migrants) creates a problem for the law in terms of resources and the impracticability of enforcement. Bolwell and Weinz document the level of child labour in tourism which they state to be 'common' in tourism:

> In the hotel and restaurant subsectors, which includes bars, children can be exposed to physical and moral hazards that damage them for the rest of their lives, due to the association of some of these enterprises with alcohol, the sex industry, violence and illicit drugs.
>   There is a clear need for social protection to eradicate this stain, in conjunction with measures to alleviate poverty, in order to attack its

root cause. An estimated 13–19 million children under 18 years of age work in an occupation tied to tourism. This represents 10–15 per cent of the global tourism workforce. A further 2 million children in the world are victims of commercial sexual exploitation. International tourism is one sector where this evil can be effectively dealt with.[38]

They refer to the ILO Worst Forms of Child Labour Convention, 1999,[39] which particularly targets child trafficking and slavery, procuring children for prostitution and pornography and other illicit activities and 'work which, by its nature or the circumstances in which it is carried out, is likely to harm the health, safety or morals of children'.[40] Their call for a social dialogue is to seek a means of prosecuting the requirements of the Convention, as clearly orthodox policing of such provisions would be insufficient globally.

Likewise they refer to migrant labour in the tourism industry as a group which has not even an accurate estimate of their numbers, although 'migrant workers are a vulnerable group and are overly-employed in the sector, concentrated in lower paid, low-skilled and less stable jobs'.[41] In such areas the 'hidden' nature of the work makes the role of the law difficult and creates an even greater need to establish a discourse which raises expectations about how workers should be treated. In part this is one reason for calls for a 'social dialogue' and enlisting corporations that operate in the tourism industry in the hope that instilling an ethic of corporate responsibility might achieve something that the law cannot. Nevertheless, this still requires the articulation of a detailed understanding and response to the areas of work within which exploitation occurs, lest the discourse generated here soon becomes as impotent as formal laws.

Death as a tourist experience

The final example of trangressive tourism we wish to examine is that of death tourism. The notion of 'medical tourism' has existed for some time while 'death tourism' probably has a more recent history, particularly as it relates to travel for the purposes of committing suicide. In the case of each of these there is probably a tendency to think of them as using the notion of the 'tourist' loosely. But on reflection one can also see how the use of 'tourism' in association with illness or death actually both challenges the boundaries of what constitutes tourism, as well as reinforcing the essence of tourism. For example, to the extent that tourism is perceived to be a way of regenerating national economies, it is said that medical tourism often involves affluent people from rich nations travelling to developing countries where they purchase access to high-quality health care.[42] This enables poorer countries to earn valuable foreign income (and possibly enrich local medical professionals) while the affluent traveller is able to avoid waiting lists in their home country and gain their treatment for a lower price. This global trade in medical care is done without regard to the broader consequences for health-care provision in the developing country. All of these features appear to represent many of the features of tourism for which codes of ethics for tourism have been designed to address.

The ethical issues raised by medical tourism are most visible when the medical procedure to be performed is illegal in the patient/tourist's home country.[43] One obvious example is travel for the purpose of abortion where that procedure is unlawful in the home country, such as Ireland.[44] In similar vein, travelling to commit suicide carries with it the similar dilemma as most countries in the world do not permit euthanasia.[45] As such cases often involve a spouse or partner travelling with the person to assist in the process, this has created a dilemma for law-enforcement authorities when people have travelled from one country to another country that permits assisted suicide for the terminally ill (such as Switzerland) with respect to whether the persons who have assisted them should be prosecuted upon their return. When this arose in 2003 in the United Kingdom in a case involving a person travelling to Switzerland for the purpose of suicide the United Kingdom Government issued a statement on death tourism:

> [S]ection 2(1) of the Suicide Act 1961 makes it an offence in this country to aid, abet, counsel or procure somebody to commit suicide. Provided that the aiding abetting etc takes place in this country, we believe (though the point is untested by the courts) that the offence under section 2(1) is committed even where the suicide occurs abroad. However, aiding, abetting etc, of suicide abroad is a matter for the authorities in whose jurisdiction the suicide occurs. It is therefore for the Swiss authorities to determine whether any offence has been committed under Swiss law. ... We are of course concerned that UK citizens, whether terminally ill or not, may be helped to die in countries where this is legal in certain circumstances. But this is a matter of law in the country concerned and not one in which the Government should intervene.[46]

The difference between this position and that of child-sex tourism should be immediately apparent. But there is a broad consensus in society about the need to protect children from sexual exploitation. On the other hand, euthanasia divides many communities equally and so prosecution of relatives for assisting in the overseas suicide of their loved ones is politically fraught.[47] Equally, the notion that one could place travel bans on those wishing to travel overseas for the purposes of killing themselves is equally controversial, even if there may be the legal precedent of doing so in the case of child-sex tourists and suspected terrorists.[48]

There is too a wider issue about how mobility affects both the concept of tourism and its impact on how we are governed. Srinivas in summarising the net effect of people travelling overseas to commit suicide in order to avoid legal prohibitions at home says:

> For now, nobody questions the ability of American states to regulate life-ending procedures within their borders. But when constitutional constraints and geopolitical concerns prevent state and federal governments from effectively curbing death tourism, as this Article has concluded, the ability to regulate internally loses much of its value. The states that have decided against legalizing life-ending procedures – forty-seven and one-half by my count may ultimately reverse course and decide that, if their residents are undergoing these procedures anyway, they might as well do so at home and under the watchful eye of local regulators. The states that would rather keep their hands clean than have them forced, though, may see their policies reduced to mere value statements. In the end, that may be the cost of living in a free and cosmopolitan world.[49]

The implication here is that *due to the ability to travel* the effect of national laws are diluted in certain circumstances. The notion that a law might be altered or even repealed to take account of the effects of citizens travelling to avoid that law affects the way in which we see the connection between law and tourism. Usually we might consider that law regulates tourism and travel, but here is an example of how tourism – and the mobility on which it depends – fashions and shapes the law. Moreover, it arises in the context of a transgressive practice, at least from the perspective of the home nation.

Death as a tourist attraction

Another connection between death and tourism is through what has become known as 'dark tourism'. This has been described as 'recreational visitation to sites "associated ... with death, disaster, and depravity"'.[50] There is also a distinction drawn between 'dark tourism' and 'darker tourism' explained as:

> ... a difference between sites *associated with* death, disaster, and depravity and sites *of* death, disaster, and depravity. If visitation to the former is rightfully characterized as "dark tourism," then journey/ excursion/pilgrimage to the latter constitutes a further degree of empathetic travel: "darker tourism."[51]

For example, the Jewish Museum in Berlin might be an example of dark tourism, while the actual site of Auschwitz concentration camp, now a memorial and museum, would be an example of darker tourism.

This form of tourism is said to have a long history.[52] Stone and Sharpley also comment that:

> It is also a phenomenon that, over the last century, has become both widespread and diverse. Smith, for example, suggests that sites or destinations associated with war probably constitute 'the largest single category of tourist attractions in the world', yet war-related attractions, though diverse, are a subset of the totality of tourist sites associated with death and suffering. Reference is frequently made either to specific destinations, such as the Sixth Floor in Dallas, Texas or to forms of tourism, such as graveyards, the holocaust, atrocities, prisons, or slavery-heritage tourism. However, such is the diversity of death-related attractions, from the 'Dracula Experience' in Whitby, UK or Vienna's Funeral Museum to the sites of 'famous' deaths, or major disasters (for example, Ground Zero), that a full categorization is extremely complex.[53]

They also raise a number of issues with respect to the phenomenon of dark tourism, including whether it is in effect a form of morbid voyeurism or more connected with remembrance – 'grief tourism'.[54] But the concern with whether it also raises issues with respect to what is ethical tourism[55] is of most interest for our purposes.

As we have discussed in previous chapters the notion that tourism may embody 'noble pursuits' or a 'just cause' has much to do with the extent that tourists consider how tourism contributes to global inequalities, poverty, environmental degradation and cultural destruction. In this sense, to act ethically is to first confront the 'realities' of tourism. Thus Craig Wight considers that 'dark tourism' may well be an honest form of tourism:

> Dark tourism (or the intimated 'dark tourist') displays some of the traits of the 'alternative tourist', particularly because encountering 'truth' and 'reality' and the search for new (or 'rare') knowledge and experiences is central to the discursive formation of dark tourism.[56]

The ethical problem, however, is to know how to determine that the 'reality' is authentic. Wight notes the extent to which tourists' expectations about certain dark tourist sites – for example, those connected with the Holocaust – are often developed from their experience of Hollywood films and that this 'hyper reality' about certain sites is not contested by tourism bodies in various locations for fear of damaging their business.[57] He provides an example from the work of Cole:[58]

> The author refers to a display in the United States Holocaust Memorial Museum and makes an interesting contribution to the 'ethical' debate in

noting the American 'repackaging' of the Holocaust (in the Holocaust museum in Washington, DC, for example, and also in Americanised narratives of Anne Frank in film and theatre). There is something surprising, notes Cole, about this adaptation of what is someone else's history and something incongruous about American Jews (disassociated through choice with Israel, and neither survivors nor the children of survivors) talking of 'Jewishness' in terms of 'Holocaust' and 'Israel'. Yet the Holocaust Museum in Washington, DC (together, of course, with Hollywood, theatre and other 'dream factories') continues to perpetuate a competing national narrative, an adapted 'Americanised Holocaust', an atrocity that took place on foreign soil and within a European historical context. The issue throws open the debate over the esotericism in the scope of what is morally acceptable to various communities of interest.[59]

Ethical codes such as the Global Code of Ethics for Tourism, which states that 'tourism policies and activities should be conducted with respect for the artistic, archaeological and cultural heritage, which they should protect and pass on to future generations',[60] provide no guidance as to how what constitutes heritage is to be determined. Wight comments that heritage, as with ethics, is a personal matter constructed from one's life experiences.[61] In his view, the heritage of tragedy in dark tourism sites is exploited for their uniqueness by the tourism industry and made interesting for those tourists who want to experience something 'different'.[62] Indeed, as he says, debates about how close they narrate the 'truth' itself makes them more attractive to tourists who, as he says in post-modern times, are uncomfortable with the notion that there is one truth in any event.[63] But it would also be folly to discount the important contribution to healing and reconciliation remembrance can play within a community. Sandercock makes this point in relation to the Vietnam War Memorial in Washington, DC and the Jewish Museum in Berlin.[64] This may also be the importance of the Twin Towers site in New York City for many people.

Yet these latter examples are spaces which have become iconic and known almost globally. Whether or not there is a role for sites which are more localised is much more problematic. For example, some city authorities have removed, or attempted to remove, roadside shrines erected near where individuals have perished in road accidents. Sometimes such shrines have also been blamed for further accidents, and it is possible that local laws or the law of public nuisance might be invoked to rid them from the landscape. It is possible that, if this is done, the law is being used here to 'beautify' the space as much as it is being called upon to remove a hazard. The point is, that for many, death is not how they want to read their city or have it placed in front of tourists.

The role of transgression in tourism

In the commercialisation of death as a tourist attraction there also exists the possibility of empathy and remembrance – a tourism that seeks the lost cause, the failure, the defeat and the souls of those departed. In this the 'death tourist' offers the possibility of a tourism based on empathy and understanding for the pain of others. In this way it could be that this form of tourism can actually come closer to an ethical form of tourism than that engaged in for pleasure and escape. Could it be that in the transgressors, the dark tourism of our fears, we may discover the true meaning of an ethical tourism? There is, though, a danger in this form of tourism as it carries the risk that it might commodify and perpetuate forms of exploitation that supposedly are the very negation of tourism. If we are to tour places of death then do we not after all require more and more of them for future journeys?

On the other hand, it seems that for there to be ethical tourism we must also know what is unethical. And so, perhaps the point of dark tourism is to enable us to remind ourselves of the less virtuous practices in the world. The risk that some may engage in it for ghoulish reasons may be the price we have to pay to gain the lessons it can provide. The problem for the law then is that criminalising and marginalising it may actually provide the basis for death tourism. Many of the death sites themselves were so created because of the prevailing legal regimes at those points in history. But this form of tourism may also then be no bad thing, as it reminds us that there is a history of injustice as well as a history of justice.

As for the connection between tourism and work, in the hidden borders of tourism lies the possibility of people who exist within the legal margins – refugees, illegal immigrants and those illegally employed – but nevertheless seeking a better place in spite of, and not because of, their legal status. This is no doubt a dark side of tourism and one often ignored, save for the occasions when immigration raids occur or child labour receives attention in the media. It is also heavily gendered, and in that dark space no doubt many forms of discrimination occur. The question is whether the law can penetrate those spaces.

Notes

1 United Kingdom Department for Culture, Media and Sport, *Winning: A Tourism Strategy for 2012 and Beyond* (London, 2007), p. 4.
2 Ibid., p. 14.
3 Ibid., p. 17.
4 Ibid.
5 Ibid.
6 Ibid.
7 Ibid., p. 64.

8 See above p. 39.

9 Ibid., p. 70.

10 Australian Government Tourism White Paper, *A Medium to Long Term Strategy for Tourism: The Future View of Australian Tourism* (Canberra, Commonwealth of Australia, 2003), p. 27.

11 Ibid.

12 Ibid.

13 G. Shaw and A.M. Williams, *Critical Issues in Tourism: A Geographical Perspective* (Oxford, Blackwell, 1994), pp. 139–40. They provide the example of the informal economy in leisure, such as doing screenprinting for friends. This may have lesser application in tourism.

14 Ibid., p. 142.

15 Ibid., p. 150.

16 Ibid.

17 Ibid., pp. 151–52.

18 Ibid., p. 152.

19 Ibid., pp. 152–53.

20 R. Parker (1999) 'Las Vegas: Casino Gambling and Local Culture', in D.R. Judd and S.S. Fainstein (eds) *The Tourist City* (New Haven, Yale University Press, 1999), p. 120.

21 Ibid.

22 Ibid., p. 121.

23 Ibid., p. 122.

24 N.A. Wonders and R. Michalowski (2001) 'Bodies, Borders, and Sex Tourism in a Globalized World: A Tale of Two Cities – Amsterdam and Havana', *Social Problems*, Special Issue on Globalization and Social Problems, 48(4): 545–71, p. 549, citing K. Kempadoo and J. Doezema, *Global Sex Workers: Rights, Resistance and Redefinition* (London, Routledge, 1998), p. 17.

25 Ibid., p. 549.

26 D. Bolwell and W. Weinz, *Reducing Poverty through Tourism* (International Labour Office Geneva, October 2008), pp. 5–6.

27 Ibid., p. 6.

28 Ibid.

29 Global Code of Ethics for Tourism, art. 9.

30 Ibid., art. 9(1).

31 Fair Work Act 2009 (Cth.), s. 3.

32 ILO/UNWTO Statement on Tourism and Employment, Geneva/Madrid, 18 September 2009, p. 1.

33 Ibid.

34 Ibid. There is also ILO Working Conditions (Hotels and Restaurants) Convention, 1991, C172 which seeks to ensure certain standards of working conditions for employees in hotels and restaurants. To date only 15 countries have ratified this Convention.

35 Ibid.

36 J. Scott 'Sexual and National Boundaries in Tourism', *Annals of Tourism Research* (1995) 22(2): 385–403.

37 Ibid., p. 401.

38 D. Bolwell and W. Weinz, *Guide for Social Dialogue in the Tourism Industry* (International Labour Office, Geneva, October 2008), p. 10.

39 ILO Convention No. 182.

40 Ibid., art. 3.

41 Bolwell and Weinz, *Guide for Social Dialogue in the Tourism Industry*, p. 11.

42 Urry gives the example of Havana and Delhi: J. Urry, *Mobilities* (Cambridge, Polity, 2007), p. 264; Srinivas gives the examples of Colombia, South Africa, Ireland and 'especially' India, noting that in 2007, 150,000 Americans travelled overseas for medical treatment: R. Srinivas, 'Exploring the Potential for American Death Tourism', *Michigan State University Journal of Medicine and Law* (2009) 13: 91–122, p. 108. See also M.Z. Bookman and K.R. Bookman, *Medical Tourism in Developing Countries* (New York, Palgrave Macmillan, 2007).
43 Srinivas, 'Exploring the Potential for American Death Tourism', p. 109.
44 Ibid.
45 Ibid.
46 Ibid., p. 110, citing The World Federation of Right to Die Societies, *Death Tourism*, http://www.worldrtd.net/node/560 (last visited 25 September 2008). The statement was made by Lord Charles Falconer, then Minister of State for the Home Office.
47 This has been evident in the United Kingdom where the DPP has issued new guidance on assisted suicide committed within the UK. See Crown Prosecution Service, *Policy for Prosecutors in Respect of Cases of Encouraging or Assisting Suicide* (released 25 February 2010, accessible at http://www.cps.gov.uk/publications/prosecution/assisted_suicide_policy.html). This guidance was released in response to a call from the House of Lords for clarification on the relevant factors for prosecution in such cases; see *R (on the application of Purdy) v Director of Public Prosecutions* [2009] UKHL 45 as cited in the document. It also follows a number of high-profile cases involving the prosecution and arrest of individuals for assisted suicide which underlined the contested nature of this area of public policy and law.
48 Srinivas, 'Exploring the Potential for American Death Tourism', p. 121. Apart from the diplomatic tensions this might give rise to such a ban would also have to overcome challenges based on breaches of human rights standards in jurisdictions where that was available as a basis for testing such a law: see, e.g., J. Coggon and S. Holm, 'The Assisted Dying Bill – "Death Tourism" and European Law' (http://www.ccels.cardiff.ac.uk/archives/issues/2006/cog on_holm.pdf).
49 Ibid., p. 122.
50 W.F.S. Miles, 'Auschwitz: Museum Interpretation and Darker Tourism', *Annals of Tourism Research* (2002) 29(4): 1175–78, p. 1175, citing J. Lennon and M. Foley, 'Interpretation of the Unimaginable: The US Holocaust Memorial Museum, Washington, DC, and "Dark Tourism"', *Journal of Travel Research* (1999) 38: 46–50.
51 Miles, 'Auschwitz', p. 1175.
52 P. Stone and R. Sharpley, 'Consuming Dark Tourism: A Thanatological Perspective', *Annals of Tourism Research* (2008) 35(2): 574–95. They give the example of the first guided tour in England being a train trip to witness the hanging of two murderers: ibid., p. 574.
53 Ibid., p. 575 (references omitted).
54 Ibid., p. 575.
55 Ibid.
56 C. Wight, 'Contested National Tragedies: An Ethical Dimension' in R. Sharpley and P.R. Stone (eds) *The Darker Side of Travel* (Bristol, Channel View Publications, 2009), pp. 129–44 at p. 134.
57 Ibid., p. 136.
58 T. Cole, *Images of the Holocaust: The Myth of the 'Shoah Business'* (London, Gerald Duckworth, 1999).
59 Wight, 'Contested National Tragedies', p. 137.

60 Global Code of Ethics for Tourism, art. 4(2).
61 Wight, 'Contested National Tragedies', p. 143.
62 Ibid.
63 Ibid.
64 L. Sandercock, *Mongrel City* (London, Continuum, 2003), p. 213.

Part IV

Tourism in law

Chapter 8

Conclusion

Tourism as a legal problem

> The special circumstance of the terrorist attack on the World Trade Center in 2001 – the shock of an aircraft attack on civilians in the United States, the targeting of one of the most recognizable symbols of U.S. power, and the location in New York, a global media capital – made the site a public space like no other in the city ... it was both ground zero as a military target and sacred and hallowed ground where heroes died to preserve the nation ... the WTC's location in New York City guaranteed that it would become a major tourist attraction.
> (Sharon Zukin *Naked City: The Death and Life of Authentic Urban Places* (Oxford & New York, OUP, 2010), p.149)

A recurring theme in the construction of tourism is how it can re-invigorate economies, regenerate cities and even ensure sustainable lifestyles. In this sense tourism is given an exalted status, where it is perceived as a noble cause in which all should participate. The invoking of religious fervour is even explicit at times. Witness the Acapulco Document in 1982 and its statement that 'domestic tourism enables the individual to take *spiritual possession* of his own country, just as it prepares him for a universal perspective'.[1] The same document also connected tourism with the achievement of world peace as it 'enables peoples to gain first-hand knowledge of each other, thus bringing them closer together'.[2] It also reaffirmed that 'world tourism can be a vital force for world peace' and that as stated in the Manila Declaration on World Tourism in 1980, tourism can lead to a 'new international economic order that will help to eliminate the ... economic gap between developed and developing countries'.[3] Thus tourism is also constructed as integral to the reduction of global poverty.

That tourism, in bringing people together, may actually create increased suspicion of others escapes consideration in many of these statements related to the role of world tourism. Likewise, the assumed connection between tourism and the creation of a new world economic order which in turn leads to a reduction in inequality and poverty makes some fatal mistakes in reasoning – that increased economic activity benefits everyone and that all people are motivated solely by economic well being. While the view that tourism is about creating economic benefits is not a necessary aspect of how tourism may be conceptualised, it appears to have become central in the tourism strategies of many so-called advanced nations. In part this makes for good local politics – for example, in selling the Olympics to potential host communities governments rush to proclaim how many jobs they will create for the local economy, including in tourism.[4] But there is no necessary connection here. A thriving tourist industry will not reduce poverty through the provision of employment in itself. As Bolwell and Weinz's paper produced for the International Labour Organization has observed:

> Economic growth is an essential but not a sufficient condition for poverty reduction. Poverty reduction involves growth with a substantial reorientation in favour of the poor. It includes changes in institutions, laws, regulations and practices that help create and perpetuate poverty. It includes targeted interventions to enable poor people to better integrate into economic processes and take advantage of opportunities to improve their economic and social well-being. It means ending harassment of the poor, and eliminating restrictions on how they make their livelihoods. This especially applies to the tourism sector. Interventions must be made to help poor people become part of the processes that drive the industry.[5]

The notion of wealth redistribution has lost popularity in present times (although the bailing out of large banks as a consequence of the global financial crisis may affect that), but in effect what the ILO paper is calling for is a strategy to ensure that the wealth generated by tourism is distributed for the benefit of all people. In particular, it seems to be calling for some scope for poorer people to participate in the industry whether by establishing their own businesses or receiving fair rates of pay for working in businesses owned by others. It also says there is clearly a role for the law in this process. What seems to be the case, however, is that although there are various international law (and 'law-like') documents relating to the importance of reducing poverty through tourism, at the national level little law is explicitly directed to this aim. Tourism laws rarely mention the social purpose of tourism but seem to be simply about facilitating the mechanics of tourism. Anti-discrimination and human-rights laws might help at times, but these also come up against laws and rhetoric which stress the importance of public safety and order, not to mention the fear of terrorism. The cacophony of laws works to blur the focus on the manner in which the rights of the poor are subverted to the needs of the tourism industry.

The other flaw in the assumption that tourism is prized by all for its contribution to economic prosperity relates to a central theme of this book, the age of uncertainty. As Benjamin Barber writes, we live in a time when we are caught between two inexorable forces, referring to William Butler Yeats's 'the two eternities of race and soul'.[6] The first (race) is described as 'a Jihad in the name of a hundred narrowly conceived faiths against every kind of interdependence, every kind of artificial social cooperation and mutuality: against technology, against pop culture, and against integrated markets; against modernity itself as well as the future in which modernity issues'.[7] The second (soul) is 'a bus portrait of onrushing economic, technological, and ecological forces that demand integration and uniformity and that mesmerize peoples everywhere with fast music, fast computers, and fast food ... pressing nations into one homogenous global theme park, one McWorld tied together by communications, information, entertainment, and commerce'.[8]

This is the age of uncertainty. As Barber says, 'the planet is falling precipitously apart and coming together at the very same time'.[9] These are the tensions that bedevil world tourism and in particular the agencies that seek to regulate it. On the one hand is the elevation of tourism as a force for mutual respect and tolerance, while at the same time the values which appear to be at the centre of tourism create hostility for those who question the lack of spirituality in those who travel. And it is not that the tensions are implacably opposed, theirs is a symbiotic relationship:

> We have seen how athletic shoe salesmanship revolves around selling American black subculture; how American Express treats global travel (a privilege of McWorld) as a safari to exotic cultures still somehow intact in spite of the visitations and depredations made possible by American Express; how McDonald's 'adapts' to foreign climes with wine in France and local beef in Russia even as it imposes a way of life that makes domestic wines and local beef irrelevant. McWorld cannot then do without Jihad: it needs cultural parochialism to feed its endless appetites. Yet neither can Jihad do without McWorld: for where would culture be without the commercial producers who market it and the information and communication systems that make it known? *Modern* Christian fundamentalists (no longer an oxymoron) can thus access Religion Forum on Compuserve Information Service while Muslims can surf the Internet until they find Mas'ood Cajee's Cybermuslim document. That is not a computer error: 'Cybermuslim *is* the title. Religion and culture alike need McWorld's technologies and McWorld's markets. Without them, they are unlikely to survive in the long run.[10]

The point here is not to understand this tension as one between East and West, or between Muslim and non-Muslim. While this is the tabloid representation of one aspect of this tension in the world, namely the 'war on terror', consider the uncertainty when it is discovered that a terrorist or alleged terrorist is in fact a citizen of the country which they are seeking to target. Of course, there will be attempts to find some other 'difference' between the person and the rest of 'us', but Barber's thesis speaks to the manner in which communities are both 'one' and 'divided' at the same time.

This in turn creates special challenges for the regulation of tourism and travel. To a certain extent the absence of law in tourism is a consequence of the difficulty of coming to a suitable response. Faced with intractable differences the law has a long tradition of constructing general statements which appear to support positive change ('promotion of mutual tolerance') but in their interpretation and application come to mean little and change nothing. There is also the problem in that having constructed tourism as rotating around 'industry' there is a simple belief that it can somehow self-regulate. This then leads to codes of conduct and the co-opting of business interests into the very groups that will then form the regulatory responses. It is then no surprise that such codes and other forms of self-regulation tend to minimise the amount of actual wealth redistribution that takes place.

Legal silence

What seems to have occurred as tourism's economic value has been seen as more and more important is an apparent silence in the law about the social impacts of tourism, with the possible exception of some international documents, such as the Global Code of Ethics for Tourism. This has also been compounded with more recent awareness about the connection between the impact of tourism on the environment and global warming. 'Sustainable tourism' seems to have been given a narrow focus in most tourism strategies to refer to the effect tourism has on the natural environment. Thus the United Kingdom's tourism strategy for the Olympics in 2012 and beyond speaks of sustainable tourism for the most part in this narrow way:

> The 2012 Games offer us a real opportunity to ensure that there is a sustainable approach to tourism. With increasing public concern about climate change and the impact of tourism on the environment, we must do all we can to improve the sustainability of the industry.
>
> That means effectively managing the interaction between the needs of Visitors, Industry, Community and the Environment – the 'VICE principle' – and ensuring that it is embedded in policy formulation.[11]

The VICE principle is explained as follows:

Visitor

Ensuring quality and making holidays accessible for all.

Quality of facilities and services, reliable information, safety and security and providing facilities that all can enjoy, including those with disabilities.

Industry

Reducing the seasonality of demand – concentration of tourism trips into certain times of the year can reduce the viability of enterprises and their ability to offer year round employment and place pressure on communities and natural resources and leave surplus capacity at other times.

Improve the quality of tourism jobs – how the sector is perceived as a career choice revolves around the quality of jobs, salary levels, the pattern, length and consistency of working hours (while recognising that these match the pattern of customer demand), the ability to offer fulltime, year-round jobs and long-term contracts, and career opportunities.

Community

Maintaining and enhancing community prosperity and quality of life – tourism has the power to change the character and prosperity of the places where it occurs. The challenge is to manage change in the interests of the well-being of the community. This might include supporting local businesses, local employment and encouraging local residents' use of tourist facilities.

Environment

Minimise resource use – tourism has the potential to use a large amount of environmental resources. Minimising energy consumption, reusing and recycling of materials, improving water and air quality, reducing water consumption and reducing and managing litter can all reduce tourism's footprint. Tourism businesses can also give back something to the environment in recognition of its impact, for example by supporting biodiversity or habitat conservation schemes.

Address the impact of tourism transport – the impact of climate change makes this a high-profile issue for tourism planning. It also impacts on the economic viability of the industry and the quality of life for local communities. DCMS will seek stakeholders' views about the appropriateness of these challenges and how progress on them should be measured, before publishing and disseminating them more widely.[12]

The value in seeing the whole VICE statement is that it is possible to assess the extent to which the social aspects of sustainability are emphasised, and in what manner. Clearly, much of the statement is concerned with the impact of tourism on the natural environment with a limited mention of matters related to 'community'. This section is arguably obscure as to its meaning for while it acknowledges the ability of tourism to 'change the character and prosperity of the places where it occurs' it then suggests that this merely presents a challenge 'to manage change in the interests of the well-being of the community'. These are the 'motherhood' clauses so well known in many areas of the law. But who will define the 'interests' and 'well-being' of the community here? The statement falls back on improving the economic returns through improving business and employment opportunities. But where is the strategy for addressing the impact from tourism on a community's character? The only non-business oriented strategy mentioned relates to providing local people with use of tourist facilities. Yet this may be the ultimate irony, for if the tourist facility is destroying local character, then is not providing access to local residents asking them to participate in their own demise?

Bolwell and Weinz attempt to provide greater substance to a much broader notion of sustainable tourism which embraces not only the business needs of the tourism industry, but also one which seeks to balance 'economics with people, culture, and environment'.[13] They refer to the notion of 'pro-poor tourism' developed by the International Centre for Responsible Tourism, the International Institute for Environment and Development and the Overseas Development Institute.[14] Pro-poor tourism (PPT) is:

> tourism that results in increased net benefits for poor people. PPT is not a specific product or niche sector but an approach to tourism development and management. It enhances the linkages between tourism businesses and poor people so that tourism's contribution to poverty reduction is increased and poor people are able to participate more effectively in product development. Links with many different types of "the poor" need to be considered: staff, neighbouring communities, land-holders, producers of food, fuel and other suppliers, operators of micro tourism businesses, craft-makers, other users of tourism infrastructure (roads) and resources (water), etc. There are many types of PPT strategies, ranging from increasing local employment to building mechanisms for consultation. Any type of company can be involved in PPT – a small lodge, an urban hotel, a tour operator, an infrastructure developer. The critical factor is not the type of company or the type of tourism, but that an increase in the net benefits that go to poor people can be demonstrated.[15]

While they are mainly concerned with the poverty experienced by people in developing countries, there seems little reason why this model should not be adopted in more affluent countries, particularly when one considers that for the poor in those countries the impact of tourism on their lives can be just as dramatic in terms of making them homeless, powerless and marginalised as in less affluent places. For example, they note that the impacts of tourism are multi-dimensional. Tourism may provide employment, but it also may increase land and food prices in a location.[16] This can be an aspect of tourism in any country.

The law can play its part at many different levels. In relation to workplaces this might be through ensuring the right to form trade unions so they can effectively negotiate wages and conditions.[17] In heritage, it can be through the careful articulation of values about what should be preserved. But a more fundamental need is for law to move beyond rhetoric and platitudes about reduction of inequality and connect more directly with the detail such as the manner in which tourism impacts on human rights, and in what ways, and seek to articulate a more detailed set of principles and processes for delivering justice to the poor. In this way, notions such as 'sustainable tourism' should be given a fuller meaning and provide a platform for challenging many decisions that seek to promote tourism at the cost to local communities.

With this in mind there are now evolving documents such as the 'Guide for Social Dialogue in the Tourism Industry', a working paper produced for the ILO.[18] That paper defines social dialogue as: 'all types of negotiation, consultation or simply exchange of information between representatives of governments, employers and workers, on issues of common interest relating to economic and social policy'.[19] This may represent an acceptance that reliance solely on laws and regulatory mechanisms is insufficient when faced with the sheer scale of global tourism. As the paper also notes:

> [t]he number of international arrivals rose from only 25 million international arrivals in 1950 to an estimated 806 million in 2005. This is an average annual growth rate of 6.5 per cent. In 2006, there were over 842 million international tourist arrivals. By 2020 that figure is forecast at 1.6 billion in 2020.[20]

However, as we have said, to turn to codes of conduct as a means of achieving some regulation also carries with it other complications. As we have argued in relation to child-sex tourism, they can be self-applauding processes that, whatever they achieve in the narrow field they occupy, also form a part of a process that hides other forms of exploitation in tourism. There is also the need to question whether such forms of 'corporate responsibility' and 'self-regulation' can retain legitimacy in the fallout of the global financial crisis. In asking for a social dialogue as a way of regulating behaviour these questions must come to the fore.

Limiting the right to travel

One obvious matter to be addressed is whether in the wake of concern with climate change there should be restrictions on the right to travel. This immediately runs foul of documents such as the Global Code of Ethics for Tourism which have embedded the notion of freedom of movement.[21] It also conflicts with the exalted view of tourism that suggests that it promotes world peace and tolerance. If that is true, then by not travelling we risk a more insular and parochial world. Of course, it could be that in an age of fear of terrorism that more travel leads to less tolerance and greater suspicion. On either count it is difficult to see any state advocating restrictions on movement. They are too wedded to the notion of tourism as economic regenerator to take that stance. We may see less travel for particular groups, or requirements to travel in particular ways (such as train instead of aircraft), but these may all happen around the margins. For the law, though, there is a larger crisis of legitimacy of its own here. If the projected growth in tourism and travel is correct, then at what point do laws which require 'sustainable transport' and 'carbon neutral' impacts seem illegitimate? Added to this will be the problem that, practised by the more affluent, tourists might be seen to indulge in consumption that others are excluded from.

Non-tourism as the new just cause

During World War II in the United Kingdom posters were erected which asked the question, 'Is your trip really necessary?' We understand that this was a means of both saving energy and the risk that spies might overhear conversations that would reveal vital information. By not travelling the consumption of energy (and the risk of passing information) was reduced. There may be the circumstances where such a campaign could gain currency today. The environmental impacts of travel alone would seem to justify such an approach, and it is the case that some organisations, probably more for cost reasons, already do so.

However, when some in the tourist industry are developing space tourism and intercontinental travel via space, there is also a risk that this new just cause will be for the poor, while the rich continue to travel, albeit in faster and more fuel-efficient aircraft (and spacecraft?) than previously was the case. It may be that for those unable to travel 'virtual tourism' could take its place. This might even have appeal as it avoids security checks and other inconveniences. Of course, it might be that the non-tourists will still form part of tourism, working in the industry servicing the needs of those who can still afford to travel.

These scenarios are perhaps fanciful and overstated. For a start, the importance placed on the economic value of tourism requires it to grow and not contract. But what we have attempted to show is that the 'right to tourism' is a right with little meaning outside the various ways in which tourism is practised. When that right is mentioned in ethical codes it is doubtful that it is meant to apply to sex tourism, dark tourism or imply the right to exploit others. Yet those forms of tourism both define the boundaries of tourism and suggest the possibilities. To the extent that social change requires transgression, perhaps the right we should be seeking to assert is the right to transgress in the context of tourism.

In seeking to understand how law thinks about tourism we must also acknowledge the extent to which the state has been captured by the ideology of the marketplace. It may be that in attempting to construct a more ethical form of tourism – however defined – a more independent state is required in order to more fully integrate social considerations into tourism regulation. At every turn it seems, the notion that tourism is a business seems to haunt the process. Of course law has a history of supporting the prevailing economic orthodoxy of the times, but it also possesses some tradition of dissent. If tourism is populated by many uncertainties as to its direction and tensions, then law too can claim to be based on many ambiguities. Perhaps in the mire this generates, law and tourism may meet.

Notes

1 World Tourism Organization, *Acapulco Document 1982*, para. 9(c)(iii). Our emphasis. See also Manila Declaration on World Tourism 1980, art. 21, discussed in Chapter 1.
2 Ibid., preamble.
3 Ibid.
4 See above, p. 160.
5 D. Bolwell and W. Weinz, *Reducing Poverty through Tourism* (International Labour Office Geneva, October 2008), p. 1.
6 B.J. Barber, *Jihad vs McWorld: How Gloablism and Tribalism are Reshaping the World* (New York, Ballantine, 1995), p. 4.
7 Ibid.
8 Ibid.
9 Ibid.
10 Ibid., pp. 155–56.
11 United Kingdom Department for Culture, Media and Sport *Winning: A Tourism Strategy for 2012 and Beyond* (London, 2007), pp. 53–54.
12 Ibid., pp. 54–55.
13 Bolwell and Weinz, *Jihad vs McWorld*, p. 9. This is based on the World Travel and Tourism Council's 2003 policy statement: *Blueprint for New Tourism*.
14 Ibid., p. 10, n. 34.
15 Ibid., p. 10.
16 Ibid., p. 11.
17 Ibid., p. 18.
18 D. Bolwell and W. Weinz, *Guide for Social Dialogue in the Tourism Industry* (International Labour Office, Geneva, October 2008).
19 Ibid., p. 20.
20 Ibid., p. 3.
21 Global Code of Ethics for Tourism, art. 8.

Bibliography

Abrahamson, M. (2004) *Global Cities.* New York and Oxford, Oxford University Press.

Adelaide City Council (2002) *The central west precinct New Directions – Capacity, Vivacity, Audacity.* Adelaide.

Australia Department of Energy, Resources and Tourism (2008) *Tourism and Climate Change – A Framework for Action* (July). Canberra.

Australia Department of the Environment, Water, Heritage and the Arts (2009) *The Australian Environment Act: Report of the Independent review of the Environment Protection and Biodiversity Conservation Act 1999* (The Hawke Report Final Report, October). Canberra.

Australian Government (1994) *Creative Nation: Commonwealth Cultural Policy* (October). Canberra.

Australian Government—(2003) *The Future of Australian Tourism: A Medium to Long Term Strategy for Tourism* (White Paper, Commonwealth of Australia). Canberra.

Australian Government (2003) *Tourism White Paper: The Future View of Australian Tourism* (Commonwealth of Australia). Canberra.

Australian Government (2004) *Transnational Terrorism: The Threat to Australia* (Commonwealth of Australia). Canberra, Department of Foreign Affairs and Trade.

Barber, B.J. (1995) *Jihad vs McWorld: How Globalism and Tribalism are Reshaping the World.* New York, Ballantine.

Beeho, A.J. and Prentice, R.C. (1995) 'Evaluating the Experiences and Benefits Gained by Tourists Visiting a Socio-Industrial Heritage Museum: An Application of ASEB Grid Analysis to Blists Hill Open-Air Musuem, the Ironbridge Gorge Museum, United Kingdom', *Museum Management and Curatorship*, 15(4): 371–86.

Boer, B. and Wiffen, G. (2006) *Heritage Law in Australia.* Victoria, Oxford University Press.

Bolwell, D. and Weinz, W. (2008) *Guide for Social Dialogue in the Tourism Industry.* International Labour Office, Geneva, October.

Bolwell, D. and Weinz, W. (2008) *Reducing Poverty through Tourism.* International Labour Office Geneva, October.

Boniface, P. and Fowler, P.J. (1993) *Heritage and Tourism in 'the Global Village'.* London, Routledge.

Bookman, M.Z. and Bookman, K.R. (2007) *Medical Tourism in Developing Countries*. New York, Palgrave Macmillan.

Brungs, M. [2002] 'Abolishing Child Sex Tourism: Australia's Contribution', *Australian Journal of Human Rights*, 17. http://www.austlii.edu.au/au/journals/AJHR/2002/17. html.

Burns, P. (1999) 'Paradoxes in Planning:Tourism Elitism or Brutalism?', *Annals of Tourism Research*, 26(2): 329–48.

Coggon, J. and Holm, S. (2006) 'The Assisted Dying Bill – "Death Tourism" and European Law' (http://www.ccels.cardiff.ac.uk/archives/issues/2006/coggon_holm. pdf).

Cohen, E. (1979) 'A Phenomenology of Tourist Experiences', *Sociology*, 13(2): 179–201.

Cole, T. (1999) *Images of the Holocaust: The Myth of the 'Shoah Business'*. London, Gerald Duckworth.

Conforti, J.M. (1996) 'Ghettos as Tourist Attractions' *Annals of Tourism Research*, 23(4): 830–42.

Crick, M. (1989,) 'Representations of International Tourism in the Social Sciences: Sun, Sex, Sights, Savings, and Servility', *Annual Review of Anthropology*, 18: 307–44.

Dann, G. (1996) *The Language of Tourism – A Sociolinguistic Perspective*. Wallingford, Oxford CAB International.

Davison, G. (1991) 'The Meanings of Heritage' in G. Davison and C. McConville (eds) *A Heritage Handbook*. Sydney, Allen and Unwin.

Editorial (1996) *Museum Management and Curatorship*, 15(4): 345.

English Heritage (2009) *PPS Planning for the Historic Environment: Historic Environment Planning Practice Guide*. Living Draft, 24 July.

Ennew, J. (1986) *The Sexual Exploitation of Children*. New York, St. Martin's Press.

Fainstein, S.S., Hoffman, L.M. and Judd, D.R. (1999) 'Introduction', in D.R. Judd. and S.S. Fainstein (eds) *The Tourist City*. New Haven, Yale University Press.

Farrell, B. and Twining-Ward, L. (2005) 'Seven Steps Towards Sustainability: Tourism in the Context of New Knowledge', *Journal of Sustainable Tourism*, 13(2): 109–22.

Feichtinger, G., Hartl, R.F., Kort, P.M. and Novak, A.J. (2001) 'Terrorism Control in the Tourism Industry', *Journal of Optimization Theory and Applications*, 108(2): 283–96.

Fisher, R. (1991) 'Nocturnal Demolitions: The long March Towards Heritage Legislation in Brisbane' in J. Rickard and P. Spearritt (eds) *Packing the Past?* Melbourne, Melbourne University Press.

Gladstone, D.L. (2005) *From Pilgrimage to Package Tour: Travel and Tourism in the Third World*. Abingdon, Routledge.

Goldstone, P. (2001) *Making the World Safe for Tourism*. New Haven and London, Yale University Press.

Grewcock, D. (2006) 'Museums of Cities and Urban Futures: new approaches to urban planning and the opportunities for museums of cities', *Museum International*, (Urban Life and Museums, proceedings of the first conference of CAMOC. ICOM'S new International Committee for the Collections and Activities of Museums and Cities), 231 (September): 32–41.

Hall, L. (2004) 'Sitting Down in the Square: Indigenous Presence in an Australian City', *Humanities Research: Cultural Politics and Iconography*, Vol. XL, NO Humanities Research Centre and the Centre for Cross Cultural Research, Australian National University, ACT, Australia.

Hannigan, J. (1998) *Fantasy City: Pleasure and Profit in the Postmodern Metropolis*, London and New York, Routledge.

Higgins-Desbiolles, F. (2006) 'More than an "Industry": The Forgotten Power of Tourism as a Social Force', *Tourism Management*, 27: 1192–1208.

Higgins-Desbiolles, F. (2007) 'Hostile Meeting Grounds: Encounters between the Wretched of the Earth and the Tourist through Tourism and Terrorism in the 21st Century' in P. Burns and M. Novelli (eds) *Tourism and Politics: Global Frameworks and Local Realities*. Amsterdam, Elsevier, pp. 309–32.

Holcomb, B. (1999) 'Marketing Cities for Tourism' in D.R. Judd and S.S. Fainstein (eds) *The Tourist City*. New Haven, Yale University Press.

Hollinshead, K. (1999) 'Surveillance of the Worlds of Tourism: Foucault and the Eye-of-Power', *Tourism Management*, 20: 7–23.

Jacobsen, J.K.S. (2000) 'Anti-Tourist Attitudes: Mediterranean Charter Tourism', *Annals of Tourism Research*, 27(2): 284–300.

Kempadoo, K. and Doezema, J. (1998) *Global Sex Workers: Rights, Resistance and Redefinition*. London, Routledge.

Kincaid, J. (1988) *A Small Place*. New York, Farrar, Straus and Giroux.

Leheny, D. (1995) 'A Political Economy of Asian Sex Tourism', *Annals of Tourism Research*, 22(2): 367–84.

MacCannell, D. (1976) *The Tourist: A New Theory of the Leisure Class*. New York, Schocken.

McKean, P.F. (1998) 'Towards a Theoretical Analysis of Tourism: Economic Dualism and Cultural Involution in Bali' in V.L. Smith (ed.) *Hosts and Guests: The Anthropology of Tourism*. Philadelphia, University of Pennsylvania Press, pp. 119–38.

Miles, W.F.S. (2002) 'Auschwitz: Museum Interpretation and Darker Tourism', *Annals of Tourism Research*, 29(4): 1175–78.

Mills, M.B. (2003) 'Gender and Inequality in the Global Labor Force', *Annual Review, of Anthropology*, 41–62.

Mordue, T. (2007) 'Tourism, Urban Governance and Public Space', *Leisure Studies*, 26(4): 447–62.

Mullins, P. (2003) 'The Evolution of Australian Tourism Urbanisation' in S.S. Fainstein, L.M. Hoffman and D.R. Judd (eds) *Cities and Visitors*. Oxford, Blackwell Publishing.

OECD Directorate for Science, Technology and Industry (2003) *National Tourism Policy Review Of Australia* (July). Paris.

Oppermann, M. (1999) 'Sex Tourism', *Annals of Tourism Research*, 26 (2): 251–66.

Parker, R. (1999) 'Las Vegas: Casino Gambling and Local Culture' in D.R. Judd and S.S. Fainstein (eds) *The Tourist City*. New Haven, Yale University Press.

Patterson, K. (1993) 'Aloha! "Welcome to Paradise"', *New Internationalist*, 245 (July): 13–15.

Pitman, J. (1997) *The Exhibitionists in the Directory*, 5–11 April.

Prott, L.V. (2006) 'The Dja Dja Wurrung Bark Etchings Case', *International Journal of Cultural Property*, 13: 242–46.

Ratz, T. (2000) 'The Socio Cultural Impacts of Tourism' (http://www.geocities.com/Paris/9842/impacts.html).

Richter, L. (1980) 'The Political Uses of Tourism', *Journal of Developing Areas*, 14: 237–57.

Rojek, C. (1993) *Ways of Escape: Modern Transformations in Leisure and Travel*. London, Macmillan.

Russell, R. ((1996) 'The Politics of Interpretation: Interest Groups, Sponsors and Exhibitions', *Museum National*, 5(2): 17.

Ryan, C. and Hall, C.M. (2001) *Sex Tourism: Marginal People and Liminalities*. London and New York, Routledge.

Sandercock, L. (2003) *Mongrel City*. London, Continuum.

Scott, J. (1995) 'Sexual and National Boundaries in Tourism', *Annals of Tourism Research*, 22(2): 385–403.

Seabrook, J. (1996) *Travels in the Skin Trade*. London, Pluto Press.

Shankland, A. (1993) 'The Natives are Friendly!', *New Internationalist*, 245 (July): 20–22.

Shaw, G. and Williams, A.M. (1994) *Critical Issues in Tourism: A Geographical Perspective*. Oxford, Blackwell.

Shaw, G. and Williams, A.M. (2002) *Critical Issues in Tourism: A Geographical Perspective* (2nd edition). Malden, Blackwell.

Shaw, G. and Williams, A.M. (2004) *Tourism and Tourism Spaces*. London, Sage.

Simpson, B. (1998) 'The Legal Boundaries of Tourism: The State versus the Marketplace in Defining the Tourist' in N. Ravenscroft, D. Phillips and M.Bennett (eds) *Tourism and Tourist Attractions: Leisure, Culture and Commerce*. LSA Publication No. 61.

Simpson, C. (1994) 'Heritage What's in a Name?', *Alternative Law Journal*, 19(4): 161.

Srinivas, R. (2009) 'Exploring the Potential for American Death Tourism', *Michigan State University Journal of Medicine and Law*, 13: 91–122.

Stone, P. and Sharpley, R. (2008) 'Consuming Dark Tourism: A Thanatological Perspective', *Annals of Tourism Research*, 35(2): 574–95.

United Kingdom Department for Culture, Media and Sport (1999) *Tomorrow's Tourism: A Growth Industry for the New Millenium*. London.

United Kingdom Department for Culture, Media and Sport (2006) *Welcome Legacy: Tourism Strategy for the 2012 Games – A Consultation*. London.

United Kingdom Department for Culture, Media and Sport (2007) *Winning: A: Tourism Strategy for 2012 and Beyond*. London.

United Kingdom Department for Culture, Media and Sport (2007) *Heritage Protection for the 21st Century* (Cm 5057, March). London.

United Kingdom Department for Communities and Local Government (2009) Planning Policy Statement: *Consultation Paper on a New Planning Policy Statement 15: Planning for the Historic Environment* (July). London.

United Kingdom Government (2006) *Countering International Terrorism: The United Kingdom's Strategy* (Cm 6888, July). Norwich, The Stationery Office.

Urry, J. (1990) *The Tourist Gaze: Leisure and Travel in Contemporary Society*. London, Sage.

Urry, J. (1991) 'Sensing the City' in D.R. Judd and S.S. Fainstein (eds) *The Tourist City*. New Haven, Yale University Press.

Urry, J. (1995) *Consuming Places*. London, Routledge.

Urry, J. (2002) *The Tourist Gaze* (2nd edition). London, Sage.

Urry, J. (2007) *Mobilities*. Cambridge, Polity.

Walsh, T. (2006) *No Offence: The Enforcement of Offensive Language and Offensive Behaviour Offences in Queensland*. Brisbane, University of Queensland.

Wearing, S. (2002) 'Re-centering the Self in Volunteer Tourism' in G.S. Dann (ed.) *The Tourist as a Metaphor of the Social World'*. Oxford, CABI, pp.237–62.

Wight, C. (2009) 'Contested National Tragedies: An Ethical Dimension' in R. Sharpley and P.R. Stone (eds) *The Darker Side of Travel*. Bristol, Channel View Publications.

Willis, E. (2007) 'History, Strong Stories and New Traditions: The Case of "Etched on Bark 1854"', *History Australia*, 4(1): 13.1–13.10. Monash University ePress.

Willis, E. (2008) 'The Law Politics and "Historical Wounds" The Dja Dja Wurrung Bark Etchings Case in Australia', *International Journal of Cultural Property*, 15: 49–63.

Wonders, N.A. and Michalowski, R. (2001) 'Bodies, Borders, and Sex Tourism in a Globalized World: A Tale of Two Cities – Amsterdam and Havana', *Social Problems*, Special Issue on Globalization and Social Problems, 48(4): 545–71.

Zhang, L. (2001) *Strangers in the City: Reconfigurations of Space, Power, and Social Networks Within China's Floating Population*. Stanford, CA: Stanford University Press.

Zukin, S. (1995) *The Cultures of Cities*. Cambridge, Mass., Blackwell.

Index

abortion 168
Abrahamson, M. 57
Acapulco Documents on the Rights to Holidays 11, 14
ACCOR and ethical standards 45
Adelaide 76–78, 92–94, 117, 127, 142
Al Qaida 121
American Express 122, 181
Amsterdam 137, 141–42, 145
Auschwitz 159, 169
Australia 5–6, 11, 38–39, 51, 64–69; 91, 121–23, 128–29, 132, 164; child-sex tourism laws 146–49, 155; tourism strategy 5, 52, 162; National Gallery 90
Australian Tourist Commission 18, 21, 37–38

Bali 120, 128–31
Bangkok 140, 142
Barber, B. 180–81
Berlin 169
Blackpool 63–64
Bolivia 34
Boniface, P. 59–61, 103–4
Brisbane 61, 62, 63
British Museum 97
Burma 114–15
Burns, P. 41–42

Canada and child-sex tourism laws 155
Canadian Tourism Commission 19
Carlson Companies 153–54
child labour 166
child-sex tourism 143–55; codes of conduct 149–52
children xi, 13, 45, 74, 90, 103, 115, 140, 143–52, 154–55

Church, A. ix, xi
climate change 46, 50–52
Coles, T. ix, xi
Crick, M. 31, 35–36, 117
crime 72–75, 126–27
cultural impacts of tourism xi, 19, 22, 32–33, 150
cultural tourism 22
Cyprus 166
dark tourism 169–71

Davos Declaration 49–50
death 167–72

Earth Summit 36
eco-tourism 41
ECPAT 140, 150
Egypt 125–26
Elgin Marbles 97
employment and tourism 33, 124
employment laws 11, 12, 162
Ennew, J. 140
environment 16–17, 23, 33, 39–40, 50–52
ethical standards in tourism 42–45
euthanasia 168
European Commission 152

Fainstein, S.S. 74
Farrell, B. 7, 8
Fowler, P.J. 59–61, 103–4

Gladstone, D.L. 17, 32, 36–37
Global Code of Ethics for Tourism 16, 17, 37, 39–42, 58, 86–87, 100, 112, 119–20, 126, 133–34, 144–45, 147, 150–52, 155, 160, 164, 171, 182, 186
global financial crisis 165, 180, 185

globalisation 119, 153–54, 164
Goa 126–27, 154–55
Gold Coast (Australia) 61, 63
Grand Prix 80–81

Hague Declaration on Tourism 15, 16
Hall, C. M., 138–40, 142, 155, 159
Hawaii 33–34, 103–4
heritage 59–60, 61–71 criteria for
  heritage listing 65–69; 95–96
  indigenous heritage 91–100
Higgins-Desbiolles, F. 8, 9, 16, 17,
  119–21
Holcomb, B. 57, 63
Hollinshead, K. 24–25
homelessness 73–76, 78–80
housing 80
Hong Kong 20

India 132
Indigenous people 34–35, 76–78,
  102–6; cultural property 87, 96–99;
  and heritage 91–100; land rights
  100–102
Indonesia 128–32
International Covenant on Economic,
  Social and Cultural Rights 14
International Convention on Apartheid
  in Sport 118
International Convention on the
  Elimination of all Forms of
  Discrimination Against Women 118
International Convention on the
  Elimination of Racial Discrimination
  118
International Labor Organization
  164–65, 167, 180, 185
Ireland 168
Islam 48–49, 72

Jemaah Islamiyah 121

King"s Cross (Sydney) 141
Krippendorf, J. 105–6

labour force 163–65
La Pigalle (Paris) 142
Las Vegas 87, 145, 159, 163
Leheny, D. 141
Leisure as a right 9, 11, 14, 38–39
Liverpool 86
London 56, 89, 163; Olympic strategy
  148

Malaysia 45
Manila Declaration on the Social
  Impact of Tourism 16
Manila Declaration on World Tourism
  9, 10, 14, 58, 179
Market and tourism 8, 13, 16, 22, 39,
  88–89, 143, 145, 187
Medical tourism 167–68
Melbourne 90, 94, 142
Melbourne Museum 94
Migration 163, 166
Museums 87–100

Newcastle-upon-Tyne 74
New Delhi 132
New Orleans 145
New South Wales 68–69
New York 56, 90, 163, 171; and
  attack on World Trade Center 120,
  122, 179

Olympics 57, 78–79, 81, 111, 124, 148,
  160–61, 182
Oppermann, H. 137

Paraguay 34
Paris 56, 142, 163
Parker, R. 163
Patterson, K. 33–34
Perth (Australia) 101
Philippines 22–23; 35–36, 113–14,
  116, 147
Poverty and tourism x, 18, 34, 36–37,
  73–76, 112, 121, 126, 134, 145
Poverty alleviation 16, 41, 51, 120, 163,
  166, 179, 184
Prostitution 36

Queensland 61–63, 69, 73, 101

Ratz, T. 32–33
Rio de Janeiro 34–35, 126
Richter, L. 23
Right to travel 10, 11, 14, 122, 186
Rojek, C. 4, 5
Ryan, C. 138–40, 142, 155, 159

SARS 52, 123
Seabrook, J. 140–41
Seoul 78, 140
Sex tourism 137–55
Sexual exploitation 45

Shankland, A. 34–35
Shaw, G. 21–22, 87, 162–63, 165
Social impacts of tourism 18–19, 20–21,
    23, 31–33, 39, 115, 123–24, 150, 182
Social tourism 21, 121
South Africa 118
South Australia 36, 68, 76–78, 92
South Australian Museum 92–94
South Australian Tourism Commission
    19, 21
Sri Lanka 140
Suicide tourism 168–69
Surveillance 73
Sustainable tourism 5–8, 17, 36, 39, 42,
    52, 70, 86, 121–22, 151, 182, 184–85
Swine flu 46, 52
Sydney 56, 78, 80–81, 141, 163

Terrorism 46, 48, 49, 72–73, 78, 80,
    119–34
Thailand 126, 138, 140
Third World tourism 17, 36–37
Tourism and authenticity 32; and crime
    126–27; and death 167–72; and
    economic and social objectives 6, 38,
    50, 69–71, 124; and employment 124;
    and heritage 59–60, 61–71; and
    indigenous culture 91–106; and land
    rights 100–102; and legal discourse
    11, 13–14, 18, 24; and modernity 4;
    and museums 87–100; and politics
    22; and public interest 20–21; and
    repression 112–15; and sex 137–55;
    and state policy 3, 12, 50, 52, 116;
    and social responsibility 5; and
    sustainability 69, 71; and terrorism
    5, 72–73, 78–80, 119–34; and women
    163–64; and work 159–67; as industry
6, 8, 9, 13, 16, 38–39, 50, 66, 162; as
    mass tourism 4, 32, 46; 53 as
    repression 115–17, 125
Tourism Australia 20, 38, 51
Tourism Bill of Rights and Tourist
    Code 14–15, 58, 152
Transportation Security Administration
    (United States) 46–48
Travel advisories 128–32
Twining-Ward, L. 7–8

Uluru 102
UNICEF 150–51
United Kingdom 6, 50, 131, 133–34,
    186; policing of child-sex tourism
    149, 155; tourism strategy 6, 124,
    160–62, 182–84; heritage and tourism
    69–71; retention of cultural property
    94–98
United Nations Convention on the
    Rights of the Child 118, 149, 153
Universal Declaration of Human
    Rights 9–13, 118
Urban planning 70–71, 75
Urry, J. 3, 6, 7, 24–25, 75, 111

Victoria (Australia) 36, 68, 80–81, 89
Victoria and Albert Museum 89

Williams, A.M. 21–22, 87, 162–63, 165
Women xi, 33, 100, 118, 137–40, 143,
    145, 153, 155, 163–66; and inequality
    in tourism 163–64
World Tourism Organization 9–11, 13,
    15, 21, 36, 42, 51, 57–58, 120,
    150–51, 165

Zukin, S. 57